Women and Nationhood in Restoration Spain 1874-1931
The State as Family

LEGENDA

LEGENDA is the Modern Humanities Research Association's book imprint for new research in the Humanities. Founded in 1995 by Malcolm Bowie and others within the University of Oxford, Legenda has always been a collaborative publishing enterprise, directly governed by scholars. The Modern Humanities Research Association (MHRA) joined this collaboration in 1998, became half-owner in 2004, in partnership with Maney Publishing and then Routledge, and has since 2016 been sole owner. Titles range from medieval texts to contemporary cinema and form a widely comparative view of the modern humanities, including works on Arabic, Catalan, English, French, German, Greek, Italian, Portuguese, Russian, Spanish, and Yiddish literature. Editorial boards and committees of more than 60 leading academic specialists work in collaboration with bodies such as the Society for French Studies, the British Comparative Literature Association and the Association of Hispanists of Great Britain & Ireland.

The MHRA encourages and promotes advanced study and research in the field of the modern humanities, especially modern European languages and literature, including English, and also cinema. It aims to break down the barriers between scholars working in different disciplines and to maintain the unity of humanistic scholarship. The Association fulfils this purpose through the publication of journals, bibliographies, monographs, critical editions, and the MHRA Style Guide, and by making grants in support of research. Membership is open to all who work in the Humanities, whether independent or in a University post, and the participation of younger colleagues entering the field is especially welcomed.

ALSO PUBLISHED BY THE ASSOCIATION

Critical Texts
Tudor and Stuart Translations • New Translations • European Translations
MHRA Library of Medieval Welsh Literature

MHRA Bibliographies
Publications of the Modern Humanities Research Association

The Annual Bibliography of English Language & Literature
Austrian Studies
Modern Language Review
Portuguese Studies
The Slavonic and East European Review
Working Papers in the Humanities
The Yearbook of English Studies

www.mhra.org.uk
www.legendabooks.com

STUDIES IN HISPANIC AND LUSOPHONE CULTURES

Studies in Hispanic and Lusophone Cultures are selected and edited by the Association of Hispanists of Great Britain & Ireland. The series seeks to publish the best new research in all areas of the literature, thought, history, culture, film, and languages of Spain, Spanish America, and the Portuguese-speaking world.

The Association of Hispanists of Great Britain & Ireland is a professional association which represents a very diverse discipline, in terms of both geographical coverage and objects of study. Its website showcases new work by members, and publicises jobs, conferences and grants in the field.

Editorial Committee
Chair: Professor Trevor Dadson (Queen Mary, University of London)
Professor Catherine Davies (University of Nottingham)
Professor Sally Faulkner (University of Exeter)
Professor Andrew Ginger (University of Bristol)
Professor James Mandrell (Brandeis University, USA)
Professor Hilary Owen (University of Manchester)
Professor Christopher Perriam (University of Manchester)
Professor Philip Swanson (University of Sheffield)

Managing Editor
Dr Graham Nelson
41 Wellington Square, Oxford OX1 2JF, UK

www.legendabooks.com/series/shlc

STUDIES IN HISPANIC AND LUSOPHONE CULTURES

1. *Unamuno's Theory of the Novel*, by C. A. Longhurst
2. *Pessoa's Geometry of the Abyss: Modernity and the* Book of Disquiet, by Paulo de Medeiros
3. *Artifice and Invention in the Spanish Golden Age*, edited by Stephen Boyd and Terence O'Reilly
4. *The Latin American Short Story at its Limits: Fragmentation, Hybridity and Intermediality*, by Lucy Bell
5. *Spanish New York Narratives 1898–1936: Modernisation, Otherness and Nation*, by David Miranda-Barreiro
6. *The Art of Ana Clavel: Ghosts, Urinals, Dolls, Shadows and Outlaw Desires*, by Jane Elizabeth Lavery
7. *Alejo Carpentier and the Musical Text*, by Katia Chornik
8. *Britain, Spain and the Treaty of Utrecht 1713-2013*, edited by Trevor J. Dadson and J. H. Elliott
9. *Books and Periodicals in Brazil 1768-1930: A Transatlantic Perspective*, edited by Ana Cláudia Suriani da Silva and Sandra Guardini Vasconcelos
10. *Lisbon Revisited: Urban Masculinities in Twentieth-Century Portuguese Fiction*, by Rhian Atkin
11. *Urban Space, Identity and Postmodernity in 1980s Spain: Rethinking the Movida*, by Maite Usoz de la Fuente
12. *Santería, Vodou and Resistance in Caribbean Literature: Daughters of the Spirits*, by Paul Humphrey
13. *Reprojecting the City: Urban Space and Dissident Sexualities in Recent Latin American Cinema*, by Benedict Hoff
14. *Rethinking Juan Rulfo's Creative World: Prose, Photography, Film*, edited by Dylan Brennan and Nuala Finnegan
15. *The Last Days of Humanism: A Reappraisal of Quevedo's Thought*, by Alfonso Rey
16. *Catalan Narrative 1875-2015*, edited by Jordi Larios and Montserrat Lunati
17. *Islamic Culture in Spain to 1614: Essays and Studies*, by L. P. Harvey
18. *Film Festivals: Cinema and Cultural Exchange*, by Mar Diestro-Dópido
19. *St Teresa of Avila: Her Writings and Life*, edited by Terence O'Reilly, Colin Thompson and Lesley Twomey
20. *(Un)veiling Bodies: A Trajectory of Chilean Post-Dictatorship Documentary*, by Elizabeth Ramírez Soto

Women and Nationhood in Restoration Spain 1874-1931

The State as Family

Rocío Rødtjer

LEGENDA

Studies in Hispanic and Lusophone Cultures 34
Modern Humanities Research Association
2019

Published by Legenda
an imprint of the Modern Humanities Research Association
Salisbury House, Station Road, Cambridge CB1 2LA

ISBN 978-1-78188-589-5 *(HB)*
ISBN 978-1-78188-590-1 *(PB)*

First published 2019
Paperback edition 2021

All rights reserved. No part of this publication may be reproduced or disseminated or transmitted in any form or by any means, electronic, mechanical, photocopying, recording or otherwise, or stored in any retrieval system, or otherwise used in any manner whatsoever without written permission of the copyright owner, except in accordance with the provisions of the Copyright, Designs and Patents Act 1988, or under the terms of a licence permitting restricted copying issued in the UK by the Copyright Licensing Agency Ltd, Saffron House, 6–10 Kirby Street, London EC1N 8TS, England, or in the USA by the Copyright Clearance Center, 222 Rosewood Drive, Danvers MA 01923. Application for the written permission of the copyright owner to reproduce any part of this publication must be made by email to legenda@mhra.org.uk.

Disclaimer: Statements of fact and opinion contained in this book are those of the author and not of the editors or the Modern Humanities Research Association. The publisher makes no representation, express or implied, in respect of the accuracy of the material in this book and cannot accept any legal responsibility or liability for any errors or omissions that may be made.

Trademark notice: Product or corporate names may be trademarks or registered trademarks, and are used only for identification and explanation without intent to infringe.

© Modern Humanities Research Association 2019

Copy-Editor: Charlotte Brown

CONTENTS

	Acknowledgements	ix
	Preface	xi
1	The State as Family: Gender, Nationalism and the Family	1
2	Julia de Asensi: A Daughter of the Century	29
3	Alternative Lineages: 'El encubierto' and the Myth of the Returning King	46
4	Blanca de los Ríos: 'More than a Daughter, Wife, Niece'	58
5	Performing Pedigree in *Melita Palma*	74
6	Women and National Mythology in *Madrid goyesco*	90
7	Carmen de Burgos: Talking with the Descendants	106
8	*La que quiso ser maja*: Creating a Female Legacy	120
9	Counterfeit Genealogies and Forged Patrimony in *Los anticuarios*	132
	Epilogue: A Bone of Contention	149
	Bibliography	155
	Index	171

ACKNOWLEDGEMENTS

There are many people and organizations without whom this book would not have been possible. Thank you to my parents for their unwavering enthusiasm for this project, even when written in a language not their own. A sincere thank you to my supervisor Daniel Muñoz Sempere for his support, faith, endless bibliographical knowledge and for always asking the right questions; to my secondary supervisor Federico Bonaddio for always asking the difficult ones. This work has benefitted enormously from their guidance and generosity.

Thank you to the Department of Spanish, Portuguese & Latin American Studies (SPLAS) at King's College London for the grants and support they have offered me throughout the years, which also enabled me to complete the research; to Professor Catherine Boyle and Dr Xon de Ros for encouraging me to embark on a PhD in the first place.

An enormous thanks to the staff of the British Library, Biblioteca Nacional de España, Ateneo de Madrid, Senate House, and UC Berkeley Library for their patience, help and skilful navigation of resources. In particular, I would like to thank Geoffrey West, recently retired curator of the Hispanic Collections at the British Library, whose humanity, warmth and astonishing encyclopaedic knowledge was invaluable; and to Claude Potts, librarian for the Romance Collections at UC Berkeley, who together with Michael Iarocci, have made me feel so welcome in California.

Many thanks to Women in Spanish and Portuguese Studies (WiSPS) for providing such an intellectually-stimulating forum and creating a safe and welcoming space for postgraduates to present their ideas. To the International Nineteenth-Century Hispanism Network (INCH) for fostering a culture of interdisciplinarity and allowing me to meet historians like María Sierra, Javier Moreno Luzón and Juan Pro Ruiz, as well as others in the field who have helped me fill out vital historiographical gaps.

Over the years, I have had the opportunity to discuss different sections of this book with numerous colleagues and peers in conversations, seminars and conferences. I am grateful to each and every one of them for their input. In particular, I am indebted to Professor Alison Sinclair for her exhaustive review of a very early draft of what would eventually become my chapter on Julia de Asensi's 'El encubierto' and to Patricia Novillo-Corvalán for her detailed feedback on my analysis of Carmen de Burgos 'Los anticuarios'.

This monograph is based on my dissertation, which was a runner-up in the annual Publication Prize for Doctoral Students sponsored by the Association of Hispanists of Great Britain and Ireland (AHGBI) and the Office for Culture and

Scientific Affairs of the Spanish Embassy. I thank them for their generosity and support. I am equally grateful to the editorial team of Legenda, particularly to Graham Nelson and to Charlotte Wathey for her diligent proof-reading.

The generosity and support shown by fellow researchers continues to be a source of joy: to my friends and colleagues at King's College London, especially Charlotte Fereday, Maite Usoz de la Fuente and Rachel Scott. Thanks to Emilie Oléron Evans for always saying the right thing at the right time; to Marta Ferrer for helping me discover forgotten women. A massive thanks to Judith Rideout for one day dropping unannounced some priceless information on Julia de Asensi into my inbox, in what would be the beginning of our epistolary friendship; to Drew Beckett for carrying the fire; to Xavier Aldana Reyes for the music; to my husband Tom Insam, whose faith, humour and impatience with sloppy syntax will always be irreplaceable. And finally to my daughter Alma, without whose constant input this book would have been finished in half the time — this is for you.

R.R., March 2019

PREFACE

> Todos, seamos nobles o no, tenemos nuestras genealogías.
> [All of us, noble or not, have our genealogies.][1]
> (Glantz 1998: 17)

A visitor to the Spanish Senate might have come across the 'Jura de la Constitución por S.M. la Reina Regente doña María Cristina' [Her Highness Queen Regent María Cristina Pledging to Uphold the Constitution] painted by Joaquín Sorolla in 1897.[2] It is the cover of this book and one of many paintings on display that narrates the origins of Spain and the consolidation of its constitutional monarchy found at the Senate. Most parliaments contain similar visual histories of the nation, a secular Book of Genesis inculcated from a young age, and illustrated by the throng of schoolchildren crowding Sorolla's monumental canvas the morning of my visit. Yet the painting depicting queen regent María Cristina of Habsburg stands out as one of the few historical episodes that features a woman at its centre. In it, a heavily pregnant María Cristina, clad in black mourning for the recently deceased Alfonso XII, swears to uphold the Constitution of 1876. Her pledge took place in the winter of 1885, less than a decade after the ascenscion of Alfonso XII to the throne. Standing with a daughter on each side and surrounded by a sea of male officials and members of parliament, the bereaved queen has been positioned so that her advanced pregnancy is clearly visible. María Cristina embodies both the continuity of liberalism with her hand on the constitution and the perpetuation of the Bourbon dynasty with her pregnant body. A male heir, the future Alfonso XIII, would be born shortly after.

María Cristina's symbolic function as a powerful yet passive guarantor of political stability serves as a springboard for this book which, as its title *Women and Nationhood in Restoration Spain 1874–1931: The State as Family* indicates, explores how family imagery both emancipated and hampered Spanish women during the historical period known as the *Restauración* (henceforth known by the English term 'Restoration'), a reference to the rehabilitation of the Bourbon dynasty in Spain under Alfonso XII in 1874 until the proclamation of the Second Republic in 1931. The name of the era itself alludes to pedigree; after all, 'restoration' implies the recovery of a legitimate lineage that had been temporarily disrupted. As a period, turn-of-the-century Spain has often been overlooked in favour of the Second Republic that succeeded it, when female suffrage was finally passed. If anything, the perceived lack of progress when compared to some of its European counterparts was blamed on the weak hold of feminism in Spain — a feminism defined by female suffrage — in the same way that an insufficiently implemented liberalism was held responsible for the Francoist dictatorship. Yet since the 1990s, studies on the Restoration have increasingly moved beyond such simplistic and overwhelmingly negative portrayals of the period (Moreno Luzón 2018: 47). Instead historians have questioned this correlation and fragmented such linear narrative, highlighting instead the ideological legacy of a foundational period in the construction of the modern nation state that still prevails today.

A similarly deconstructive impulse informs my choice of source material. I have selected three women writers who provide a snapshot of the different ways in which women used genealogical imagery in their work to signal either their inclusion in or exclusion from nation building, often both. To show the reach and different manifestations of the state as family metaphor, the women chosen hail from different ideological standpoints. In this way the republican Carmen de Burgos y Seguí forms part of the same continuum as the less vocal Julia de Asensi y Laiglesia, a monarchic supporter best remembered for her moralistic children's tales and, placed even further across the political spectrum, the conservative Blanca de los Ríos Nostench, who would even collaborate with the Primo de Rivera regime (1923–30).[3] More conservative writers like Asensi and Ríos have been included in an explicit effort to expand the parameters that measure female political engagement during this time. Their incorporation reflects the inclusive aspirations of a study aimed to showcase the variety of approaches chosen by women who, regardless of political orientation, were not eligible to vote, be members of parliament or join other key institutions that underpinned the liberal project.

The Restoration period constitutes a key period for the consolidation of the state as family rhetoric. With the rise of the nation-state in the nineteenth century, family became a pervasive trope, used to evoke more figurative lineages that bound people to a common political project, such as a common language, traditions and a shared past, rather than just the blood bonds of yore. As we will see, the family tree expanded to include not only the actual bloodlines that had upheld the aristocracy, but also more *figurative* lineages that justified the ascendant bourgeoisie as heirs to these new state models. Isabel Burdiel observes how 'viejos lenguajes, tradiciones, valores y sentimientos de pertenencia previos se reelaboraron y reorganizaron hasta construir algo tan solo parcialmente nuevo' [old languages, traditions, values and previous feelings of belonging were re-elaborated upon and reorganized, building something only partially new] (2018: 28). Such imagery helped illustrate the concept of national sovereignty in which allegiance to a king or other powerful individual was being replaced by loyalty to the more abstract idea of a state. Benedict Anderson (1983) christened these new bonds 'imagined communities' in his eponymous study of nationalism.

A decade after Anderson, Anne McClintock foregrounded the gender dimension of the family metaphor in the equally important essay *Family Feuds: Gender, Nationalism and the Family*. Frequent allusions to the family in state constructs fulfil two important functions according to McClintock (1993: 63). Firstly, they lend representative government an 'organic' atemporal quality inherent to kinship — any resulting hierarchy within this unit is labelled 'natural'. Secondly, comparisons to family furnish liberalism with its own ancestral tree and provide it with the gravitas of a long history of continuous presence. Family is thus a powerfully malleable metaphor that can imbue a subject with both a transcendental quality and, paradoxically, a time-specific traceable lineage.

It is also the family tree in which women are notably absent. Women are left out of national genealogies, and as the painting of the regent queen María Cristina shows, they are instead often relegated to the role of mother of the nation and guardians of morality. Writing of Argentina in the nineteenth century, Francine Masiello (1992: 5) observes how 'women were brought into the political imagination of men to represent the virtues of nationhood'. Precisely by focusing on the family, this study aims to go beyond these bonds of kinship, and recover nineteenth-century women from the roles as mothers, sisters and wives that often overshadow them. Many of them — including Julia de Asensi, Blanca de los Ríos and to a certain extent Carmen de Burgos — have been forgotten or have been cast as passive participants at a foundational period for modern democracies.

Faced with a patria family trope that, on the one hand, conceived the nation as a mother but, on the other, undermined this mother by associating the female with passivity and powerlessness, how do women inscribe themselves into these new emerging lineages and national narratives? The results reflect the complex negotiations of women with their ideological inheritance and available paths to cultural clout. As Kirsty Hooper has remarked in her study of contemporary writer Sofía Casanova (1861–1958), 'to read women simply as victims of essentializing patriarchy [...] is to disregard the evidence of their own texts; the realization that women participated in nationalist and imperialist projects' (Hooper 2008: 20). What emerges instead is a complex patchwork of discourses that sometimes follow dominant narratives, sometimes tacitly or openly questioning them, or as, to quote Hooper again (2008: 20), the texts studied are 'a site for multiple, often contradictory, representations of power relationships'. *Women and Nationhood in Restoration Spain* seeks to recover a complexity sacrificed in the name of cohesive narration, and the romanticized vision of a male hero fighting against the odds in a solitary quest that characterizes traditional tales of nation formation.

Notes to the Preface

1. All translations are the author's own, unless otherwise stated.
2. The painting was started by Francisco Jover in 1890 but completed by Sorolla in 1897 after the former's unexpected demise.
3. Julia de Asensi y Laiglesia, Blanca de los Ríos Nostench and Carmen de Burgos y Seguí will be referred to by their first surname only. This is more a question of style, as the few scholars who write about these authors — both in Spanish and English — do not agree on how to address them, some writing 'de Asensi', 'de Ríos' or 'de Burgos', although most simply stick to the first surname 'Asensi', 'Ríos' or 'Burgos'. I am aware of the potential irony in using only the paternal surname in a study that criticizes the excessive attention to paternal lineages at the expense of maternal ones.

CHAPTER 1

The State as Family: Gender, Nationalism and the Family

In the beginning there was the family. The practice of arranging events and people into familiar patterns has a long genealogy. 'Storytelling is family, Family is story,' writes Noël M. Valis (1989: 367), concluding that it 'is perhaps the only story told over and over'. Family constitutes an enduring and expanding epistemic space that helps us catalogue the world. In their introduction to *A Cultural History of Heredity*, the authors observe how:

> Genealogy is the oldest kind of logic. Humans have always made use of kinship and descent in mythology, in philosophy, and in the sciences to describe the constitution of the world. Key concepts of ancient logic such as genus and species possess genealogical connotations, and the relationships among these concepts were modelled on relations of parentage. (Müller-Wille & Rheinberger 2012: 1)

The German scholar Sigrid Weigel labels this mental disposition towards conceptual kinship 'Genea-Logik', that is, 'genealogic', as she explores the connections and overlaps between the pleasingly alliterative *Genealogie* [genealogy] and *Geschichte* [history]. Tracking the origin of the origin myths, Weigel maps out the discourse surrounding the three 'G's — *Gattung* [genus], *Geschlecht* [gender] and *Genealogie* [genealogy] — of nineteenth-century Germany, a period steeped in the genealogical imagination (Weigel 2006: 145–61). It is not the only country to succumb to the ancestral fever, spreading to its European neighbours and other colonial powers like the United States. In the nineteenth century, these discussions of genealogy and pedigree — ancestral byword for legitimacy — reveal the insecurities that afflicted the West as it grappled with modernity and the ongoing effects of industrialization. To look at evolving definitions of pedigree and other related kinship terms can therefore provide an insight into the ideological hierarchy of a period. They reflect any significant political and cultural shifts that society might be undergoing. This is partly because changing power structures and the struggle for political authority are often articulated in the language of legitimacy that underpins blood lineages. It owes this rhetorical popularity to the semiotic accessibility of family, a useful metaphor furnished with an equally accessible field to articulate more abstract concepts like nation or cultural traditions.

Much has been written about nationalism and liberalism as the two main forces that shaped Europe, both advanced by its nineteenth-century architects and disseminators as movements with long established lineages. Such primordial representations have in recent decades gradually been replaced with more instrumental interpretations. The nationalist liberal project — they often went hand in hand — is now generally regarded in academic circles as an artificial creation moved by political interests. The now classic *Imagined Communities: Reflections on the Origins and Spread of Nationalism* foregrounds the narratological disposition of nationalism. Anderson (1983) conceptualizes this imagined community as an ancestral plot with historical continuity and a recognizable national conscience. *The Invention of Tradition* (1983) by Eric Hobsbawm and Terence Ranger, published the same year as *Imagined Communities* constitutes another key title in the dissection of nineteenth-century nationalism and the collective traditions that sustain it, many formed for the express purpose of cohesion. Uptake in Spain was originally slower, with a greater focus on Basque, Catalan, Galician nationalisms. Yet the last two decades in particular have witnessed a profusion of studies on the emergence of a Spanish nationalist sentiment and its different manifestations.[1] An emerging sense of nationhood is seen as an ersatz — a sociological necessity — that fills the void left by blood hierarchies that had sustained smaller communities, but that suffer the strain of massive mobilizations to larger industrial centres with no such kinship framework in place (Ichijo & Uzelac 2005: 9).

A dissection of the discursive practices surrounding the national liberal project can also throw some light on the exclusion of women from the resulting narratives. Yet for a long time, many of these accounts remained gender blind, even though a strict separation of the sexes is one of its underlying axioms. In an early intervention, McClintock (1993: 63) posits that 'nationalism is thus constituted from the very beginning as a gendered discourse, and cannot be understood without a theory of gender power'. Similarly, Inmaculada Blasco Herranz concludes more recently that:

> Que la identidad nacional española no se definiera de la misma manera para los hombres y para las mujeres se explica porque, como en otros países europeos, los procesos de nacionalización desarrollados a lo largo del siglo XIX fueron de la mano de la consolidación de la diferencia sexual moderna. (Blasco Herranz 2013: 168)

> [That Spanish national identity was not defined the same way for men and for women can be explained because, as in other European countries, the nationalization processes developed throughout the nineteenth century went hand in hand with the consolidation of modern gender differences.]

That is, national identity was forged at the same time as women and men were defined in opposition to each other in an enduring gender binary. Consequently, the two sexes were entrusted different responsibilities depending on physical and intellectual qualities seen as intrinsically related to their biology. Whilst men occupied political positions and partook in military campaigns, the field of operations allocated to women was plotted along more domestic lines, bound above all by their maternal role.

The identification of women with the mother country afforded them a certain leeway. As Catherine Davies has observed in her study of gender in the rhetoric that underpinned South American independence claims in the nineteenth century:[2]

> Literary women not only cemented the conventional patria-family trope but turned it into their advantage; if the patria was thought of as a family, so the family might be thought of as a *patria chica* [little homeland], in which women played a major part. Women's writing reshaped the patria to fit the family model. Purposefully or not, their imaginative literature resisted and undermined the dominant gender order (Davies 2006: 274).

At the same time, this new-found status did not translate into a substantial presence in the ancestral plots being assembled, nor did the trope of the mother country materialize in direct participation in the new constitutional project. As Davies also points out, in her edition of Gertrudis Gómez de Avellaneda's *Sab*, 'women's gain in moral status did not mean their inclusion in the legal, commercial and political arena' (Gómez de Avellaneda 2001: 18). This is not a surprising outcome given the gendered logic that coloured all fields from historiography, literary studies and biology. Noting the marked absence of women from what Joan Wallach Scott calls 'narratives of the "rise of civilization"' (1999: 9), she reminds us how historians, particularly nineteenth-century ones, did not merely record past events or any disruptions to gender nomenclatures. 'I assume,' she writes, 'that history's representations of the past help construct gender for the present' (1999: 2).

Under the auspices of the rise of liberalism, the entrenched legitimacy of monarchy had started to be questioned, particularly after the onset of the French Revolution in 1789 and its aftermath (Anderson 1983: 21). In its place, the concept of a sovereignty that resided in the people and was embodied in a parliamentary system started to gain traction. Similarly, hereditary privilege no longer constituted the only source of political legitimacy but had to compete with merit and the legal framework of citizenship that conferred, in theory, the same rights to all *men*. It was thus a system founded on the separation of sexes and the exclusion of women from the public sphere. Guadalupe Gómez-Ferrer lucidly outlines this inequality at the heart of liberalism in a passage that is worth quoting at length:

> Pero conviene tener presente que el discurso liberal de género conllevó una diferencia fundamental entre los sexos; por una parte, proclamó la igualdad ante la ley y manifestó el rechazo de los privilegios que se derivaban del nacimiento; pero al mismo tiempo, quedó establecida, también en función del nacimiento, una clara discriminación, si bien en esta ocasión no fue el estamento sino el sexo la fuente de privilegios, llamados ahora derechos. (Gómez-Ferrer Morant 2011: 12)

> [But it is worth remembering that the gender discourse of liberalism carried a fundamental difference between the sexes; on the one hand, it proclaimed equality before the law and expressed a rejection of any privilege derived from birth; yet at the same time, a clear discrimination was established, also based on birth, although in this case it was not class but one's sex that was the source of privilege, now called rights.]

Gómez-Ferrer features amongst a growing list of historians who present gender as a central building block in the discourse of liberalism and nationalism, the two collective creeds that shaped the nineteenth century and continue to do so.[3] That sexual difference plays a fundamental role in the forging of modern nation-states is an aspect that has in the last couple of decades spawned an illuminating bibliographical body.[4] Recent years have also witnessed a steady stream of works that focus explicitly on the significance of gender in the Spanish liberal project.[5] The so-called cultural turn has also seen a widening in our understanding of political participation not determined merely by the ability to vote, but by a whole series of practices and beliefs that underpin the emergence of constitutionalism and sustain representative democracy (Yetano Laguna 2013 and Cruz Romeo 2014).

This initial absence in Spanish scholarship can be partly attributed to the peripheral role occupied until recently by Spain in the narrative of liberalism, seen as a late adopter of new political ideas, or for not having implemented its ideals sufficiently (Burguera 2012: 18). Recent attempts to reframe Spanish liberalism within European political cultures (Paquette 2015) have also contributed to a reevaluation of the role played by women in its construction and dissemination. Other maxims have been questioned, crucially the traditional division between the public and the domestic, or as Anne K. Mellor suggests, 'at the very least, the conception of a hegemonic "domestic ideology" [...] must be fundamentally revised to include women's active role in the discursive public sphere' (2000: 7). As mentioned earlier, such demarcation was often more of a prescriptive one rather than a true reflection of reality, undermined most visibly by the many working-class women compelled to contribute to the household. Rebecca Haidt (2011) argues for different parameters that also measure women's economic output as shown in her study on women and work during the eighteenth century. Not only has the stability of such categories as the public and the domestic been undermined but also their associations. In doing so, these early efforts to recover female presence unwittingly contributed to the portrayal of passive women and the existence of clearly demarcated domains. Women were excluded from the liberal project at its foundational stage by the reserving of suffrage to men and the barring of women from public office. One cannot deny such marginalization, yet the domestic sphere is not bereft of impact. Given its centrality in national and liberal discourses, some suggest that by making domestic bliss a bourgeois ideal, the private becomes public and women become national subjects (Cruz-Fernández 2014: 254). Similarly, María Cruz Romeo makes the domestic political in a recent essay wherein she observes that:

> El molde constrictor de la ideología de la domesticidad no impidió, sin embargo, la ampliación hacia la sociedad de las funciones de la madre, figura por excelencia de la mujer. Como tampoco cerró las vías para la disensión y para propuestas alternativas en el modo de entender lo femenino y lo masculino. (Cruz Romeo 2014: 90)

> [The ideology of domesticity's constraining mould did not prevent, however, the social expansion of the duties of the mother, the par excellence figure of woman. Neither did it block the path for dissent and for alternative proposals in understanding the female and the masculine.]

Parameters of participation in the liberal project have traditionally measured representation in government and other official institutions (criteria that after all adhere to the founding principles of liberalism). Yet such a framework overlooks other ways to exert influence or take part in nation-building, those cultivated by women. These include the establishment of philanthropic associations, the funding and editing of women's magazines, the creation of schools and teaching, as well as the cultivation of domestic literature that affirms the maternal duty of women and their vital role in the moral make-up of the nation. Whilst it does not provide an impression of gender equality, it shows that women did not resign themselves to a passive role. The private was also political, or as Cruz Romeo (2014: 109) puts it, 'los escritos sobre mujer y familia eran políticos, a pesar de la aversión liberal a confundir ambos planos' [the writings on women and the family were political, in spite of the liberal aversion to mixing up these fields].

The centrality of the mother nation trope and the genealogical imagination that furnishes new civic constructs with such evocative and relatable imagery are both beneficial and detrimental to women. Such rhetorical strategies reveal the many layers of inclusion and exclusion in the nation. With the focus no longer exclusively on female suffrage and other overt signs of political engagement, this analysis suggests a more plural account of the different ways by which women sought to gain agency or visibility, recovering previously neglected contributions. This is the starting point of many recent re-evaluations, including that of Mónica Burguera in her survey of female participation in the first half of the nineteenth century. In her study, Burguera in turn refers to the influential work of the historian Mary Nash (1994), an early advocate of a more diffuse take, who:

> Llamaba la atención sobre la pluralidad histórica de los feminismos (no siempre vinculados a la tradición liberal sobre la igualdad política) y aportaba mecanismos interpretativos nuevos sobre la tardía aparición del sufragismo en España revalorizando, a su vez, las primeras manifestaciones feministas del último tercio del siglo. (Burguera 2012: 18)
>
> [Drew attention to the historical plurality of feminisms (not always linked to the liberal tradition of political equality) and provided new interpretative mechanisms for the late appearance of the suffragette movement in Spain, revaluing at the same time the first feminist manifestations in the last third of the century.]

In a more a recent essay, Joyce Tolliver (2011) similarly urges revisionist efforts not only to recover works or writers more amiable to our own contemporary sensibilities, but also those who espouse models that seemingly contradict them. While Carmen de Burgos has been the object of increased scholarly attention during recent years partly due to the openly feminist stance in some of her writings, Julia de Asensi and Blanca de los Ríos remain relatively forgotten. This oversight is partly due to a tendency within certain feminist quarters to disqualify some writers from an alternative canon for being too timidly emancipatory, or for not living up to certain expectations held by the critic (Hooper 2008: 17–20). Some scholars have fallen into the teleological trap that places pioneering feminists in the future for being 'ahead of their time' and conservatives like Asensi or Ríos in the past, for clinging on to old conventions or ideologies. The concept of a literary critic retroactively judging a writer for not 'being of her time' because she does not fit into our vision of the past is as problematic as praising an author for being 'ahead of their time' because they concur with modern sensibilities, as if there were some preordained path of progress. As a result, preceding women writers are not so much placed in an ahistorical context as not allowed to function in their own present time. Thus, Tolliver reminds us that:

> Not only must we consider the particular development of feminist thought firmly within the context of the particularities of Spanish culture, we must also be careful not to impose a twenty-first century model of feminism upon our readings of works from earlier periods. (Tolliver 2011: 244)

Remarks like these echo Lou Charnon-Deutsch's (2004: 461–69) reassessment of the value of domestic fiction as one of the few platforms available to explore and voice the concerns faced by many women, rather than as just a medium to disseminate a stifling cult of domesticity, as put forward by earlier feminist readings. It is a thesis espoused by others like Hooper (2008: 17), who observes that 'the reality that *fin de siglo* women frequently base their works on domestic or sentimental models and take the private as their starting position has led to the swift dismissal of their works — even by feminist critics — as melodramatic, conventional and idealized'.

Such was the fate of Asensi, Ríos and even the progressive Burgos. In the same way that female suffrage has overshadowed other calls for increased female visibility, certain genres like the Realist novel and later avant-garde streams have been consecrated as the preferred mediums to reflect social change at the expense of others. I will elaborate on the creation of these literary genealogies as I go along. For the moment it will suffice to point out how most women were excluded from these canons, for cultivating genres deemed apolitical or too domestic. Any textual analysis demands not only the dissection of the family imagery employed by Asensi, Ríos and Burgos, but also a reframing of the chosen vehicle for expression. Only then can the impact of their texts and the paratextual engagement be better assessed. In this way, Asensi's preference for penning historical legends during the apogee of the Realist novel in the 1880s does not necessarily translate into political disengagement. Likewise her decision to revisit the myth of the returning king in the aftermath of the third and final Carlist War, an ongoing dynastic dispute that also pitted constitutionalism against absolutism, cannot simply be brushed off as apolitical. Similarly, the novella, a genre favoured by Ríos and Burgos, languished for a long time in the shadow of other formats considered more legitimate. Although at almost opposite ends of the political spectrum, Burgos and Ríos have more in common than one would originally assume. In some respects, Burgos is more traditional than her portrayal as a trailblazing republican reflects, whilst the orthodox Ríos displayed a relentless drive to include women in the national genealogies created by liberalism.

All three writers are deeply invested in the legacy of the liberal project and its genealogical imagination, partly due to their own family connections. Women have been routinely defined by their relationship to men as wives, sisters or daughters. The irony that I introduce each woman to the reader by highlighting their blood relations is not lost. However, instead of relegating them to a secondary role, the family connections serve to repoliticize them and see their writings as yet another product of liberalism, rather than as removed from public debate. Asensi, Burgos and Ríos all came from well-off families that formed part of the new political regime. All three authors benefitted from these networks of influence. In addition to the possibilities for intervention afforded by the cult of domesticity, women took advantage not only of the family metaphor, but also of their family contacts as a less transgressive way to transition into the public eye. In other words, 'the power and advantages one gains from having a network of contacts as well as a series of other more personal or intimate personal relations', as Toril Moi (1999: 293) remarks on the bargaining power of the extended family.

Like all revisionist endeavours, and following the family metaphor, this study is an attempt to expand or create family trees, whether it be the literary canon or the participation of a certain group in a collective past that ultimately led to our present. In this way both the new narratives that emerged in the nineteenth century and revisionist studies such as this claim legitimacy for their subjects. The crucial difference, of course, is that while past discourses portray these lineages as natural, present studies — including mine — attempt to dismantle their claims and question dogmatic definitions of legitimacy that kept certain collectives like women out. Positing it as the overarching theme, these readings conceive genealogy broadly as a narrative that ties the individual to a wider community, as a blood bond or the more figurative ones championed by nationalism. Its chaperone 'pedigree' offers equally flexible possibilities of definition, as exemplified by the succinct yet accommodating definitions, 'a person's lineage or ancestry' and 'the history or provenance of a person or a thing' (*OED*). This pliability leads to conflicting interpretations of exactly what constitutes 'the history of a person' in order to attain the desired legitimacy associated with 'pedigree'. Eviatar Zerubavel summarizes this semiotic shorthand as 'we basically use pedigree to establish descendants' genealogical credentials and therefore legitimacy' (2012: 25). Ongoing debates on who belonged to these new nations are codified in the dialectics of legitimacy or as Sophie Gilmartin writes: 'which pedigrees are assimilated or included, which are seen as alien or excluded, in a nation's definition of itself and in a narrative's structure' (1998: 21).

The Spanish Nation as a Family in Decline

In the assembly of these new family trees, Spain in particular seemed haunted by the shortcomings of its pedigree, and this insecurity is couched in gendered terms. With a fading imperial star, theories of degeneration attributed this decline to the country's loss of masculinity at the expense of more virile nations like the United States (Kirkpatrick 2003: 91). Following such logic, the geopolitical influence of Spain had faded because it had lost its virility, that is, it had become feminized or enfeebled, which essentially meant the same thing. When once it led, now Spain followed other countries and adopted their cultural trends rather than originating them, a phenomenon that further diluted its essence and own native legacy according to prevailing logic. If taking the initiative was a male trait, then the opposite must apply to the female sex. To make the feminine a byword for imitation is a corollary of this gendered essentialism, whilst authenticity, that is *legitimacy*, seems to be associated with the masculine sphere. Many fretted about the perceived stagnating development of the country compared to its more precocious neighbours. Even enthusiastic patriots like the Spanish writer and diplomat Juan Valera laments in 1887 that 'no por esto me atreveré yo a negar nuestra decadencia y nuestro atraso, cada día mayores, desde fines del siglo XVIII hasta ahora' [nor would I deny our decadence and our backwardness, more marked every day, starting at the end of the eighteenth century until the present] (quoted in Ezama Gil 2008: 357).

Within the same pages Valera bemoans the fact that Spanish authors are obliged to adopt foreign fashions to remain relevant. This preoccupation with national decadence is not only the remit of men, it also concerns female intellectuals like Carmen de Burgos or Blanca de los Ríos. Seeking to boost Spain's presence and colonial might, Ríos appeals to the shared history between a now independent Latin America and the mother country with rhetoric that owes much to the genealogical imagination: 'para los hispanoamericanos el punto de partida y de apoyo, la base histórica y moral, el abolengo, la herencia, la estirpe, la raíz de la vida y del espíritu, somos nosotros, es España, la heroica, la excelsa madre' [for Latin Americans, the point of departure and of support, the historical and moral base, their ancestry, their heritage, their lineage, the root of life and of spirit, is us, is Spain, the heroic, sublime mother] (Ríos 1911: 9).

Ríos invokes the maternal trope, regards Spain as an unchanging metaphysical entity to which Latin America can trace back its roots and crusades for national regeneration. A wish for renewal, an essentialist view of Spain and a search for the true character of the nation also fuel the existential ruminations of writers like Miguel de Unamuno or Ramiro de Maeztu. They are all traditionally linked with the so-called 'Generation of 98', an ex post-facto literary ensemble characterized by a concern for the perceived decadence of Spain. Unsurprisingly neither Blanca de los Ríos or Carmen de Burgos feature in this androcentric generation despite overlapping concerns about national decline. Labelled by Michael Ugarte (1994) as the 'generational fallacy', the model has been consistently criticized throughout the decades (Gullón 1969, Butt 1980, Soufas 1998). In addition to Ugarte's seminal study, the gendered dimension of generations, a genealogical label if there ever was one, has been addressed by several scholars including Johnson (1999, 2003) and Leggot (2008: 24) who remarks that despite this questioning, the generation fallacy continues to be an enduring episteme in assessment of literature 'particularly that of the pre-Civil War period'. Similarly Kirkpatrick remarks how the predominantly masculine nature of the Generation of 98 excluded the work of Carmen de Burgos, who like many of her male contemporaries, also called for national regeneration (2003: 21).

Feelings of decay and degeneration are — it should be pointed out — not the sole property of Spain but echo the intellectual climate of *fin de siècle* Europe (Blasco Pascual 1993: 61; Uría 2008: 145–46), epitomized in the works of Friedrich Nietzsche and Max Nordau. The latter popularized the link between femininity and social involution in his book *Degeneration* (1892), in which Nordau diagnoses artists who cultivate symbolic, decadent or mystic imagery in their art as lacking virility, and suffering from such effeminate symptoms as hysteria — Kirkpatrick (2003: 91) notes for example how some followers of Nordau use 'virile' and 'vital' interchangeably. It is a more extreme and distorted version of what Charles Darwin had proposed in *The Descent of Man* (1871), wherein he claimed that certain traits such as imitation and intuition, both traditionally associated with women, characterized inferior races at an earlier evolutionary stage. Darwin would infamously claim that 'it is generally admitted with woman the powers of intuition, of rapid perception, and perhaps of imitation, are more strongly marked than in man, but some, at least, of the faculties are characteristic of the lower races, and therefore of a past and lower state of civilization' (1981: 326–27). Such declarations would only serve to provide scientific validation to long-held prejudices on the intellectual capacity of women.

The consideration of such prejudices is crucial. This is because the centrality of genealogy in the cultural landscape of the period cannot only be ascribed to the ancestral plots drawn by liberal historiography or the emerging literary canons. It owes part of its ubiquity to the growing influence of scientific discourse, particularly of Darwinism, as well as emergent language-based disciplines such as philology. As observed by Stephen G. Alter, both biological and human sciences during the late nineteenth and early twentieth century showed a marked tendency to adopt a 'comparative research method and produced a genealogical arrangement of their data, thereby mirroring the Darwin tree of life' (1999: xii). The theory of natural selection formulated in *On the Origin of the Species* had a particular impact on the epistemic framework of the period, even though philology already conceptualized and assembled linguistic families into genealogical trees. Far from offering alternatives, scientific discourse emphasized the procreative role of women, implying decadence should they deviate from their biological duties (Scanlon 1986: 170–73). It is what Tess O'Toole (1997: 122) calls the difference between women being portrayed as a passive ancestral body and authorial hand. In other words, also in the biological realm women continued to be portrayed as passive vaults for the propagation of the race rather than agents of change.

Such gendered appraisals also colour a conception of culture that leads to a split between high and low culture in the last part of the century — roughly overlapping with the Restoration in Spain — referred to as the 'Great Divide' by Andreas Huyssen. In this segregation, the feminine becomes codified as popular derivative culture, whilst the masculine stands for a more elitist, distilled version:

> It is indeed striking to observe how the political, psychological, and aesthetic discourse around the turn-of-the-century consistently and obsessively genders mass culture and the masses as feminine, while high culture, whether traditional or modern, clearly remains the privileged realm of male activities. (Huyssen 1986: 47)

However, the dwindling influence of Spain in the new geopolitical order and the loss of its last significant colonies in 1898 significantly accentuate this sensibility of decline, as the historian Juan Pan-Montojo describes:

> Si se ha tendido a leer el 98 en términos españoles, como excepción y desvío respecto a la trayectoria del conjunto de la sociedad europea, es porque la crisis finisecular adquirió entre las élites culturales hispanas una dimensión especial: la derrota fue vivida en términos de fracaso del proyecto nacional español y con el tiempo esa dimensión acabaría tiñendo por completo su significado. (Pan-Montojo 1998: 9–10)
>
> [If there has been a tendency to read the events of '98 in Spanish terms, as an exception to and deviation from the common trajectory of European society, it is because the *fin de siècle* crisis acquired a special dimension amongst Hispanic cultural elites: the loss was experienced as a failure of the national Spanish project and with time this dimension would end up completely colouring its significance.]

Consequently, a preoccupation with authenticity permeates Spanish cultural production. Jesús Torrecilla (1996: 19) observes how it is difficult to establish exactly when the tenet of originality became so central to our appraisal of cultural artefacts. He links it to two phenomena: the emergence of political liberalism and the individual, together with the idea of progress. Similarly, Kathy Bacon (2007: 27) points out that the concept of the individual lauded for its uniqueness as championed by Romanticism left a deep imprint, so that 'imitation could be seen as stifling creativity and independent thought and hence condemning people to mediocrity'. Both agree that definitions of authenticity are porous, unstable and arbitrated by those with most discursive authority — a privileged group that does not include Spain during this period, leading to its marginal position. Michael Iarocci locates the country on the periphery of ideological impact when he remarks of Spain that: 'a country that had been one of the privileged sites for the enunciation of European history in the early modern era had by the eighteenth century increasingly become an object of representation — and symbolic subordination — for a newly dominant northern Europe' (2006: xi). Andrew Ginger (2007a: 16; 2007b: 121–22) concurs that the displacement is an inevitable consequence of this relocation of discursive parameters to other countries like France or England, against whom Spain, with its different trajectory, will always remain an incomplete copy. Valis (2002) localizes this feeling of inadequacy and belatedness in the phenomenon of *cursi,* a key word to understand the culture of the country and its discursive patterns. Lacking an English equivalent, *cursi* denotes misguided cloying pathos, unfounded pretensions, excess and mimicry. Although also levelled against men, *cursi* remains a heavily gendered word intrinsically linked with the feminine. It complements the similarly non-translatable word *castizo,* meaning purebred in a dichotic dyad that encapsulates the insecurities and conflicting agendas of the period. It is a localized Spanish version of the low/high culture posited by Huyssen and other critics.

The contribution of women writers is then buried under two widespread assumptions: the equation of women with popular culture and lack of aesthetic innovation, together with the perceived marginal role of Spain in the development and spread of modernity. Over time these two discourses settled as an imperceptible sediment in the cultural landscape, their original intent of discrediting the cultural production of women and Spain now eroded, and their claims disguised as detached, neutral observations.

Spain not only had to grapple with the disruptive transition to modernity, it also had to endure the impression of trailing behind its more precocious neighbours. On the one hand there is the fear of cultural dilution and decadence elicited by a progressively consuming and engulfing mass culture that defines the modern experience. On the other we have an insecure Spain anxious about its perceived arrested development and simultaneously despondent of its aping of more advanced nations. The massification of culture, a sense of delayed modernity, together with an urge to remain faithful to an elusive national spirit, led to ideological configurations that would prove particularly disadvantageous to women, who were accused of all these ills: cheapening culture, obstructing progress and blindly following foreign fashions at the expense of more genuine *castizo* alternatives. Women writers were thus haunted by accusations of imitation translated into a discursive disenfranchisement. And yet at the same time they were hailed as embodiment of the nation and regenerative force against decadence.

Such dynamics are explored in the literary production of Asensi, Ríos and Burgos. Each of the texts selected explores the ability of women to obtain legitimacy against a cultural hegemony that disenfranchises their production. This search is expressed through a fixation with pedigrees, both blood and more figurative ones. The different approaches and interpretations that emerge from these readings testify to the complex interactions between gender, nationalism, and modernity that feed into the genealogical imagination in the last decades of the nineteenth century and beginning of the twentieth.

To help contextualize the dialogues each chosen author establishes and appreciate their significance, the following sections expand the socio-historical backdrop. The lineage of Spanish liberalism is traced as it eroded the default status of absolutist monarchy and redefined mechanisms of legitimacy. This overview itself is purposely framed as a family saga as it traces the dwindling fortunes of monarchy, not because it sees it as a natural progression, but rather to show the undeniable narratological appeal of dramatizing historical change. My aim is to show to what extent the genealogical imagination permeates the nineteenth century, and in particular the Restoration. In this respect liberalism was aided in its effort to create a competing pedigree by the emergent fields of historiography and literary criticism, and in art most notably by the *Exposiciones Nacionales de Bellas Artes* [National Exhibitions of Fine Arts] (Reyero 1989, Labanyi 2005). Held annually and sponsored by the state, painters were encouraged to produce vast canvases recreating past episodes to fuel the public imagination. A good example of this is Sorolla's painting of the queen regent María Cristina pledging to uphold the constitution. Yet neither liberal historiography nor more conservative reimaginings of the past — written or visual — contain many female protagonists, nor is room made for them in the nation-building of the day. Already in 1846, the poet Carolina Coronado had highlighted the exclusionary nature of the liberal project in her ironically titled poem 'Libertad' [Freedom]:

> Pero, os digo, compañeras,
> que la ley es sola de ellos,
> que las hembras no se cuentan
> ni hay Nación para este sexo.
> (Coronado 1991: 390)
>
> [But, I tell you, fellow women,
> that the law is only for them,
> that females do not count
> nor is there a Nation for this sex.]

An overview of the family trees drawn during this period, all dominated by men, serve to highlight the absence of women from the ancestral plots crafted by politicians, historians, writers and painters alike. The void is articulated by the writer and journalist Sofía Casanova more than half a century later after the laments of Coronado. In a 1910 lecture at El Ateneo de Madrid, a forum in which she was still a minority, she denounces the fact that 'la mujer española *está borrada* de la *cosmogonía intelectual* de Europa, cual Atlántida que devoró el mar, flotador epitafio de solo dos nombres: Isabel la Católica y Teresa de Jesús' [the Spanish woman has *been erased* from the *intellectual cosmogony* of Europe, like Atlantis swallowed by the sea, an epitaph with only two names floating: Isabel the Catholic and Teresa of Jesus] (Casanova 1910: 5). It is onto this relatively barren panorama with few female predecessors that Asensi, Ríos and Burgos attempt to inscribe themselves at the turn of the century.

Founding Fathers and Maligned Mothers: The Ancestry of Spanish Liberalism

Like the Book of Genesis, the lineages produced by liberalism seem to be heavily patrilineal. The canonical example is the United States, a nation traditionally conceived as having been founded, not on blood allegiances, but on a set of self-evident truths. That the authors of these pledges are known as the 'Founding Fathers' testifies to the role the genealogical imagination played in conveying these new power structures. Even today, the expression 'founding fathers' occupies a central place in Americans' conception of their own past, and a contentious source of political, legal and historiographical debates (Bernstein 2009: 3–4). Precisely because the requirements for becoming an American citizen are not directly correlated to ancestry, but rather dependent on embracing certain values outlined at the incept of the country, the authors of these values are ascribed great significance.

The founding myths of Spanish liberalism lack such clearly identifiable figures, yet a similar genealogical imagery informs them, exemplified by works such as *Vidas de españoles célebres* [Lives of Famous Spaniards], a series of patriotic biographies started in 1807 by the statesman and writer Manuel José Quintana. Instead of founding fathers, the emergence and consolidation of Spanish liberalism is marked by what one could call 'maligned mothers', that is, the symbolic value ascribed to the Queen Regent María Cristina of Boubon-Two Sicilies — who shared a name with the later Queen Regent and mother of Alfonso XIII — and particularly her daughter Queen Isabel II. As Mónica Burguera (2006: 85) puts it: 'la transición del absolutismo a la monarquía constitucional y la consiguiente relegitimación simbólica de la monarquía se construyó en España a través de las imágenes y los significados políticos asociados a la figura de Isabel II' [the transition from absolutism to constitutional monarchy and the subsequent symbolic re-legitimation of the monarchy was built in Spain through the images and political meanings associated with the figure of Isabel II]. Both mother and daughter failed to conform to the ideals of domesticity and the public dimension of the private that informs liberal discourse. María Cristina acted as regent following the death of her husband Fernando VII in 1833 until she was forced to give up the role in 1840, whilst her daughter Isabel II was crowned in 1843 and ousted in 1868. Following such gendered logic, the political legitimacy of liberalism and the role of monarchy were coloured by the morality, or absence thereof, in two women who did not conform to the mechanisms of legitimacy laid out by liberalism. Such new assessment criteria are central to understanding the leverage of liberalism. Most historians now dismiss traditional claims that power merely seeped from a weakened nobility to businessmen and members of the liberal professions, and that the free market supplanted feudal economies. Capitalism and the middle classes did not merely replace all previous power structures and practices (Cruz 1996). Yet as Isabel Burdiel (2000: 17) points out, liberalism did catalyze a crucial paradigmatic shift responsible for a 'new political arrangement of the mechanisms of social and economic power, and of the sources of cultural legitimacy, which had already undergone substantial change during the eighteenth century'. The concept of constitutionalism — the regulation of all government by a defined body of law — becomes an essential axiom in the vocabulary of legitimacy. It underpins liberalism's claim to be recovering historical rights lost to the greed of absolute monarchy and the nobility, and is what gives it its historicist character.

All these changing sources of cultural legitimacy are articulated in the language of pedigree and reflect ongoing contests for influence between different groups as absolute monarchy loses its status as sole repository of authority. In Spain, the reign of Carlos IV (1788–1808) spanned two decades punctuated by military defeats and economic mismanagement, a toxic combination that significantly dented the credibility of the Crown. Napoleon took advantage of this instability and placed his brother Joseph on the throne, supplanting the Bourbon line with his own family tree. The popular opposition that this dynastic coup provoked led to what would be known as the *Guerra de la Independencia Española* [Spanish War of Independence] (1808–14), read a posteriori by both progressive and conservative parties alike as the awakening of national consciousness and the glorious uprising of a unified people against the foreign invader. Before historiography settled on its definitive epithet, the conflict went by many different names including the War of Usurpation, a label that emphasized its dynastic dimension, while those more liberally inclined preferred the more modern term 'revolution' (Alvárez Junco 2001: 126). Very few of those involved referred to it as the 'War of Independence', an ex post facto label that instead gained currency during the second part of the nineteenth century.[6] It reflects the changes that had taken part in historiography, now with a new set of patriotic priorities better served by the term 'independence' and its implication of unified resistance against a foreign invader. The country had come to be portrayed as 'una sola y gran familia, gobernada por un solo cetro' [a single large family, ruled by a single sceptre] (Lafuente 1850: 11).

The war becomes an essential founding myth for new national narratives, particularly for Spanish liberals who identify 1808, the year it started, as the inception date of the liberal tradition and the genesis of its ancestry. Its founding document is the Constitution of 1812, the first of its kind in Spain and one of the more progressive documents in Europe at the time with its radical provisions on division of powers and national sovereignty. This liberal manifesto had been drafted by the Cádiz *Cortes* [Cádiz Courts], a national assembly who took over administrative duties in the absence of the Bourbon monarchy during the war with Napoleon. Although Ferdinand VII attempted to reinstall absolutism after the end of the conflict, his reign would be disrupted by attempts to dismantle this royal despotism — no longer seen as the default mode of government.

With the implosion of the old regime, liberalism in its many different guises, whether disruptive or more Burkian in its attitude to insurgencies, would become the main legitimizing force in these new state prototypes. As Burdiel (2000: 18) so succinctly summarizes it, 'the liberal revolution was not anything other than the ongoing attempt to appropriate it and define it'. As progressive and conservative factions jousted for power, the past became a discursive battlefield to justify competing visions of the nation patent from the beginning of the liberal revolution. The authors of the constitution of Cádiz had faced the challenge of furnishing their new model of polity with a pedigree that conceived of parliamentary representation as the natural default state of Spain. They located these roots in a romanticized Middle Ages, where assemblies known as 'courts' ensured that the king did not overstep his remit, most prominently presented in *Teoría de las Cortes* [Theory of the Courts] (1813) by Francisco Martínez Marina, a text officially endorsed by the Cádiz *Cortes*. Its author claimed absolutism to be an export introduced to Spain by the equally foreign Habsburg dynasty in the sixteenth century and alien to the natural inclinations of the nation. This narrative found favour amongst members of the modern day *Cortes*, named after its medieval predecessor, and a nod to this historical continuity: 'El Parlamento, en su acepción moderna, nació en España sin legitimidad histórica: de ahí el empeño de los hombres de 1812 en fundamentar las Cortes y la Constitución de Cádiz en la propia tradición española de las cortes medievales' [Parliament, in its modern sense, emerged in Spain without historical legitimacy; hence the determination of the men of 1812 in laying the foundations for the Courts and the Cadiz Constitution within the Spanish tradition of the medieval courts] (García Delgado, Fusi Aizpurúa & Sánchez Ron 2008: 35–36). It echoes Julie des Jardins's observation that after the American Civil War 'constitutional and political historians believed their narratives could induce national cohesion if democratic institutions seemed rooted in history' (2003: 21). A similar cohesive impulse characterizes the Spanish constitutional project. Álvaro Flórez Estrada, a member of the new assembly, summarizes this strategy of legitimacy when he claims that:

> Las Cortes de Cádiz no han hecho otra cosa que restablecer alguna parte de nuestra antigua Constitución, que en mejores días formaban el paladín de nuestra libertad y cuya mayor parte estaba destruida por el no uso y otras lo habían sido por el fraude y la violencia durante los reinados de Fernando V, Carlos I y Felipe II. (Quoted in Maravall 1977: 561)
>
> [The Cadiz Courts have merely reestablished part of our old Constitution, which in better days championed our freedoms, a large part of which having been destroyed due to neglect, other parts having been destroyed by the fraud and violence during the reigns of Fernando V, Carlos I and Felipe II.]

The Constitution of 1812 would become a symbolic referent particularly for more progressive strands of liberalism in later attempts at a constitution. With this archaeological excavation for the roots of liberalism, proponents also wanted to demonstrate the homegrown status of a movement that had nothing to envy in similar, earlier stirrings in countries like England or France. Years later, the journalist and writer Joaquín Belda (1922: 52) would satirize this origin story as '¡Patria gloriosa del parlamentarismo, que supo convertir unos concilios apestosos, que solo olían a potaje, en unas espléndidas Asambleas de la verdadera democracia, que luego nos han fusilado vilmente otros países para darse tono de innovadores!' [Glorious homeland of parliamentarism, which knew how to turn a foul-smelling council, which stank of stew, into the splendid Assemblies of true democracy, which have been vilely shot down later by other countries claiming to be pioneers!].

The narratological nature of history and the consecration of the medieval period as a locus for authority finds another exponent in the Royal Statute of 1834, the pseudo-constitution that was the brainchild of Francisco Martínez de la Rosa, a short-lived pragmatic compromise drafted to appease more moderate factions. When not engaged in matters of state, Martínez de la Rosa penned successful plays, most notably *La conjuración de Venecia* [The Conspiracy of Venice] (1834), set in a mythical Middle Ages coloured by a Romantic nationalism (Fontana 2007: 141–42). Like his more progressive counterparts he also searched for medieval etymology in his political projects and insisted, for example, that members of the lower house be called *procuradores*, as 'el nombre procurador del reino es más español, más castizo; nos recuerda que no hemos ido a mendigar estas instituciones a las naciones extranjeras' [the name of *procurador* is the most Spanish one, the purest one; it reminds us that we do not have to go borrowing these institutions from foreign lands] (quoted in Álvarez Junco 2001: 226).[7]

Martínez de la Rosa also perfectly embodies the symbiotic relationship between historiography, literature and politics in the nineteenth century. Both an author and statesman, he exemplifies exactly how the liberal project used history and historical fiction to envision Spain as an unchanging metaphysical entity. Men like Martínez de la Rosa provide liberalism with its own family charts and form part of a lineage of historians and authors turned politicians (or vice versa) who shape the trajectory of the nation and contribute to its genealogical imagination.

The failed Royal Statute marked the beginning of the regency of María Cristina of Bourbon, last wife of Ferdinand VII, while their daughter, the future Isabel II, came of age. Before his death, the king had annulled the so-called Salic Law that prevented women from occupying the throne. The succession rules reverted instead to those laid out in the *Siete Partidas* [Seven Divisions], a statutory code compiled during the reign of Alfonso X of Castile (1252–84), another initiative that, whether intentionally or not, relied once more on the Middle Ages as its legitimizing source. Isabel II's ascension to the throne in 1833 was opposed by the pretender Don Carlos, brother of Ferdinand, who as the next male in line claimed to be the legitimate heir. Liberals gathered behind Isabel II, and Absolutists sided with Carlos, and the clash resulted in the first of three civil conflicts — the Carlists Wars — that would plague Spain during the nineteenth century.[8] Framed superficially as dynastic disputes, it was clear from the start of the First Carlist War (1833–40) that behind family feuds over lineage legitimacy lay the *political* legitimacy of competing visions of the nation. The liberal state emerged victorious from all three conflicts and was split into two main streams: the *progresistas* [progressives] to the left and the *moderados* [moderates] to the right.

It was a further blow to absolutism, no longer considered a viable model by many influential social groups, including the army. Yet the language of consanguine credibility frames the debate despite rejecting a form of sovereignty based exclusively on kinship. In this way, the pro-Isabel *La Revista española* [The Spanish Magazine] (1832–36), founded during the first Carlist conflict (1833–40), would frequently pair any mention of the Queen Regent María Cristina with the title 'verdadera Madre de la Patria' [true Mother of the Homeland], until the two may as well have become synonymous. Yet her right to don such an honorific became increasingly questioned due to her private conduct. Her main sins included an alleged emotional distance from her daughter in conflict with the maternal devotion promoted by domestic ideals, as well as her morganatic marriage to a low-ranking officer mainly motivated by lust, according to her growing number of critics. The Queen Regent was also accused of corruption, in particular the privatization of some royal patrimony, 'anteponiendo el interés de su "familia privada" (e ilegítima) al interés de la "familia nacional"' [prioritizing the interests of her 'private (and illegitimate) family' over the interests of the 'national family'] (Burguera 2006: 90). María Cristina eventually resigned as a regent, a role subsequently held by General Baldomero Espartero until her daughter Isabel II was declared of age and crowned queen.

Christened after her predecessor Isabel the Catholic, whom Sofía Casanova had identified as one of the two survivors from the erasure of women from history, the shared name aimed to evoke historical continuity for a past monarch admired by all. Despite this matronymic aura, the successor proved to be a far less popular figure. The disappointing outcome constitutes another strand that feeds into representations of women and legitimacy during this period and later on, as the legacy turned sour, with the growing disenchantment and final demise of the constitutional monarchy of Isabel II in 1868. Some historians have reflected on how the indecorous conduct of an increasingly vilified Isabel II would have affected gender politics and the morals of a middle class who increasingly regarded the whole enterprise as a failed project.[9] As Burdiel has remarked in her biography of the infamous queen:

> El hecho de que el primer monarca netamente constitucional de la historia de España fuese una mujer con una vida *privada* considerada, de forma creciente, como escandalosa, no puede ser contemplado como un hecho neutro o sin significación política relevante. (Burdiel 2004a: 21)
>
> [The fact that the first clearly constitutional monarch in the history of Spain was a woman with a *private* life considered, increasingly, as scandalous, cannot be regarded as something neutral or devoid of political meaning.]

The figure of Isabel II became firmly entrenched in the liberal imagination as a symbol of religious fanaticism, greed and corruption that had betrayed the constitutional dream (2004a: 813).[10] In the backlash that ensued, palpable in the popular press, Alison Sinclair (1977: 28) observes that 'the naïve assumption made in many violent pieces of this period was that, in ridding itself of Isabel and the multiple immoral practices ascribed to her, Spain was ridding itself of its political problems'. However, despite the disputes and troubles that characterized her reign (1833–68), Isabel, unlike her father Ferdinand, had no other choice but to have her powers curtailed as a return to absolutism seemed now impossible. Yet her tainted image, transformed from mother of the nation to fallen woman and fickle tyrant, started to be seen by many as a threat to the newly founded liberal state. Isabel II was eventually ousted in 1868 by *La Gloriosa* [the Glorious Revolution], a revolt led by General Prim, inaugurating a six-year-period that would later be known as the *Sexenio Democrático* or *Sexenio Revolucionario* [the six democratic or revolutionary years]. This period encompasses the brief reign of Amadeo I de Saboya (1871–73), another bid for constitutional monarchy but with an imported king, followed by an even shorter republican interlude (1873–74). Spain's first attempt at self-governance without a monarch at its helm lasted barely a year before the Bourbons returned to the throne in the form of Alfonso XII, son of the deposed Isabel II. As the trust in the regime of Isabel II crumbled, the paternity of the heir had been increasingly challenged. These accusations of illegitimacy did not disappear with the proclamation of the republic. As Sinclair points out, 'if anything, the question of paternity gained more importance after the revolution, because of the possibility that the Bourbons might be restored to the throne in the person of Alfonso XII' (1977: 44). This double inheritance, both biological and ideological that a son of Isabel II might carry, allegedly led the politician Fernando Fernández Córdova to exclaim: '¡El Príncipe arrastra una herencia fatal!' [the Prince carries a fatal legacy!] (quoted in Sinclair 1977: 44). Fernández Córdova was amongst those who had supported a dynastic renewal in the form of Amadeo I of Savoy, an experiment that did not last long.

What would be known as the Restoration was mainly orchestrated by Antonio Cánovas del Castillo (Espadas Burgos 2000: 5), an historian turned politician, demonstrating once more the crucial role played by historiography in dictating new standards of legitimacy. Cánovas also drafted the so-called *Manifiesto de Sandhurst* [Sandhurst Manifest] signed by the then prince, wherein Alfonso pledges that 'ni dejaré de ser buen español ni, como todos mis antepasados, buen católico, ni, *como hombre del siglo, verdaderamente liberal*' [I will not cease to be a good Spaniard nor will I stop being a good Catholic, as were all of my ancestors, or, *as a man of the century,* will I not be *truly liberal*] (quoted in Villares & Moreno Luzón 2009: 637–38, my emphasis). The new charter, the Constitution of 1876, counted Cánovas as its principal author in a system wherein the Liberal party led by Práxedes Mateo Sagasta and the Conservative party headed by Cánovas himself alternated in power in a controlled process known as 'el turno pacífico' [the peaceful turn]. The early death of Alfonso XII in 1885 led to the regency of his consort — the other María Cristina — until the heir Alfonso XIII came of age in 1902. His abdication in 1931 and the ensuing declaration of the Second Republic marks the end of the Bourbon Restoration and the end of half a century of creating an historical collective imagination.[11] Such was the level of penetration amongst all social classes in the closing years of the nineteenth century, that Clarín could parody the national mythos product of a century of liberal proselytism in his sketch 'El rana' [The Unlucky One]. Asked to define Spain and the homeland, a barely literate ageing soldier itemizes liberal landmarks:

> ¿Qué era España? ¿Qué era la patria? No lo sabía... Música... El himno de Riego, la tropa que pasa, un discurso que se entendió a medias, jirones de frases patrióticas en los periódicos... Pelayo... El Cid... La francesada... El Dos de Mayo. (Alas 2002: 941–42)
>
> [What was Spain? What was the homeland? He didn't know... Music... The Hymn of Riego, a passing troop, a half-understood speech, shreds of patriotic sentences in newspapers... Pelayo... The Cid... The War of Independence... The Second of May.]

Narrating the Nation

The previous overview of the rise and consolidation of the liberal state might follow the fortunes of the Bourbon dynasty, yet monarchs lose part of their protagonism in chronicling efforts of the period. Instead the liberal maxim of national sovereignty leads to an increased focus on a totemic *pueblo* [the people], guardian of a new legitimacy. This new philosophy is echoed by the royal academician José Zaragoza who claimed that 'desde que los reyes no son los únicos árbitros de las naciones, desde que los pueblos han aspirado también a ser absolutos, la historia debe escribirse para todos, porque todos tienen que aprender en ella' [since kings are no longer the only arbiters of nations, since the people have aspired to govern themselves, history should be for everyone, because everyone has to learn from it] (1858: 5). The quotation appears in *Historia Patria: Politics, History, and National Identity in Spain, 1875–1975,* in which Boyd emphasizes the legitimatizing function of historiography during the nineteenth century, a teleological vision of the past often articulated as a family saga.[12]

National history provided a justification for the new order of things — in the words of Joseph Fontana, "a genealogy of the present" — that explained the inevitable historical process by which the liberal state and its ruling class had come into being and defined their historical mission (Fontana 1982: 9).[13] Once more, this lineage mostly resembles a patrilineal one, partly due to the separation of private and public spheres in the nineteenth century. Thus in her study of female participation in the historical enterprise of shaping America, Julie des Jardins observes how the professionalization of the historian in the second part of the nineteenth century leads to the exclusion of many women from the field. Traditionally, women had been seen as repositories of local and familial history, but as Des Jardins points out 'scholars no longer believed that national character was bred in the private sphere alone. Women lost their historical authority once they were perceived to occupy a place so distant from the public and political seats of action' (2003: 23). The historian Carole Berkin reaches a similar conclusion in *Revolutionary Mothers*, her attempt to recover the input of women in the founding of the United States: 'The new professional historians turned their attention to great men and formal politics, to generals and diplomats, to public figures and political institutions' (2006: xiv).

Following this pattern we find the lineage of Spanish historiography dominated by the labour of male historians such as Antonio Cánovas del Castillo, Modesto Lafuente or Marcelino Menéndez y Pelayo. This new breed of historian who enthusiastically assembled family trees for the nation often belonged to liberal professions: lawyers, journalists and politicians who pursued a political agenda very different from that of the clerics who had as late as the eighteenth century made up the bulk of chroniclers (Boyd 1997: 68). None of these earlier accounts covered the rise of the liberal state, and the new genealogies that supported it. Older history books lacked this new nationalist focus, or, as Roberto López-Velaz puts it, the previous production 'no podía satisfacer las necesidades de dotar con un andamiaje histórico al liberalismo histórico' [could no longer satisfy the need to equip historical liberalism with a historical framework] (2004: 198).

This gap was eventually covered by the ambitious thirty-volume *Historia general de España desde los tiempos más remotos hasta nuestros días* [General History of Spain from Immemorial Times to Our Days] published by Modesto Lafuente between 1850 and 1867, with a second edition of thirteen volumes between 1874 and 1875. Lafuente, who toiled as a journalist, fits the profile of the new liberal historian. This new saga became one of the most read works in the second part of the nineteenth and even at the beginning of the following century, a success that turns it into a key reference during the Restoration 'tanto en la fijación de los grandes tópicos de los manuales escolares como en la construcción del imaginario histórico de la España liberal' [in establishing the main themes for school manuals as well as in building the historical imaginary of liberal Spain] (Fontana & Villares 2007: viii).[14]

The emergent field of literary criticism performed a similar function to historiography, through its creation of cohesive ancestral plots and the promotion of homogeneous national identities. The coevality is highlighted by Álvarez Junco, one of many critics to remark that it was not until the middle of the eighteenth century that literary histories started to be branded with national markers like English, French or Spanish, and conceived of as the cultural diary of an entire uniform national spirit (Álvarez Junco 2001: 228). Influential intellectuals like Marcelino Menéndez y Pelayo, were aware of the short genealogy of literary history as a 'scientific' objective discipline (Fitzmaurice-Kelly 1901: viii). Yet this did not compromise the immutability of the canon itself, merely awaiting to be recovered by scholars like Menéndez y Pelayo. He thus declares in his own ambitious multivolume study *Historia de las ideas estéticas en España (1883–1891)* [History of Aesthetic Ideas in Spain (1883–1891)] that:

> Pero entiéndase siempre que estos cánones no son cosa relativa y transitoria, mudable de nación a nación y de siglo a siglo, aunque en los accidentes lo parezcan, sino que en lo que tienen de verdadero y profundo, se apoyan en fundamentos matemáticos inquebrantables. (Menéndez y Pelayo 1890: xiv)
>
> [But let it be understood that these canons are not a relative or transitory thing, changeable from nation to nation and from century to century, even though it might occasionally seem so, their truth and depth are supported by unbreakable mathematical foundations.]

This metaphysical conception of literature as the mirror of an unchanging national ethos coincides with a commensurate patriotic turn in historiography that interpreted rebellions and uprisings as the will of a homogeneous people. It spawned numerous new national pedigrees that claimed roots in the Middle Ages or the early modern period, which in literary terms became known as the Golden Age. The literary version of Modesto Lafuente arrives in the shape of Amador de los Ríos — uncle of Blanca de los Ríos — who in 1861 publishes the first volume of his *Historia crítica de la literatura española (1861–1865)* [Critical History of Spanish Literature (1861–1865)]. Considered the first comprehensive literary history penned by a Spaniard, the dedication to Isabel II openly declares its instrumental role in the consolidation of the liberal regime:

> Traigo a los pies del trono constitucional de la Reina de España la Historia crítica de la literatura española, donde se revelan vivamente los conflictos de la patria, templan y endulzan sus dolores las pacíficas glorias de sus preclaros hijos. (Ríos 1861: n. p.)
>
> [I bring to the foot of the constitutional throne of the Queen of Spain the critical History of Spanish literature, wherein the conflicts of the homeland are vividly revealed, the peaceful glories of its illustrious sons calming and sweetening their sorrows.]

Patrilineal Canons: The Lady Vanishes

Despite fawning dedications like these, the growing unpopularity of the queen would translate into cultural delegitimization. Following the ever-present gendered logic, previous cultural production is tainted by the decadence of a crumbling Isabeline regime and identified as feminine. As we have seen, the first attempt at a constitutional monarchy in the form of Isabel II ended acrimoniously with an exiled queen, the whole enterprise regarded as a resounding failure. Even with the restoration of the Bourbon line in 1874, many liberals distanced themselves from the recent past as they recalibrated lineages to view this episode as a deviation. The revolution of 1868 and subsequent political developments invalidated the work of many previously successful women writers like Pilar de Sinués (1835–93), Angela Grassi (1823–83) or Faustina Saéz Melgar (1834–95), who had all started their careers under Isabel II. Iñigo Sánchez-Llama remarks how 'el colapso del régimen isabelino en 1868 origina criterios artísticos alternativos en la configuración de la cultura oficial española' [the collapse of the Isabeline regime in 1868 gives rise to alternative artistic criteria in the configuration of official Spanish culture] (1999: 756) — the mechanisms for cultural legitimacy were completely overturned and new ones created to represent the new reality. In literary terms, the legitimacy criteria changed drastically to favour the novel cultivated by the likes of Benito Pérez Galdós, a genre now masculinized, highlighted by Catherine Jagoe in her pioneering study 'Disinheriting the Feminine: Galdós and the Rise of the Realist Novel in Spain' (1993). Similarly, Maryellen Bieder (1992) and Alda Blanco (1995) feature amongst early critics who convincingly show how the emergent field of literary studies in the nineteenth century produced a gendered language of appraisal that equated the masculine with originality and the *castizo*, while the feminine became associated with the emulation of imported trends and *cursi*.

Two years after Isabel II's abdication, Pérez Galdós himself would famously promote the Realist novel as the quintessential *castizo* expression, in opposition to what he regarded as foreign forms and genres, in his 1870 essay 'Observaciones sobre la novela contemporánea en España' [Observations on the Spanish Contemporary Novel]. Pérez Galdós gave his preferred mode of narrative an impeccable pedigree with roots traceable to Miguel de Cervantes himself, hailed during this period as a hallmark of Spanishness. Just as the authors of the 1812 Constitution had identified an established democratic tradition in the medieval *cortes*, literary historians like Amador de los Ríos — often also historians — found in past authors like Cervantes the origins of alleged native genres like Realism, thus providing it with a similar legitimacy and historical continuity (Close 1978: 246–47).The parallels in these two pre-lapsarian tales are palpable with both Realism and national sovereignty hailed as the return to a natural default state. It is a narrative encapsulated by the Cervantist Julio Cejador y Frauca in his monumental *Historia de la lengua y literatura castellana* [History of the Castilian Language and Literature], written between 1915 and 1922 at the tail-end of the Restoration, wherein he presents the Spanish pedigree of the Realist mode as a cultural axiom: 'Cervantes, español hasta los tuétanos, al parodiar los descabellados libros de caballerías, no hizo más que volver por el realismo castellano contra los idealismos, fantasías y sueños de aquella literatura extranjera' [Cervantes, Spanish through and through, by parodying the preposterous courtly romances, did nothing more than return to Castilian realism against the idealisms, fantasies and dreams of that foreign literature] (1915: 218).

It also entailed some aggressive pruning of the literary family tree, as many authors were now excluded from the canon for not meeting the new admission criteria laid out by Realism. Women in particular were affected by this discursive shift. It can be seen in Pérez Galdós dismissing Cecilia Böhl de Faber, better known by her pseudonym Fernán Caballero, as being 'afectada de una mojigatería lamentable' [affected by a lamentable sanctimoniousness], whereas similar male writers like José María de Pereda merely get berated for being a tad too parochial (1957: 234). Leopoldo Alas 'Clarín' mocks Pilar Sinués in a similar vein in an 1885 column for her perceived sentimentality and self-appointed role as defender of decorum: 'En el número anterior de *Gil Blas* me pedía mi amigo Blasco que le ayudase en la penosa tarea de desmoralizar a nuestro público, entiendo por desmoralizar, como quien dice despilarsinuesdesnarcotizar' [In the previous issue of *Gil Blas* my friend Blasco asked for my help in the laborious task of demoralizing our public, by demoralizing I mean to depilarsinuesdesensitize as it were] (1885: 209). The name of a woman author actually becomes a synonym for sentimentality, a literal example of the discursive strategy identified by feminist critics whereby certain qualities, deemed negative by a culture, become associated with women — language becomes gendered.

Even nowadays such conceptions of the role of women in nineteenth-century cultural production persist. In a recent survey on the cultural panorama of nineteenth-century Spain, Cecilio Alonso (2010: 215) mentions traditional exceptions such as Fernán Caballero, Concepción Arenal, Rosalía de Castro and Pardo Bazán as literary representatives of the period, and concludes that it is 'escaso residuo si se observa que, en el XIX, no menos de medio millar de escritoras españolas podrían calificarse de literatas, por haberse aproximado, con poco éxito, al concepto de creación artística' [scarce remains given that in the nineteenth century, no less than half a thousand Spanish women writers could be labelled *literata*, for having come close, with little success, to the concept of artistic creation].[15] Remarks like these reveal the reach and repercussion of nineteenth-century narratives that continue to colour the judgment of modern critics, often due to accumulated inertia rather than any underlying misogyny.

Intrinsically linked with the practice of nation-building, literary canons became another predominantly masculine space. It leads Ríos-Font to conclude that 'despite the grammatical gender of the word *España*, the emblem of the Castilian warrior prevails from the beginning over that of the nurturing motherland (*la madre patria*)' (2004a: 32). Such a gendered perspective translates into a marginalization of women in the canon, their works considered derivative and not true heirs to the national narrative. Unlike men, women can more easily prove biological legitimacy but had to frequently defend their literary output from accusations of imitation and unoriginality. The lack of female presence in canons reflects this dominant discourse that associates women with another type of reproduction, understood as a copy, rather than a process that results in an original creation. It leads Blanco (1995: 128) to conclude that 'the representation of woman as imitator permeated the discourse of literary criticism from its earliest days and would resonate well into the 1920s'.

As a result very few women remain in the literary canon, but instead form an alternative group whose common denominator seems to be sentimentality and a lack of originality, as claimed even nowadays. The exclusion of writers like Julia de Asensi and Blanca de los Ríos who, despite a varied opus, did not cultivate the novel, is closely linked to the rise of this genre as the emblematic repository of nineteenth-century cultural production. Carmen de Burgos, mostly a practitioner of the novella like Ríos, did not produce her first full novel, *Los inadaptados* [The Misfits], until 1909, by which time the momentum for this mode had faded. Her remaining nine novels, including *Los anticuarios* [The Antique Dealers] (1918) and *El tío de todos* [Everyone's Uncle] (1925), were all written at the tail end of the Restoration, after the end of the First World War, when events had once again renewed the parameters of literary legitimacy. The Realist novel no longer seemed fit to represent the reality of early twentieth-century Spain. Benito Pérez Galdós, stalwart of the genre, became dismissively referred to as 'Benito el garbancero' [Benito the bumpkin] by the modernist writer Ramón del Valle-Inclán. Johnson (2001) and Kirkpatrick (2003) feature amongst those critics who point out how Spanish *modernismo* and other avant-garde streams prioritized aesthetic innovation, again branded as a masculine trait, over societal shifts triggered by the changing role of women. Such dynamics will be looked at in more detail in the chapters dedicated to Carmen de Burgos, a woman closely associated with practitioners of these new streams, but never considered one of them. Although the sweeping panoptic sagas associated with Realism had fallen out of favour, they were by then firmly ensconced in the national canon. But with the exception of Pardo Bazán, very few women are included in either past or present literary lineages.

This gendered logic manifests itself in the exclusion of women from a country's literary patrimony that still has repercussions today. In a recent study into the required reading-lists of American postgraduates studying Spanish, only Pardo Bazán appears in over three quarters of those syllabuses surveyed (Brown & Johnson 1998: 5–6). Furthermore, the nineteenth century trailed not only behind the twentieth century, which one presumes has been shaped by more recent inclusive criteria, but also behind the sixteenth century. In other words, the period that witnessed the most fervent canon construction is also the one that omitted a large number of women. The figures speak for themselves. María del Carmen Simón Palmer (1991) catalogues over seven hundred writers in her pioneering *Escritoras españolas del siglo XIX* [Spanish Women Writers of the Nineteenth Century]. Recent research by Hooper has further bolstered this figure in a project that looks at female input between 1890 and 1936.[16] With a narrower and slightly different chronological demarcation than that of Simón Palmer, Hooper records over five hundred women who contributed to the cultural landscape of turn-of-the-century Spain, either as writers, journalists, translators or authors of different educational manuals. Although of varying quality, it is still startling how few women make the canonical cut given a larger pool of candidates available than in any previous centuries.

The Ubiquity of the Genealogical Imagination

The ways in which the genealogical imagination manifests itself are manifold and varied, sometimes to the benefit of women, sometimes to their disadvantage. It consecrates them as mothers of the nation and regenerators of the race yet at the same time limits them to their biology, turning them into transcendental bodies unaffected by temporal vagaries such as politics. It imbues them with an inherent sense of moral superiority yet makes the feminine a byword for degeneration. It envisages their bodies as repositories of the national spirit yet their intellectual output is corrupted by sentimentality, foreign influences or commercial interests. Such is the malleability of the genealogical imagination, such its ubiquity, that it risks encompassing everything. Everything can be assembled into a lineage: languages, the evolution of humanity or the emergence of nations — the Indo-European language family, the descent of Man, the mother country. Its epistemic ubiquity blends into the background, makes its gendered logic invisible. The following chapters highlight this ubiquity and plasticity, from the historical legends of Asensi, passing through the domestic melodramas of Ríos and finishing with the picaresque tales of Burgos. None of the texts selected follow dominant formats for discussing the fate of the nation. As we have seen, such political rumblings were traditionally relegated to the Realist novel, a premium vehicle for such pursuit, until it was replaced by the aesthetic experiments of the avant-garde.

Chapter Two provides a brief overview of Asensi, presenting her as an agent of change rather than merely passively patrolling the borders of morality. With this new vantage point, Chapter Three recasts her historical legend 'El encubierto' [The Covert/ Cloaked One] (1883) as a timely reflection on the limited platforms of power available to women, rather than a belated manifestation of a now residual apolitical Romanticism. A variant on the myth of the returning king, the figure of El Encubierto had attracted the imagination of writers who either supported or undermined his claim to descend from the Catholic Monarchs and indirectly, in turn, the legitimacy of the reigning Isabel II. What role befalls the monarch in a constitutional system? A loaded subject, Asensi was aware of the cultural currency El Encubierto had accrued in the new political vocabulary that accompanied the rise of liberalism. In her version, a disagreement over the true ancestry of the eponymous Encubierto divides a family and pits female members against male ones, revealing a gendered preoccupation that often colours her historical legends. The men emerge victorious but the narrator remains less convinced in this retelling of the legend in which political legitimacy is explicitly articulated in genealogical terms and frustration is felt by the female characters' inability to ascertain their version.

Chapter Four looks at Blanca de los Ríos, an author often defined by her kinship to men, focusing instead on how she shaped national genealogies and tried to make them more inclusive to women. Chapter Five looks at *Melita Palma* (1901), one of the many novellas penned by Ríos, another genre often dismissed as minor in comparison to its lengthier counterpart. Like 'El encubierto' the work deals with impostors: in this case the eponymous protagonist is compelled to feign a noble pedigree after the mother of her aristocratic lover, scandalized by her profession, opposes the union. Melita proves adept at performing whichever feminine role her surroundings project onto her, to the point that her suitor starts to feel wary about her talent for pretence. The publication date of this melodrama proves equally suggestive, appearing in the aftermath of the Disaster of 98, but also in the first months of the reign of Alfonso XIII, upon whom many had pinned their hopes for the desired national regeneration. Melita, on the other hand, pines to be accepted into a noble household that has seen better days, presided over by a well-meaning yet out of touch matron and the heir she wishes to marry off. The novella can be interpreted as a reflection on how women, represented by a Melita troubled by her own precarious claims to legitimacy, can help regenerate the equally decaying household that was the Spain of Queen Mother María Cristina and the recently-crowned Alfonso XIII.

Chapter Six deals with forged lineages in *Madrid goyesco* [Goyaesque Madrid] (1907), another novella by Blanca de los Ríos, and the completely fictitious family tree fabricated by Doña Aurora — a relentless social climber. Her aristocratic ambitions lead her to concoct a mythos that links her lineage to the main patrician bloodlines in Spain as she attempts to marry her beautiful niece Maravillas Reinaldos to the raffish Paco, the most sought-after bachelor in Madrid, and heir to the Marquis of Villena. However the young girl has fallen for Pepito León of Castile, the youngest son of the destitute Duke of Sansueña. Framed as a melodrama, Ríos populates the story with archetypes from national narratives that are the product of nineteenth-century historiography. Maravillas resembles one of those so-called *majas* immortalized by Goya, hailed as an archetype of Spanish womanhood before it allegedly became contaminated by European mores. Yet this identification of the female protagonist with an unpolluted yet decadent Spain implicitly condemns women to a passive if not sacrificial role in national mythology. This narrative cul-de-sac is at odds with the author herself, who actively participated in the cultural landscape of her time both as an author and as a historian. Ríos mocks the aristocratic pretensions of Doña Aurora and her penchant for counterfeit genealogy, which ultimately lead to disaster. Yet the more she ridicules characters with an overactive imagination and a penchant for storytelling — a recurrent motif in her work — the more attention she draws to her own precarious position as a woman and professional spinner of yarns.

Chapter Seven introduces Carmen de Burgos — almost diametrically opposite in political leanings to the conservative Ríos — but who also expressed an interest in the maxim of legitimacy, reflected in the interactions between gender and genealogy in her narrative. Celebrated for her unwavering commitment to the rights of women, such activism has occasionally led to the neglect of less overtly feminist texts that nonetheless form part of Burgos's persona. Her labour as an art critic for example provides us with a complex legacy: on the one hand she joins in the sacralization of Goya, Velázquez and other painters hailed as the embodiment of the Spanish soul, and on the other hand, she worries about the marginal space afforded to women in such a monolithically male space. Thus a preoccupation with leaving an imprint and the growing clout of museums in curating the national canon is explored in Chapter Eight, which is devoted to the novella *La que quiso ser maja* [The Woman Who Wanted to Be a *Maja*] (1924), in which Burgos follows the failed attempts of Carola to insert herself into a national genealogy by becoming a totemic Goya figure. Her frequent visits to the Prado Museum lead to a fascination with Goya and a plan to be immortalized in a great work of art. However, her dreams to embody a national archetype and be inducted within the walls of the Prado remain unfulfilled. The resulting painting, rejected by a conservative jury, does not receive the institutional acceptance for which she longs. It ends up instead displayed within the domestic confines of her home, much to her chagrin. Her genealogy seems condemned to remain private and without descendants.

Chapter Nine covers the little-studied *Los anticuarios* [The Antiques Dealers] (1918), the only novel included in this study, written by Burgos in the era of the avant-garde, when the emblematic nineteenth-century vehicle had lost its clout. Whilst not following modernist aesthetics, *Los anticuarios* addresses a very modern subject, the commodification and commercialization of the past. A century of liberal historiography has produced a set of collective myths ripe for exploitation. Based in Paris, the former civil servant Fabián de las Navas y Marchamalo and his enterprising wife Adelina run a shop that specializes in Spanish antiques. Fabián similarly boasts an impeccable *castizo* pedigree through his alleged patrician ancestry that, like the objects he sells, he delights in recounting in detailed narratives. However, like much of his merchandise, very little of this is true but serves instead to cement his image as a quintessential Spaniard. His wife Adelina does not share his passion for this counterfeit genealogy — populated mainly by male *castizo* ancestors — but is more excited by the possibilities a modern metropolis like Paris offers to build more inclusive lineages. Whereas Fabián fixates on a past ancestry, her focus lies on a future legacy.

Notes to Chapter 1

1. The following works have been of great help in mapping my own understanding of the role of liberalism in shaping Spanish nationalism in the nineteenth century and first three decades of the twentieth: Fox (1997), Núñez Seixas (1997; 1999), Fusi Aizpurúa (2000), Álvarez Junco (2001), Forcadell Álvarez & Cruz Romeo (2006), Moreno Luzón (2007), Quiroga (2007), Archilés (2008), Núñez Seixas & Moreno Luzón (2013), Quiroga & Archilés (2013) and Morales Moya, Fusi Aizpurúa & Blas Guerrero (2013). Against this prevalent modernist take on nationalism, other historians trace an early form of nationalist sentiment that predates the rise of liberalism. See for example *La nación antes del nacionalismo en la monarquía hispánica (1777–1824)* [The Nation Before Nationalism in Spanish Monarchy (1777–1824], in which its editors José Cépeda Gómez and Antonio Calvo Maturana (2002) defend a third historiographical approach. Away from both modernist and primordial conceptions of the nation, the volume's contributors find manifestations of a proto-nationalism in the eighteenth century.
2. There was also another side to this idealized mother trope. As Davies (2006: 270–71) also observes, for South American colonies seeking independence, Spain was sometimes portrayed as an oppressive matriarch and new nations the rebel sons.
3. The gender binarism entertained by liberal ideology finds some of its roots in the Enlightenment, particularly Rousseau's ideas on the inability of women to hold political positions, as expressed in his educational novel *Emile* (1762). See Outram (2013: 84–98) for a helpful exposition of gender constructions by influential eighteenth-century thinkers such as Rousseau and Voltaire.

4. My own readings benefit greatly from the insights of Linda K. Kerber on the role of women in Revolutionary America (1980), the pioneering efforts of Nira Yuval-Davis and Floya Athias in their *Woman, Nation, State* (1989), as well a later solo effort by Yuval-Davis (1997), the explicit genealogical angle adopted by Anne McClintock in another foundational text (1993), Joan Wallach Scott on the gendered politics of early historiography (1999), Ida Blom, Karen Hagemman and Catherine Hall's *Gendered Nations* (2000), Joan B. Landes on Revolutionary France (2001) and Catherine Davies on the independence of Latin American colonies (2006).
5. These studies include Mónica Burguera (2012) on the role of women in shaping liberal discourse in the first half of the nineteenth century, as well as more specifically that of Isabel II (2006). Burguera is also responsible for the collection of essays *Género y modernidad* [Gender and Modernity] with Mónica Bolufer (Bolufer & Burguera 2010). Inmaculada Blasco Herranz has written about the political participation of women in discourses of national regeneration in a Spain affected by the loss of its colonial clout (2013), whilst Xavier Andreu Miralles has studied the evocative power of family imagery in articulating the emerging liberal project (2009; 2011). Guadalupe Gómez-Ferrer (2005) has edited the third volume of Isabel Morant's *Historia de las mujeres en España y América Latina* [The History of Women in Spain and Latin America], *Del siglo XIX a los umbrales del XX*, with important contributions by major exponents of this revisionist wave, as well as provided her own take on the role of women in the new nation-state (2011).
6. In English the 'Spanish War of Independence' is normally referred to as the 'Peninsular War'.
7. *Procurador* in its modern meaning is 'attorney' but there is no direct translation for its reference to a member of parliament.
8. Historians disagree on whether the war that took place between 1872 and 1876 should be the second or the third Carlist conflict. It depends on if the so-called *Guerra dels Matiners* [War of the *Matiners*], which unfolded mainly in Catalonia between 1846 and 1849, is considered part of the Carlist canon. Some sources identify it as the second Carlist conflict, so that the later war in 1872 becomes the third. Others, such as the historian Jordi Canal (2000: 128), consider the 1872–76 war to be the second.
9. For other studies on the role of Isabel II in Spanish liberal discourse, see Burdiel (1998; 2004b), Pérez Garzón (2004) and Burguera (2006).
10. Burdiel also reminds us that Isabel II was mocked by prominent figures like Gustavo Adolfo Bécquer, who together with his brother Valeriano produced a series of pornographic caricatures depicting the queen and her circle. These are also analyzed by Lou Charnon-Deutsch (1996: 274–93). Ramón del Valle-Inclán also famously satirized the court of Isabel II in *La corte de los milagros* [The Court of Miracles] (1927).
11. Historians disagree on the limits of the Restoration period, mainly on when it concludes, due to the seven-year dictatorial spell of General Primo de Rivera between 1923 and 1930 which had the consent of Alfonso XII. Some point to 1923, the beginning of the Rivera regime, as the end, whereas others identify 1931, the year Alfonso XIII officially steps down, as the final curtain call of the house of Bourbon (Villares & Moreno Luzón 2009: 544).
12. In addition to the growing number of studies on Spanish nationalism, the importance of history in the emergent national curriculum is an angle explicitly addressed by Boyd (1997), Cuesta Fernández (1998), and Peiró (1995), among others.
13. History as an instrument of legitimation has spawned its own critical tradition, a 'historiografía de la legitimación' [historiography of legitimacy] (2006: 181) as Oscar Moro Abadía calls it in a recent monograph wherein he traces the functions of history throughout history, rather fittingly titled *La perspectiva genealógica de la historia* [The Genealogical Perspective of History]. Moro Abadía's use of genealogy here alludes to a historical technique traditionally associated with Friedrich Nietzsche's *On the Genealogy of Morals* (1887), in which the German philosopher historicizes morality as a product of power struggles, rather than a fixed atemporal concept that transcends history. In the twentieth century Michel Foucault expands the family tree with his own influential genealogies where he maps out the trajectory and evolution of dominant ideologies as shaped by power.
14. Although the most popular, Lafuente's version was not the only best-selling one, nor did it offer the only vision of Spain, as demonstrated by Vega in his brief overview of the idea of the nation in other popular history manuals (2013: 435–49).

15. Although not used here in such a way, the term *literata*, which could be translated as a 'literate woman', was originally used in a pejorative manner to denote women writers. Some of its negative connotations still linger nowadays.
16. See Hooper's comprehensive online resource that aims to record women writers, intellectuals and educators between 1890 and 1936, *The Atlantis Project: Women and Words in Spain, 1890–1936*, <https://web.archive.org/web/20130516094807/http://atlantis.kirstyhooper.net/> [accessed 11 January 2019].

CHAPTER 2

Julia de Asensi:
A Daughter of the Century

Julia de Asensi, who lived between 1849 and 1921, nowadays features as a footnote in Spanish literary annals if mentioned at all, mainly known for her didactic children's tales redolent with Victorian sentimentality. This reduces Asensi to a stern, sepia-coloured matron policing the borders of morality, rather than someone *expanding* the horizon of women, as she took full advantage of the new opportunities that the liberal regime opened up to her. The overview given in this study aspires to recast her as an agent of change rather than just a guardian of the status quo. In other words, it aims to foreground her as both a product and a participant of the liberal project. Yet it was also this level of involvement that made her aware of her limitations. The daughter of a politician, Asensi was born into a family comfortably entrenched within the new political system, but who had to remain at the margins because of her gender. A feeling of discontent with the passive roles allocated to women in shaping these new legislative dynasties thus pervades her writing, yet very few studies highlight it.

Her career as a successful children's writer should be understood within this context, particularly the education reforms that created a new market for pedagogical literature. In a study that explores women's strategies to carve out a space in the genealogical imagination, Asensi's labour as a children's writer can be read as her attempt to influence discourse. If the nation was envisioned as a mother and its citizens as a family, then her authorial voice could reach the nation's children. Seen from this angle, Asensi ceases to be a timid contributor to the period and becomes instead a woman eager to establish her own discursive authority through the means available.

All liberal factions prioritized state education and saw its value, not only in combating dismal illiteracy figures but also as a powerful tool for propaganda. In her *Historia Patria*, Boyd remarks that:

> Realizing that the battle for cultural hegemony between liberalism and Catholic traditionalism involved both institutional and ideological power, liberals prepared draft legislation as early as 1814 creating a national educational system that would reinforce the claims of the liberal state to the primary allegiance of Spaniards. (Boyd 1997: 3)

In this vein, the *Ley de Instrucción Pública de 9 septiembre de 1857* [Public Education Law of 9 September 1857], popularly known as the 'Ley Moyano' [Moyano's Law] after its main sponsor Luis Moyano, established compulsory schooling for girls for the first time (Castro Antonio 2010: 12). It led to the founding of the Escuelas Normales de Maestras [Teacher Training Colleges for Women] in 1858 (Scanlon 1986: 18), as the new law catalyzed demand for female teaching staff, and was, according to Davies, Brewster & Owen (1998: 17), 'the first serious effort to provide training for women teachers'. The Moyano motion had been passed by the moderate government, of which Asensi's father formed part, and incorporated significant chunks of an earlier draft by the previous progressive cabinet. Despite this early attempt at expanding the intellectual and professional horizons of women, the uptake was still slow. Even with the passing of the Ley Moyano, most overviews agree that education of women only gained prominence after the revolution of 1868 (Scanlon 1986: 21; Ballarín Domingo 1989: 255). In her 1868 work *La mujer del porvenir* [The Woman of the Future] the writer and activist Concepción Arenal criticized the meagre options available to women, and her campaign is partly responsible for the founding in 1869 of the Escuela de Institutrices [School for Governesses]. This was followed by the Ateneo Artístico Literario de Señoras [Artistic Literary Atheneum for Ladies] (1870) and the Asociación para la Educación de la Mujer [Association for the Education of Women] (1870).[1] The latter had links to the Instituto Libre de Enseñanza [The Free Educational Institution], started by Gíner de los Ríos — a prominent Krausist — the same year. Named after and inspired by the German philosopher Karl Christian Friedrich Krause (1781–1832), the Krausists were a group of progressive intellectuals who championed education as a key ingredient in the regeneration of the nation. Fellow Krausist Fernando de Castro was amongst those who enthusiastically campaigned for the increased participation of women in the national project, proclaiming that their education was 'una de las cuestiones capitales que el progreso de la civilización ha traído al debate en las sociedades modernas' [one of the main issues that the progress of civilization has brought to the debate in modern societies] (1869: 3). Measured by modern standards, this female visibility was sometimes achieved by rather indirect means. Thus in a series of lectures held in 1868 to promote female education, Castro advises his audience to 'influid en el hombre para que valga y sea algo en la vida e historia de su tiempo' [intervene so that the man becomes worthy and influential during his life and time] (1869: 16). As Ballarín Domingo points out, the education of women was not an end in itself, but rather a means of spreading this social regeneration through their maternal roles (1989: 255). It shows that even a progressive intellectual like Castro subscribed to the idea of women as mothers and educators of future generations rather than out for their own personal development.

Modest or not, these attempts to expand and standardize education led to greater demands for teaching personnel and accompanying instruction manuals, both of which were met eagerly by women. Francis Cough observes how towards the middle of the nineteenth century new paths opened for Spanish women with literary aspirations, allowing them to produce children's literature within a conservative and Catholic framework (2007: 481). Cough includes Asensi amongst the ranks of women who embraced this pedagogical platform to shape public discourse, together with the likes of Pilar Sinués, Pilar Pascual de Sanjuán and Fernán Caballero. Like their male counterparts, history plays an essential part in their output, seen in the legends penned by Caballero, Asensi and Sinués, or the exempla produced by Pascual de Sanjuán with self-explanatory titles such as the successful *La Moral en la Historia: Colección de cuadros históricos con su aplicación al alcance de los niños* [Morality in History: Collection of Historical Tableaus with Its Application Within the Reach of Children], first published in 1869 and re-edited several times, even once posthumously in 1910. That Pascual de Sanjuán appeals to historical continuity as a major source of legitimacy can be seen in the earlier *Preceptos morales para la infancia basados en hechos históricos* [Moral Precepts for Childhood Based on Historical Events], wherein she reasons that:

> Más si nos apoyamos en la autoridad histórica tendrán nuestros discursos la fuerza de la verdad, y aún antes de que nuestros alumnos estén bien instruidos en la Historia, sacaremos para ellos el fruto principal de ésta, que es enseñar con la irresistible lógica de los hechos. (Pascual de Sanjuán 1864: 8)

> [But if we rely on historical authority our speeches will have the power of the truth, and even before our students are properly instructed in History, we will provide them with its main benefit, which is to teach the irresistible logic of events.]

Similarly the author invokes the matriarch metonym that envisions the country as a mother and invests women with a certain authority, exhorting readers to 'Acostúmbrese a designar a la patria con el nombre de segunda madre' [Become accustomed to referring to the homeland as the second mother] (1864: 29). Asensi justifies her own literary incursions with similar tropes, and even shared the same publisher, Editorial Bastinos, which would become one of the main providers for this newfound demand for pedagogical literature.[2] The genre would in turn become a popular platform for women to influence discourse. Forged in this cultural landscape, Asensi is then *una hija del siglo* [a daughter of the century], the title of an 1873 novel by Pilar Sinués, another author whose conservative persona has overshadowed a more complex engagement with her time.

However whilst Sinués was writing her last works, Asensi was taking her first footsteps. Again, Sinués, Pascual de Sanjuán and even Caballero had started their literary careers during the reign of Isabel II, whilst Asensi had witnessed her abdication, a republican interlude and another attempt at constitutional monarchy with a new dynasty before a return to the Bourbons. Asensi should not just be indiscriminately grouped with her Isabelline counterparts under the common denominator of domestic sentimentality. Such generalization is found Francisco Blanco García's influential *La literatura del siglo XIX* [Spanish Literature in the Nineteenth Century] (1894–1903), in which he remarks as a dismissive side note that:

> De intento he reservado para terminar este capítulo la larga y no gloriosa serie de escritoras más o menos consagradas a la imitación y al cultivo de un género

> [la novela romántica] que tanto se adapta a las fogosidades y los arrebatos del sentimentalismo femenino. (Blanco García 1899: 388–89)
>
> [I have tried to save for the end of this chapter the long and unremarkable number of women writers more or less devoted to imitation and to the cultivation of a genre [the romantic novel] so well suited to the passions and outbursts of female sentimentalism.]

Although not sharing this latent misogyny, contemporary critics like Cough run the risk of accidentally demoting the work of these women by identifying their work as neatly fitting the conservative box. This does everyone a disservice and glosses over them as responses to specific historical circumstances. A closer look at the work of Asensi reveals that neither her children's literature nor her other fiction fits neatly into any boxes, revealing layers of meaning that clash with her traditional portrayal as a custodian of domesticity. Asensi avoids hagiography and her stories contain very few heroes and heroines. Instead a more flexible pragmatism informs these stories, guided by economic necessity rather than a strict moral code. Significantly, counterfeit genealogies crop up in some of her output, deceptive orphans in her children's stories and dubious monarchs in her adult fiction. Such a precarious sense of legitimacy stems perhaps from Asensi's interstitial position, being a member of the establishment, yet at the same time a woman. The tale of 'El encubierto' forms the basis of the following chapter, in which Asensi questions origin myths with a historical legend, a genre traditionally associated with the consolidation rather than the unravelling of national mythology. However, to contextualize Asensi's exclusion from the literary genealogies, we need to look closer at her trajectory and her ancestry, which illustrate the narrow narratological possibilities available to women like Asensi, despite her solid education in a liberal tradition, and the equally narrow parameters by which her work is judged by posterity.

The Asensis: A Liberal Dynasty

Born in Madrid in 1849, Julia Asensi y Laiglesia was the third child of Tomás de Asensi y Lugar and María Rosario Laiglesia. Her father, an illustrious diplomat, had been born in Tangier and later became the Spanish consul for Tunisia. This background contributed to his interest in antiquities and his reputation as a preeminent Egyptologist, with some of the pieces he collected now on display in the Spanish National Archaeological Museum. In addition to his diplomatic duties, Don Tomás held other influential posts during the reign of Isabel II, most significantly as a Director of Commerce in the Ministry of State and Secretary of State, a position to which he was appointed in 1856. Asensi's father occupied the more moderate fringes of liberalism, a solid representative of the new political order and accompanying mechanisms of legitimacy. His four children, three girls and one boy, received an excellent education, with a particular emphasis on literature, following the family tradition initiated by his father Manuel de Asensi, Julia's grandfather and General Consul of Spain in his day. In a letter from 1834, a year after the outbreak of the first Carlist War, Don Tomás writes with liberal nationalist fervour that his father aimed to instruct him:

> De un modo que pudiese, a ejemplo suyo, ser útil a su patria: sus servicios casi no fueron recompensados, ni intentó que lo fueran, creyendo que el mejor patrimonio que podía legarle era una esmerada educación literaria, para la cual tuvo que hacer inmensos sacrificios. (quoted in Díez Ménguez 2006: 21)

> [In such a way that he could, through setting an example, be useful to the homeland; he was barely compensated for his services, nor did he seek to be, believing that the best legacy that he could leave was a polished literary education, for which he had to make enormous sacrifices.]

This family narrative fashioned by Julia's father encapsulates the increasingly strong links between literature, the liberal project and the genealogical imagination as the century progressed. Julia's father envisions the education received from his own progenitor at great expense as a patrimony that he must pass on to his descendants. It is this legacy that Julia and her siblings receive, whilst at the same time being bonded by blood to a liberal dynasty of men who occupied key positions within the new regime.

Don Tomás seemed to have fully supported the literary aspirations of his daughter, who already as a precocious seven-year-old produced her first verses. In a brief biography sketched for *Las mujeres españolas, americanas y lusitanas pintadas por sí mismas* [Spanish, American and Lusitanian Women Painted by Themselves] (1886), a volume that counts Asensi amongst its collaborators, Matilde Gómez has left us with the only biographical account of the writer, in which she remarks on this early vocation: 'y desde esta misma edad olvidaba las muñecas y los juegos propios de la infancia por dedicarse a la lectura de libros didácticos, enemigos encarnizados de casi todos los niños' [and from this age she would forget her dolls and other childhood games to dedicate herself to the reading of didactic books, sworn enemies of nearly all children] (1886: 639). Gómez similarly portrays Asensi as an avid reader with an omnivorous taste 'las largas noches de insomnio y las muchas noches que se levantó con el alba para devorar con deleite, ya los sucesos de la historia, ya las poéticas y fantásticas páginas de mitología' [the long sleepless nights and the many times she would get up at dawn to devour with delight historical events or poetic and fantastical pages of mythology] (639). It suggests that Asensi had access to an extensive library, probably one assembled by her father in his cultural crusade. Similarly his passion for collecting antiquities must have imbued his children with a heightened sense of historical awareness. Such a privileged access to the literary stock that fed the historical imagination of the nineteenth century, together with the material artefacts collected by her father — physical repositories of this past — makes Asensi a child of her time, or at least typical of the privileged circles in which she spent her formative years. As Davies, Brewster & Owen (1998: 21) reminds us, in practice only a small percentage of women belonging to the upper echelons of society benefitted from any educational reforms.

Just as Alfonso XII had declared himself in the Sandhurst Manifest to be 'como hombre del siglo, verdaderamente liberal' [as a man of the century, truly liberal] (quoted in Villares & Moreno Luzón 2009: 637–38), Asensi inherits this liberal legacy from her father. She would discreetly revisit it in her precarious position as a woman writer reflecting on an essentially patrilineal legacy — the patrimony described in her father's letter — to which she in practice barely had rights. Her position as an educated woman translated into very little actual power and agency, despite the enthusiastic backing of her family. In real terms, Asensi occupied a marginal branch in the new family trees dreamed up by her father and other liberals.

This gendered straight-jacket must have been a source of frustration for Asensi, as can be gathered from the presence of the highly literate yet socially immobile women who populate her fiction. Such lack of mobility often takes the form of actual spatial constraint, as in her 1889 short novel 'El aeronauta' [The Aeronaut], wherein the protagonist falls in love with the eponymous aeronaut who crashes into her home town, a small hamlet she despises. The inequality is observed by the explorer, free to leave at any time unlike his female counterpart: 'Usted y yo hemos nacido con alas; pero a usted se las cortaron desde que vino al mundo y no cruzará jamás el espacio' [You and I have been born with wings; but yours were clipped at birth and you will never cross the sky] (Asensi 1905: 86).

The added obstacles she faced as a woman did not deter Asensi from pursuing a literary career and carving herself a niche in genres deemed more appropriate for her gender. By 1880, Asensi had amassed sufficient cultural clout to be approached by Emilia Pardo Bazán, who had yet to become the grande dame of Spanish letters, for another short-lived publication *La Revista de Galicia* [The Magazine of Galicia].[3] The year 1880 also marked the beginning of a long and fruitful collaboration with the publishers Biblioteca Universal, where she was the only contemporary woman to contribute an entire volume. That Asensi features in such collection is further proof of the literary renown she had attained. But it also hints at connections with the establishment that might have helped fulfil her literary ambitions at a time when talent far from guaranteed the admission of women into the field. Subsequent reviews of her output that emphasize her modesty and detachment from politics remind us of her peripheral position as a *female* author regardless of flair or connections. As we have seen, Asensi descended from a family who actively contributed to the foundations of this new political legitimacy, but to which she had restricted access due to her gender. She occupies an interstice that, on the one hand, has her entrenched within the establishment and on the other hand relegates her to a marginal position.

Bibliotecas universales: Constructing Literary Lineages

Her involvement with the collection Biblioteca Universal [Universal Library] is of particular interest, partly because 'El encubierto' is published therein. It is a collaboration that previous studies, more interested in her labour as a children's writer, have so far neglected. These so-called 'universal libraries' proliferated in the nineteenth century, product of a liberal nationalism that sought to establish and disseminate a common cultural heritage. In fact, this particular *biblioteca universal* was in turn related to the better known Biblioteca de Autores Españoles [Library of Spanish Authors], which became so intrinsically linked with the national project that it received state sponsorship. Both the genre of 'El encubierto' and its publishing medium lend the story a destabilizing irony. Whilst legends are traditionally linked with the creation of foundational myths, *biblioteca universales* are curated collections that help assemble and disseminate literary genealogies. Yet 'El encubierto' is a tale haunted by its own questioned legitimacy and unresolved ancestry.

Biblioteca Universal had started Colección de los Mejores Autores Antiguos y Modernos Nacionales y Extranjeros [Collection of the Best Writers, Old and Modern, National and Foreign] in 1872 to capture a growing market of readers. Editions like these, which aimed to make cultural milestones more affordable, and were driven by a mixture of patriotism and bourgeois capitalism, reflect the consolidation of the liberal revolution.[4] The collections catered to a growing demographic which recognized the importance of a literary education so ardently endorsed by the father of Asensi a generation earlier. Now ingrained as a status signifier the way coats of arms signalled legitimacy, the tomes that adorned their bookshelves implicitly signalled the importance of literature in the construction of a collective Spanish identity. They became secular bibles that traced the new national genealogies. This is not a coincidence. As pointed out by Gregory Jusdasnis 'though the literary canon functions like the Bible, it actually emerged in western societies when the Bible itself lost its authority as privileged text' (1991: 61). Similarly, José María Jover remarks how the kind of national narrative popularized by the likes of Modesto Lafuente could be seen as 'una especie de biblia secularizada, de libro nacional por excelencia, llamado a ocupar un lugar preferente en despachos y bibliotecas de las clases media y alta' [as a type of secularized bible, the national book per excellence, destined to occupy a special place in the offices and libraries of the middle and upper classes] (1984: 8).

Like the instrumentalization of literary history, the first *bibliotecas universales* were founded in the eighteenth century, informed by the didactic spirit of the Enlightenment. Thus we read in the 3 April 1790 issue of *Correo de Madrid* [The Madrid Mail] about the success of a 'Biblioteca universal o/catálogo abundante de los escritos griegos, latinos y hebreos, publicados y no publicados' [Universal Library or rich catalogue of Greek, Latin and Hebrew writings, published and unpublished]. However, just like literary histories, the *biblioteca universal* format booms in the following century as an efficient vehicle for disseminating liberal nationalism. Although they retain the name, these collections lose the universalist aspirations of the Enlightenment, narrowing their focus to the national. The most famous of these, the Biblioteca de Autores Españoles desde la Formación del Lenguaje hasta Nuestros Días [Library of Spanish Writers from the Formation of Language Until Our Days] (BAE), was launched by Manuel Rivadeneyra in 1846 and continued by his son Adolfo Rivadeneyra until 1880 (Pozuelo Yvancos & Aradra Sánchez 2000: 208). A very conscious attempt to construct a canon and make it available to a wider audience, it can be seen as part of the zeitgeist for national genealogies. Modesto Lafuente would publish the first volume of his *Historia general de España* only four years later, in 1850, with José Amador de los Ríos starting his *Historia crítica de literatura española* in 1861.

The BAE ran out of funds, an incident that, as Guillermo Carnero writes (1998: xxxiv), turned into a matter of state when some members of parliament started to campaign for a government rescue. The state finally agreed to contribute towards the funding of the BAE through the purchase of copies which were then distributed to all national libraries, an act that further legitimized the canon assembled by the Rivadeneyras. The first volume published in 1846, *Obras de Miguel de Cervantes Saavedra* [Works of Miguel de Cervantes Saavedra], follows the now widespread narrative that claims the author of *Don Quixote* to be the epitome of Spanishness, and as remarked by José Carlos Mainer (1994: 36) in the self-explanatory article *La invención de la literatura española* [The Invention of Spanish Literature]: 'abre la colección el tomo dedicado a las novelas de Cervantes, testimonio de una hegemonía que se ha ido asentando desde mediados de la centuria anterior' [the volume dedicated to the novels of Cervantes opens the collection, proof of an hegemony that had been building from the middle of the last century].

In 1872, Rivadeneyra's son published what would be the first two volumes of the Biblioteca Universal: Colección de los Mejores Autores Antiguos y Modernos Nacionales y Extranjeros. The volumes that inaugurate the collection, the medieval epic *Romancero del Cid* [Poem of the Cid] — divided into two parts — similarly follow the literary genealogies forged during this period. The genesis of the nation and the manifestation of its character, that is, its literature, were both located in a mythical Middle Ages and Early Modern period. It was in this *biblioteca universal*, which saw itself as 'destinada a popularizar las obras más notables de la literatura de todas las Naciones' [destined to popularize the most significant literary works of all nations], that Julia de Asensi would publish her *Leyendas y tradiciones en prosa y verso* [Legends and Traditions] in 1883.[5] Asensi's volume joined translated works by the likes of Shakespeare, Dickens, Schiller, Goethe, Petrarch and Dante, selected from the canons of other western countries such as England, Germany and Italy.

The Spanish selection curated by the editors of Biblioteca Universal follows the pattern laid down by the BAE and literary historians, and devotes much space to 'rediscovered' medieval masterpieces such as the various *Romanceros* [Collection of Ballads], together with Golden Age dramatists such as Lope de Vega, Calderón de la Barca and Tirso de Molina. Predictably, the collection features *Obras de Santa Teresa de Jesús* [Works of Saint Teresa of Jesus], one of the few women included in such canons.[6] The female presence is further bolstered by the volume of *Escritoras españolas contemporáneas* [Contemporary Spanish Women Writers] in 1880, a compilation of poetry by women writers edited by Julia de Asensi herself, and with poems by Blanca de los Ríos, Emilia Pardo Bazán and Sofia Casanova, together with older Isabelline writers such as Carolina Coronado, Enriqueta Lozano and Joaquina Balmaseda. With this compilation of over thirty women authors, one could say Asensi is curating her own female genealogy.

Aside from this lyrical anthology, Asensi is the only contemporary female author to contribute to the nearly two hundred volumes published by the Biblioteca Universal between 1872 and 1935, in a trajectory that almost overlaps with that of the Restoration itself.[7] Aside from her *Leyendas y tradiciones*, Asensi has three other works in the collection: the novella *Tres amigas* [Three Female Friends] (1880) which inaugurated her collaboration with the collection; her anthology *Novelas cortas* [Novellas] (1889), some of which had been published in different periodicals; and in 1890 a translation of the epic *Ahasvérus* [Ahasverus] from the 1833 French original by Edgar Quinet.

Her Spanish version of *Ahasvérus* for Biblioteca Universal is one of the many translations done by Asensi throughout her career and which helped readers become familiar with the works of Schiller, Théophile Gautier and the Italian Olindo Guerrini amongst others.[8] It reveals a knowledge of German, French and Italian, languages she must have taught herself and which display the scope of her literary formation championed by her father.[9] Yet ironically, the liberal project's preoccupation for identifying works intrinsic to a particular nation and a shared culture at the expense of foreign influences, meant that many of these translated texts were forgotten. As Henriette Partzsch puts it:

> In other words, the relevance of imported texts is solely judged by their importance for today's literary canon. This perspective continues to ignore the majority of texts that circulated among and were used by historical readers, thus effectively impeding a better understanding of the history of literary culture. (Partzsch 2014: 282–83).

The translation efforts of Asensi, together with those of many other women (and men), continue to be neglected.

The partnership of Asensi with Biblioteca Universal confirms her position within the cultural establishment that emerged from liberal nationalism and its attempts to implant a collective homogenized literary lineage. Whether her involvement with the Biblioteca Universal was based on literary merit alone, or she benefitted from being the daughter of a former Secretary of State, the publishing medium shows that Asensi was not a daughter merely of her father, but also of the liberalist project he helped consolidate. The significance of *Leyendas y tradiciones*, of which 'El encubierto' forms part, must be understood in the light of the medium in which they were published. As part of a collection specifically assembled to enlighten readers on the most representative writers of each country and age, Asensi advances the cultural catechism preached by her father and grandfather on the centrality of literature in the formation of a national conscience.

'The Discreet Authoress' and the Apolitical Asensi

This overview of Asensi's literary trajectory demonstrates how she contributed to the collective historical imagination despite a conscious effort to not broach the subject of politics, and how she was destined to be seen as apolitical both by her contemporaries and by modern critics like Díez Ménguez. The reception of her legends shows that her stories did not incite debate, perhaps intentional on the part of an author wary of criticism. Instead she shields herself in a modesty topos, as was customary of many women writers at the time.[10] In a rare candid moment, or perhaps a textbook example of this modesty topos — it could be read as both —

Asensi alludes to the predicament that affected many of her female contemporaries in her poem 'Tus cantares' [Your Songs]. Written in 1890, when Asensi was already an established writer, she confesses to a male friend that:

> Quieres saber amigo, qué he pensado
> del libro que estos días me enviaste,
> y del que un ejemplar me has dedicado,
> que Más notas perdidas titulaste.
> Porque mi atrevimiento no comenten
> nunca quise escribir nada profundo,
> mas tu libro es de aquellos que se sienten
> y que puede juzgarlos todo el mundo.
> Gracias te doy por él por vez primera,
> y faltando a una idea en mí arraigada,
> ofrezco mi opinión franca y sincera,
> aunque tal parecer no valga nada. (Asensi 1890: 209)

> [You want to know my friend, what I thought,
> of the book you sent me recently,
> and one of the copies of which you dedicated to me
> that you called More Lost Notes.
> So that my audacity is not commented
> I never wished to write anything profound,
> but your book is one of those that are felt
> and that can be understood by everyone.
> I thank you, which is a first for me,
> and disregarding an idea deeply entrenched within me,
> I offer my frank and sincere opinion,
> even if it might not be worth anything.]

The following extracts from two reviews in the wake of the publication of *Leyendas y tradiciones* illustrate on one hand the success she enjoyed, and on the other hand, her portrayal as a demure and politically detached writer. The first one appeared in the 7 May 1883 edition of the long-running centrist daily newspaper *La Época* [The Times], where another legend within the volume, 'El Caballero de Olmedo' [The Knight of Olmedo], had graced its pages earlier in the year. The second review can be found a few weeks later in the 1 July issue of *La Ilustración de la Mujer* [Woman's Illustrated Magazine], a fortnightly publication and one of the many magazines dedicated to the illustration of a growing female readership. Its author is another female peer, the well-known writer and journalist Josefa Pujol de Collado. Both reviewers emphasize the prudent nature of the author by the constant invocation of 'discreta autora' [discreet authoress], a particularly popular combination used to describe women who had transgressed the domestic sphere. Thus *La Época* opens its review with: 'La discreta autora de la novela *Tres amigas* y otras composiciones literarias, el mérito de alguna de las cuales han podido apreciar los lectores de *La Época*' [The discreet authoress of the novel *Three Female Friends* and other literary compositions, the merits of some these having already been sampled by the readers of *La Época*] (Anon. 1883: 4), whereas *La Ilustración de la Mujer* closes its review with the conclusion that the stories collected 'harán justicia a las dotes eminentemente literarias que adornan a su ilustrada y discreta autora' [will do justice to the clear literay talent of its learned and discreet author] (Pujol de Collado 1883: 22).

Similarly, both appraisals emphasize in the opening paragraph the prestige associated with Biblioteca Universal, as Asensi joins the illustrious company of Cervantes and Shakespeare, at least in its catalogue. *La Ilustración de la Mujer* introduces the writer as 'la joven y ya conocida escritora D.ª Julia de Asensi, en uno de los tomos que componen la acreditada Biblioteca Universal ha publicado recientemente una preciosa colección de *Leyendas y tradiciones*' [the young and already known writer Julia de Asensi, in one of the volumes that form part of the prestigious Biblioteca Universal, has recently published a lovely collection of *Leyendas y tradiciones*] (Pujol de Collado 1883: 22). This is echoed by *La Época* that remarks that Asensi:

> Ha merecido la honra de figurar en la 'Colección de los mejores autores antiguos y modernos, nacionales y extranjeros', que hace años publica con éxito muy favorable y a ínfimo precio la 'Biblioteca Universal' en la cual se ha refundido la Biblioteca de Autores Españoles. (Anon. 1883: 4)
>
> [Has had the honour of featuring in the 'Collection of Best Authors, Old and New, National and Foreign' that the 'Biblioteca Universal' has now been publishing for years and for an insignificant price, and of which the Collection of Best Authors is now part.]

Here the main difference between the two publications lies in the emphasis *La Ilustración de la Mujer* puts on the feminine qualities of the writer, whereas *La Época* prefers to highlight the shared parentage of the Biblioteca Universal and Biblioteca de Autores Españoles. The more extensive piece in *La Ilustración* is thus punctuated by variants of the mollifying 'delicadeza' and 'dulzura' as if to absolve Asensi from any potential subversion, and in turn *La Ilustración* itself for endorsing her work. The newspaper *La Época*, on the other hand, mouthpiece of the Conservative party of Cánovas and thus staunch supporter of the Restoration, feels more confident in its social status. It chooses instead to highlight the institutional stamp of approval achieved by being part of the Biblioteca Universal. This had also been mentioned by *La Ilustración* — yet further proof of the discreet credentials of Asensi — but it is expanded by *La Época* to emphasize the connection of the Biblioteca Universal with the now well-known Biblioteca de Autores Españoles ('and of which the Collection of Best Authors is now part'). Since the state had agreed to support the latter financially, it would also be of interest to *La Época*, platform for the Conservative government, to advertise the now sponsored Biblioteca de Autores Españoles.

The presence of Asensi in the newspaper not only orients us towards her position within the literary landscape, but also reveals her family connections. Several of her stories graced the pages of *La Época* between 1880 and 1885, amongst them the previously mentioned 'El caballero de Olmedo' that would later be included in *Leyendas y tradiciones*. Whether *La Época* reflects her own views, on paper she aligns herself with the moderate liberalism espoused by her father, former Secretary of State under Isabel II. *La Época* and *La Ilustración de la Mujer* are both illustrative examples of the kind of publication that hosted the writings of Asensi and have contributed in turn to shape her apolitical profile. None of these publications was neutral of course, as part of the establishment papers like *La Época* sat comfortably within the status quo. Initiatives like *La Ilustración de la Mujer* on the other hand, felt compelled to reassure readers that they had no intention of disrupting this status quo whilst contributing to the platforms available to women to express themselves publicly.

Asensi continued to be a fixture in the press throughout the 1890s, particularly in *El Álbum Iberoamericano* [The Iberian-American Album], a transatlantic weekly founded by the indefatigable writer and journalist Concepción Gimeno y Flaquer, another contemporary who swelled the ranks of women in the public arena. However, whereas the deaths of Ríos and Burgos were widely reported in the press, when Asensi died in 1921 her passing went almost unnoticed and at no point was she inducted into the canon.

Thus despite her association with a genre that fostered the pedagogical role of women, and the mother in particular, as an educator of her children, Asensi, herself childless, failed to conform to the conventional patterns of domesticity, dedicating some of her stories instead to her nieces (Diéz Ménguez 2006: 41). This can be seen in her work too — seemingly straightforward children's stories contain unexpected genealogies. 'El retrato vivo' [Spitting Image] (1897) and *La hija de Villoria* [Villoria's Daughter] (1901) are two examples that illustrate this departure from traditional tropes. The orphan protagonist of 'El retrato vivo' conforms initially to the archetype of the Dickensian urchin forced to navigate the harsh realities of a period with little institutional support, but whose unshakable moral compass attracts the charity of a private benefactor. Gustavo, however, unlike Oliver Twist, does not turn out to be of gentle birth, and undermines the idea that a noble character must reflect a noble birth, or as Gilmartin (1998: 12) summarizes this trope: 'Pedigree is often restored retroactively, and this formula is repeatedly employed in eighteenth and nineteenth-century novels'. Asensi's character, on the other hand, finds happiness through complicit mutual deception by pretending to be the deceased child of his wealthy patron, who wants to *believe* her child never died and finds in Gustavo his spitting image. A short children's tale, 'El retrato vivo' might lack the length associated with the emblematic Realist saga preoccupied with social ills and inequalities, but it nevertheless reflects how morality might be compromised by the effects of indigence and extreme poverty. The opposite happens in *La hija de Villoria*, where the young protagonist lies about her origins when it transpires that she hails from privileged stock, preferring instead to remain with her loving foster family and revoke her inheritance: 'No encontró nunca a su familia, pero ¿Qué le importaba?' [She never found her family, but why would she care?] (Asensi 1901: 16). None of these children seem particularly attached to their place of origin. In 'El retrato vivo', the young Gustavo, an orphan displaced by war, hears the distant ring of church bells as he is dozing off, and laments his destiny: 'Así sonaba la de mi parroquia cuando yo, tenía patria' [That's how the bells of my parish church rang when I had a country] (Asensi 1897: 2). Yet Gustavo is not allowed to dwell further on his rootlessness, and Asensi follows this yearning with the remark 'pero como Gustavo era un niño, aquella preocupación le duró poco, y al fin se durmió profundamente' [but because Gustavo was a child, such worry did not last, and he finally fell into a deep sleep] (2). This observation, which deflates any potential melodrama, seems to contradict the patriotism Pascual de Sanjuán wishes to instil in students in her *Preceptos morales para la infancia*: 'Como amáis las paredes de vuestro hogar, amareis después el hogar que os vio nacer' [As you love the walls of your home, you will love the home that saw you being born] (1864: 28). Such examples show that even the children's stories Asensi penned should not be easily dismissed as mere propaganda for a simplified conservative agenda.

Yet she remains a footnote, and this peripheral positioning translates into a dearth of bibliographical work on her literary output that continues to the present day. The few studies on Asensi, whilst foregrounding the socio-economic changes that opened more platforms for women, still paint Asensi with a rather conservative brush. Castro Antonio, whose study focuses on Asensi's production as a children's writer concludes that despite her female protagonists often taking the initiative, they still do not deviate from the status quo (2010: 15). Asensi's main biographer, Isabel Díez Ménguez, reaches similar conclusions. Hamstrung by traditional nomenclature, so often ill-equipped to reflect the female experience, Díez Ménguez pegs Asensi as a 'romántica rezagada' [arrested Romantic] (1999: 1353), and thus implicitly writes her out of her own time, an accidental exclusion further addressed in the following chapter on her historical legends. A complex legacy has thus been reduced to a few children's stories re-edited in recent times as part of a modest effort to mark the 150th anniversary of her birth.[11] Some of her works are also available on the state-funded online repository Cervantes Virtual, an institutional nod to a woman with a family tree so deeply rooted in the liberal establishment that catalyzed the infrastructure of the modern state.

Tres amigas: Looking for Female Literary Genealogies

However amongst the slim bibliographical pickings, Mark R. Malin (2003) bucks the trend, and offers a suggestive reading of the short novel *Tres amigas* (1880), wherein the three eponymous friends are hampered not only by societal conventions, but also by genres deemed suitable for women. It seems fitting to conclude this overview with Malin's conclusions on *Tres amigas*, a work written at the beginning of her career that already clearly shows how Asensi, like many of her contemporaries, struggled to find a narrative that accommodated her subjectivity but that did not transgress the strict limits imposed by patriarchy. Malin's reading foregrounds the little room women had for manoeuvre and their imposed domesticity expressed literally through spatial restrictions: the female protagonists often find themselves confined to interiors from which they look longingly through windows to the outside world. Approaching the text from a genealogical perspective provides a similar conclusion to that of the spatial angle employed by Malin: the discursive disenfranchisement of women.

Thus one could say that the three friends establish a secular sisterhood outside the convent in which they have been educated, as they search for a place in the new national genealogies taking shape. Again, like in many of her works, this dimension was overlooked, beginning with Luis Alfonso, author of the book's preface, who sees *Tres amigas* merely as 'un estudio de mujer, por mujer y para mujer' [a study of women, by a woman, for women] (Asensi 1880: iv), removing it completely from any political reality. Once more, Asensi is placed in a separate matrilineal tree with gender and sentimentality as distinguishing traits, overshadowing any other preoccupations.

In a narrative structured as an epistolary exchange between three former school friends, Teresa, Susana and Luisa, we follow their travails as they go their separate ways after leaving the convent where they had been educated. Teresa remains within its walls as she takes her vows. Susana finds herself embroiled in a storyline reminiscent of a Gothic romantic novel, involving gloomy castles and cursed bloodlines, before she marries and enters placid domesticity. Luisa's fall from grace, on the other hand, resembles a Naturalist narrative. Forced to return to a life of squalor and an alcoholic father, Luisa, fearing for her virtue, rejects the advances of a wealthy libertine and duly succumbs to a broken heart. Asensi might dabble with the conventions of Romanticism or Naturalism, yet Malin notes that 'in *Tres amigas*, de Asensi includes scenes which through their formalistic qualities, border on the romantic and naturalistic, yet she does not fully cross the threshold, subtly and perhaps unconsciously symbolizing women's exclusion from the dominant ideology and discourse of these movements' (2003: 106). *Tres amigas* can be read as a search for a literary tradition that would legitimize the experiences of women who find themselves ideologically bereft in the new political order. That all three women are orphans becomes a suggestive coincidence — excluded from male discourse, they lack a mother and a female genealogy to look back on. From this perspective, it is no coincidence that Teresa shares her name with her illustrious predecessor Saint Teresa of Jesus, one of the two women who together with Isabel the Catholic, according to Sofía Casanova, had not been erased from historical memory. Like her namesake, she chooses the convent, and unlike her two other correspondents, Teresa seems content from the outset with her place. After all, she can look back on a literary tradition embodied by Santa Teresa — identified as *castiza* and inducted into the canon. Leading a tranquil life away from worldly matters, she becomes instead the mostly silent recipient of epistles from Susana and Luisa, as they grapple with life post school, each one engaged in a narrative that does not fully convince them. All three of them have been the recipients of an excellent education that, particularly in Luisa's case, only draws attention to the gender gap. It echoes the situation faced by Asensi, educated on par with her brothers, yet often reduced to role of onlooker as her male relatives shaped national affairs. The more outspoken Pardo Bazán explicitly addresses this widening gap between the sexes in nation-building in an article originally published for the English publication *Fortnightly Review*:

> Repito que la distancia social entre los dos sexos es hoy mayor que era en la España antigua, porque el hombre ha ganado nuevos derechos y franquicias que la mujer no comparte [...]. Cada nueva conquista del hombre en el terreno de las

libertades políticas, ahonda el abismo moral que le separa de la mujer, y hace el papel de ésta más pasivo y enigmático. (Pardo Bazán 1999: 89)

[I repeat that the social distance between the two sexes is larger today than it was in the Spain of the past, because men have gained new rights and privileges that women do not share [...]. Each new gain by the man in the terrain of political freedoms widens the moral chasm that separates him from the woman, and makes her role even more passive and enigmatic.]

Pardo Bazán's article had appeared in 1890, a decade after *Tres amigas* and the year universal suffrage was finally passed in Spain, a step that further widened this gender chasm. However not even the more progressive republican interlude had considered extending the female vote or field of operations outside the domestic realm. Speaking to a female audience in 1869, future president of the republic Francisco Pi i Margall, warned that women should abstain from 'mezclarse en nuestras sangrientas luchas civiles' [getting mixed up in our bloody civil wars], and instead they should 'influir en la política, sin separarse del hogar doméstico' [exert their influence in politics, without leaving the domestic confines] by being a moral compass to their husbands and children (quoted by Espigado Tocino 2010: 160).

In *Tres amigas*, the two unsatisfied friends receive letters of consolation from Teresa that the reader never sees but has instead recounted in the replies of Susana and Luisa. The absence of the original source begs the question of what were Teresa's exact words and how much of it is the interpretation or projection by Susana and Luisa to justify their own conclusions.[12] The end of *Tres amigas* already reveals an author concerned with the narrow range of options available to women, which, as Pardo Bazán had remarked, the more meritocratic liberal regime had only seemed to accentuate. After Luisa dies, the story concludes with Teresa telling her remaining friend Susana: 'Tú casada, Luisa muerta, yo monja... ¿cuál será la más dichosa de las tres?' [You married, Luisa dead, I a nun... who is happiest of all three?] (1880: 78). It is a startling comparison that gives death an equal footing with marriage and religious vocation in the pursuit of happiness available to women (Malin 2003: 104). Such dramatic reasoning does not sit well with the image of an author content with her role in society, as claimed by Luis Alfonso in the preface. One cannot escape the fact that Asensi seems to imply — accidentally or not — that marriage is commensurate with death.

Well received by the press, the dissatisfaction in *Tres amigas* was never picked up by any of the critics who reviewed the work. Yet interestingly enough, the imagery employed by the newspaper *El Globo* [The Globe] reminds us once more of how entrenched the genealogical imagination was in nineteenth-century culture. Although the three friends were educated equally, they endured disparate fates, and are envisioned as 'el tronco del pomposo árbol, varias y diversamente inclinadas las ramas que lo forman' [as the trunk of the magnificent tree, the branches that form it being varied and differently inclined] (Anon. 1880: 3). For a now forgotten book that addresses the difficulty for women to participate in dominant discourses and to produce works within genres deemed representative of the political reality, it is ironic that the anonymous critic should hail *Tres amigas* as a perfect example of the

Spanish novel. In his conclusion, one reads that:

> Por lo demás, esta última ha venido a confirmar también esta vez, una opinión que ha tiempo teníamos formada; la novela española existe, pero con rarísimas excepciones, y dígase lo que quiera, no la conoce el público ni aciertan a dar con ellas nuestros editores. (Anon. 1880: 3)

> [As for the rest, this last one has confirmed this time too, an opinion we already have formed; the Spanish novel exists, but with very rare exceptions — and one can say what one will — the public has no knowledge of it nor can our editors manage to find these novels.]

Tres amigas remains a work little-known by readers, which gives the closing remarks a prophetic fatalism:

> No olviden estos y aquel, que las perlas no flotan de ordinario en las superficies de las olas; se hallan en el fondo del mar o en las cavidades de las rocas, encerradas en sus conchas de nácar, y es forzoso bucear para cogerlas. (Anon. 1880: 3)

> [Neither he nor they should forget that pearls do not normally float on top of waves; they are found at the bottom of the sea, or in the cavity of rocks, locked within their mother-of-pearl shells, so that diving is required to get them.]

The image involuntarily brings to mind Casanova's 'cuál Atlántida que devoró el mar' [like Atlantis swallowed by the sea] (1910: 5), her complaint that only Saint Teresa and Isabel the Catholic remained in the cultural cartography of the nation. *Tres amigas,* a rare pearl according to the critic, would be swallowed by the sea. Asensi herself did not follow the paths open to her three protagonists: the convent, marriage or early death. Instead, like other women, she attempts to forge different paths to legitimacy, whether this is through her labour as a children's writer or her collaboration with the Biblioteca Universal in a bid for discursive authority. Analysis of 'El encubierto' shows an Asensi deeply acquainted with the political landscape of her time in spite of her claim that 'nunca quise escribir nada profundo' [I never wished to write anything profound] (1890: 209).

Notes to Chapter 2

1. For an overview of the education of women during the second half of the nineteenth century and first decades of the twentieth, see Davies, Brewster & Owen (1998: 16–21).
2. In addition to the publishing house, Juan Bastinos also founded *El Monitor de la primera enseñanza* [The Guide to Early Education] (1859–1928), which would become the longest running magazine of its kind. His son Antonio J. Bastinos would take over the publishing house as well as launching the Biblioteca Rosa, which counted Julia de Asensi amongst its contributing authors. For more information on Editorial Bastinos, see Infantes de Miguel, López & Botrel (2003) and Durán i Sanpere (1952).
3. This collaboration between Pardo Bazán and Julia de Asensi is barely known. A later, established Pardo Bazán would gloss over this youthful foray into publishing that no longer fitted with her persona (Freire López 1999).
4. Antonio Palau y Dulcet's *Manual del librero hispanoamericano* [Manual of the Hispanic-American Bookseller] testifies to the popularity of this format, with over thirty pages dedicated to different *bibliotecas*, from literary ones to scientific ones (1949: 227–50).
5. Quotation taken from an advertisement that ran in several publications, including the 1 June 1895 issue of *El Nuevo Régimen* [The New Regime].

6. Even nowadays, Saint Teresa is one of the few women present in canons. In a survey of the reading lists provided to postgraduates at American universities, Saint Teresa ranks second after Emilia Pardo Bazán. Together with Rosalía de Castro, they feature as the three women who appear in over fifty percent of syllabi (Brown & Johnson 1998: 1–19). The revival of Saint Teresa in the nineteenth century as a hallmark of the Spanish soul is further addressed in the introduction of Blanca de los Ríos, an author who enthusiastically contributed to her myth.
7. Palau y Dulcet's *Manual del librero hispanoamericano* lists 187 in total (1949: 247), although the catalogue of the Biblioteca Nacional de España holds up to volume 191, Lope de Vega's *Los comendadores de Córdoba* [The Knight-Commanders of Cordoba] published in 1935. No volumes have been found from 1936, the year the Palau y Dulcet manual claims to be the last publication date of this collection.
8. The Italian poet Olindo Guerrini (1845–1916) published under different pseudonyms, including Lorenzo Stecchetti, under which he appears in Simón-Palmer's bibliographical compilation.
9. It is also possible that Asensi translated Schiller from a French translation instead of the German original. Many English and German works in the nineteenth century were often made accessible through a French translation.
10. The strategic function of the modesty topos in the writing of women has itself become a popular object of study by feminist scholars, more recently by Shira Wolosky who defines its texture as 'instead of being viewed only as self-effacement in polar opposition to positive self-assertion, modesty within nineteenth-century female culture represents a complex negotiation between these two poles in ways that redefine both' (2010: 2).
11. Trymar, the publisher of Castro Antonio's *Julia de Asensi: el camarada* [Julia de Asensi: The School Friend] (2010), had earlier in 2007 commissioned a Galician translation of the collection *Las estaciones, cuentos para niños y niñas* [The Stations, Tales for Boys and Girls], with the financial support of the Ministerio de Cultura. Similarly *Cocos y hadas* [Bogeymen and Fairies] (1897) received the same treatment, and a Galician version came out in 2011. They constitute the only two books to have been reedited since the 1920s, when the Biblioteca Universal republished parts of its catalogue, including titles by Asensi.
12. In this respect, Teresa enjoys a similar semiotic status as the historical Santa Teresa who between 1880 and 1930 becomes a national symbol and convergent point for often contradictory discourses on gender, spirituality and the nation (Dupont 2012).

CHAPTER 3

❖

Alternative Lineages: 'El encubierto' and the Myth of the Returning King

This chapter explores the myth of the returning king in 'El encubierto' [The Shrouded/ Cloaked One], the opening tale in *Leyendas y tradiciones en prosa y verso* [Legends and Traditions in Prose and Verse] written by Julia de Asensi in 1883. The story takes its name after the eponymous Encubierto, a mysterious figure who in the sixteenth century maintained himself to be the long-lost grandchild of the Catholic Monarchs. Although he never succeeded in his attempts to be acknowledged as the legitimate heir, his claims enjoyed a long afterlife. Nearly two hundred years later, his story would gain traction amongst nineteenth-century writers and historians. As one of the stories that feeds into the myth of the returning king, 'El Encubierto' became a useful locus for exploring the role and function of the monarch in the framework of the modern nation-state (García-Cárcel 1981: 6). Furthermore, El Encubierto's uncertain origins provided perfect fodder for reimaginings and would be revisited during the 1800s, particularly during the reign of Isabel II. As Muñoz Sempere (2011: 69) has remarked, the profusion of works centered on alternative royal lineages bears witness to the growing disenchantment with the first constitutional Spanish sovereign in both the liberal and conservative camps. Well-known examples include the historic novel by Patricio de la Escosura, *Ni rey ni roque* [Not a Single Living Soul] (1835), José Zorrilla's play *Traidor, inconfeso y mártir* [Traitor, Unconfessed and Martyr] (1849) and *El cocinero de Su Majestad o El pastelero de Madrigal* [His Majesty's Cook or the Baker from Madrigal] (1862) by Manuel Fernández y González. As we will see, 'El Encubierto' spawned its own subgenre yet Asensi's contribution remains overlooked. My aim here is, therefore, to recast the story as a product of liberal nationalism. Whether it is a conscious move or not, the choice of subject reveals the immersion of Asensi in the ideological landscape of the time. Within this socio-historical context, two aspects in particular stand out in her version of such a loaded figure. Firstly, and mirroring real events, the identity of El Encubierto is never established. It remains unresolved whether he was the returning rightful heir to the throne or just an impostor. Secondly, El Encubierto is unable to contest or defend any of these claims, as he has been dead for years by the time the story starts. With no physical presence, he has been reduced to an abstract construction that fits into whichever vision the different narrators espouse. If anything, he embodies history, his memory a contested site for the pronunciation of different visions of the past. In this way, both the unresolved ending and the absence of the main character, who still takes centre stage through his supporters and detractors, raises interesting points on the dynamics of historical construction. Incorporating elements from past re-imaginings of the episode, Asensi's adaptation stands out for its complete lack of closure. It defies the cohesive impulse and search for meaning that characterizes the act of storytelling. Furthermore, El Encubierto takes on a literal significance and remains hidden from the readers too, unable to offer his own version and only present in the memory of other characters.

The story of the returning king remained a popular platform to discuss the legitimacy of monarchy throughout the century, and yet Asensi's version has been depoliticized and labelled as a belated manifestation of a now residual Romanticism. In the only study dedicated to Asensi's legends, Díez Ménguez (1999: 1385) identifies historical fiction as a genre favoured by women writers long after its peak, and which she sees as partly responsible for prolonging Romanticism until the closing decades of the nineteenth century.

It is a sentiment repeated by Castro Antonio, who like Díez Ménguez labels *Leyendas y tradiciones* a strand of belated or arrested Romanticism (2010: 59) and in turn quotes another critic who similarly concurs that 'creo que el influjo más claro y notorio del romanticismo en la época que le sigue es la persistencia de la tradición legendaria' [Romanticism's clearest and most obvious influence in the period that follows is the persistence of legends as a genre] (Cossío 1960: 117). These readings reduce Asensi to a peripheral role within a feminine genealogy united by the common denominator of a *timeless* sentimentalism rather than a *timely* response, product of a specific socio-economic context.

El Encubierto had accumulated a long literary tradition by the time Asensi decided to compose her own version in 1883. The dubious monarch had an extensive literary lineage to his name, with adaptations traceable back to the sixteenth century. Diego Jiménez de Enciso (1585–1634), a Golden Age playwright, had already dramatized the story in his *El encubierto*, of unknown date. Written during the reign of Felipe II, descendant of the Catholic Monarchs, Enciso presents El Encubierto's claims as ultimately false. This is partly because any validation could have questioned the legitimacy of the ruling monarch Felipe III and cast doubt on the loyalty of Enciso himself.

We have to wait until the nineteenth century and the rise of the liberal project before the often-conflicting versions of El Encubierto, his significance and his legacy start to multiply. Similarly, the conflict associated with him, the *Rebelión de las germanías*, or 'Revolt of the Brotherhoods', also experienced a subsequent instrumentalization in conceptions of history at variance with each other. The revolt unfolded between 1519 and 1523 in the Kingdom of Valencia against the government of Carlos I. As with many confrontations, it was driven by clashing economic interests; reduced to its most simplified form it was mainly a confrontation between two factions: the landed nobility, who controlled agriculture and the countryside, and the *germanías*, or guilds, who controlled light manufacturing, crafts and the cities.

The war, which took place at the beginning of the reign of Carlos I, coincided roughly with the uprising of the so-called *comuneros* in neighbouring Castile.[1] Both conflicts would later be romanticized by liberals as early manifestations of the ascendancy of the bourgeoisie and its rebellion against the despotic absolutism of the decadent Habsburg House, held as partly responsible for the stagnation and decadence of Spain (Pérez Viejo 2013: 486). The instrumentalization of the pretender's pedigree in this new political climate can be seen in *El encubierto de Valencia, drama en cinco actos y en verso* [The Cloaked One from Valencia, a Play in Five Acts in Verse] written by Antonio García Gutiérrez in 1840, who backs El Encubierto's claims as genuine. The sympathies of García Gutiérrez did not lie with the regime of Isabel II, as is made patently clear in his poem '¡Abajo los Borbones!' [Down with the Bourbons!] composed after the dethronement of the queen in 1868. In his *El encubierto de Valencia,* a character alludes to the tarnished legacy the protagonist, having just uncovered his royal roots, might inherit: 'Sí; más de una corona, profanada — por la frente de un déspota' [Yes, but it is a crown desecrated — by the brow of a despot] (1840: 47). It is a clear swipe at another Bourbon, Fernando VII, the father of Isabel II, whose absolutist tendencies repeatedly obstructed the agenda of liberals like García Gutiérrez desirous of implanting a constitutional model.

Some regionalists also rallied around the figure of El Encubierto, now fashioned as a Romantic hero who defends the downtrodden burghers and peasants of Valencia against an oppressive aristocracy and the centralist attempts of Carlos I. This version is found in the historical novel *El encubierto de Valencia, leyenda histórica del siglo XVI,* [The Cloaked One from Valencia, Historical Legend from the Sixteenth Century] written by Vicente Boix in 1852. Other historians saw a historical resonance between this revolt and more current insurrections, such as the so-called 'Cantonal Revolution' of the 1860s, which also unfolded in part of the Levantine region.[2] This school of thought is illustrated by Manuel Fernández Herreros, who in 1870 published *Historia de las germanías de Valencia: breve reseña del levantamiento republicano de 1869* [The History of the Valencian Guilds: Brief Summary of the Republican Uprising of 1869].

El Encubierto's portrayal as a champion of regional rights against a centralist government, together with his claims to descend from the legitimate male line, did not make him a popular figure amongst the historians of the later Restoration. They were uncomfortably close to the claims held by supporters of the first pretender Carlos V and his heirs who had refused to accept that the throne could be succeeded to by a woman, even after Fernando VII changed the law in favour of his daughter, the future Isabel II. Disputes over succession led to the Carlist wars that would shadow the first footsteps of the constitutional monarchy inaugurated with Isabel's ascension and later that of her son Alfonso XII.[3] Similarly some conservative regionalist factions aligned themselves with Carlists to defend their interests and regional privileges against centralist policies. Given this background, it makes sense that those affiliated with the government would wish to undermine the myth of the regional redeemer. Official portrayals of El Encubierto that claim him to be a fraud stem from a desire to cement the legitimacy of the newly reinstalled Bourbons after the tumultuous republican interlude and the perpetual Carlist threat. The historian Manuel Danvila y Collado chose to corroborate this version in his 1884 inaugural speech as a member of the Real Academia de la Historia [Royal Academy of History]. To assert his own credentials, Danvila y Collado claims that 'los novelistas y autores dramáticos, al apoderarse del episodio histórico de la Germanía de Valencia, han desnaturalizado los tipos de sus hombres atribuyéndoles proporciones y calidades imaginarias según el pensamiento cardinal de sus obras' [novelists and playwrights, by claiming the historical episode of the Valencian guilds, have stripped these men of context claiming for them dimensions and imaginary characteristics that reflect the main ideas of their own works] (1884: 47).

The historian Ricardo García Cárcel's summing-up of the competing discourses on the figure of El Encubierto and his role in the Revolt of the Brotherhoods is worth quoting at length:

> La historiografía del XIX se fragmenta en dos tendencias contrapuestas: la corriente romántico-liberal que mitifica las Germanías paralelamente a las Comunidades a través de un liberalismo que tiene mucho de liberal, con nacionalismo xenófobo y un antiaustracismo militante, y la revisionista que pretende con aparato científico erudito justificar su ideología claramente conservadora. (García Cárcel 1981: 16)

> [Nineteenth-century historiography splits into two opposing tendencies: the romantic-liberal stream that mythologizes the *Germanías* in parallel with regional movements through a liberalism that is largely liberal, together with a xenophobic nationalism and a militant anti-Habsburg stance, and on the other end a revisionist stream that pretends to justify a clearly conservative ideology under the guise of a scientific and erudite cloak.]

Los encubiertos: The Many Pasts

The legend of El Encubierto, as told by Asensi, takes place in 1526 and narrates the return of the fictitious Don Lorenzo Valdés to his hometown of Valencia after years of absence during which he has amassed a fortune in the New World. On his journey home, he notices that the local inn has changed owner and upon enquiry is told by a group of children that this is due to a recent war, a reference to the Revolt of the Brotherhoods: 'Ha habido una guerra que dice mi padre se llama nacional o cosa así, entre pobres y ricos, nobles y plebeyos' [There has been a war that my father says is called national or something like that, between rich and poor, nobles and plebeians] (Asensi 1883: 7–8).

Don Lorenzo also learns about the death of Vicente Peris, real life historical figure and a leader of the band of *germanías*. His death had represented a great blow to the fortunes of the warring guilds until a new leader emerged in the form of the enigmatic figure of El Encubierto, whose origins were uncertain although he proclaimed himself to be of noble descent. The Royalist authorities placed a large reward on his head, and eventually had him caught and executed. His true identity still remains a mystery, both in reality and in fiction. As some historians point out

(Salle 2002, García Cárcel 1981), very little is actually known about the real life El Encubierto due to a scarcity of reliable records. On the one hand there is the dubious objectivity of overwhelmingly negative portrayals circulated by the authorities. On the other hand we have accounts by authors who were more invested in the dramatic potential of El Encubierto's exploits than in historical accuracy.

Asensi does not commit herself to any single version of the story, and hers is the only known adaptation to avoid doing so. In her take, two different family members — sympathizers of each faction — present their stories to Lorenzo, recently returned from the colonies and neutral in the conflict, having neither been in the country at the time nor affected by the events narrated. First his older brother Antonio, one of the men who captured El Encubierto and brought him to justice, lays out his version. But before Antonio begins his tale, he pre-emptively discredits any other potential interpretations: 'la historia novelesca, en la que yo no creo [...] ya te la contarán mi mujer, mi nuera o mi nieta; la real, hela aquí' [the novelesque story, the one I don't believe [...] my wife, daughter-in-law or niece will surely tell you; the real version you'll find here] (Asensi 1883: 13–14). By explicitly identifying his wife and other female relatives as acolytes of El Encubierto, Antonio claims objectivity at the expense of portraying these women as easily seduced by novelistic figures. Undermining female objectivity, Antonio insists that El Encubierto was just a conniving charlatan who sought power and who, despite messianic delusions of grandeur, was actually a Jewish convert, a rather damning allegation during the height of the Inquisition. 'Convert' in this context should be read as a byword for 'impostor' rather than a deeper reflection on the alleged Jewish origins of El Encubierto. That is, in the eyes of his enemies, he does not descend from Christian lineage but from an alternative counterfeit genealogy that only has a veneer of Christianity (the irony of course remains that Christ was of Jewish descent). Antonio attempts to delegitimize El Encubierto by dragging this suspect pedigree into his version, an act that tarnishes the bloodline of El Encubierto. At the time the story takes place, the difference between so-called Old Christians and the recently converted New Christians was not only a social demarcation but also a legal category (Roth 2002: 230).

However, to the contemporaries of Asensi, references to his alleged Jewish heritage might reveal instead the familiarity of the author with the literary pedigree of El Encubierto. It features in some versions of the myth that has him as a learned Jew, who had served the merchant Juan de Bilbao in Oran, before resigning due to an affair with the wife or daughter, or a similarly dishonourable act (García Cárcel 1981: 133). This is the case for example in the earlier mentioned *El encubierto de Valencia* (1840) written by Antonio García Gutiérrez, one of the most prominent adaptations of the myth, and a work that might have formed part of Asensi's literary education. In this version, El Encubierto, named Enrique, has been adopted by Juan de Bilbao, unaware of his royal roots. Asensi echoes this version when she has Antonio tell his recently arrived brother Lorenzo that: 'Era muy niño cuando entró a servir a un comerciante llamado Juan Bilbas [...]. Le faltó en todo, hiriéndole en sus afecciones y en su honor, y Juan Bilbas le despidió ignominiosamente de su casa' [He was a child when he entered the service of a merchant called Juan Bilbas [...]. He disgraced himself entirely, snubbing his master's affections and honour, and Juan Bilbas dismissed him ignominiously from his house] (Asensi 1883: 16–17). Here Juan Bilbao has become 'Juan Bilbas', but apart from a single deviating letter, his description matches that of the trader of Oran and foster parent of El Encubierto.

When Lorenzo, intrigued, queries the apparent familiarity of his narrator with the background of El Encubierto and his family tree — his brother had earlier alleged that nobody could ascertain the identity of the controversial leader — Antonio becomes agitated, a reaction that reveals his biased point of view and own emotional investment. Defensively, he replies 'nunca falta una persona que busque antecedentes y los halle' [there is always someone who can dig up dirt] (Asensi 1883: 16).

Antonio, as one who does not support El Encubierto, engages in vague innuendo, and avoidance of direct questions. The sixteen-year-old Inés, by contrast, a niece of Lorenzo, aligns herself as a fervent supporter of the now deceased leader. Her version is at odds with that of her grandfather Antonio, and she paints a completely different picture of El Encubierto, a depiction that resembles a hagiography, in which he appears as a martyr and protector of the poor. Inés also refers to him by his name, Don Enrique Enríquez de Rivera, rather than his sobriquet. Again, the introduction of this name for El Encubierto reveals the familiarity of Asensi with the myth, or at least testifies to detailed documentation. Enrique Enríquez de Ribera (rather than 'Rivera') and Enrique Manrique de Ribera are two of the names given to the enigmatic figure in later chronicles, and are both according to García Cárcel 'de reconocida falsedad' [patently false] (1981: 135).

Inés, like her grandfather Antonio, opens her story by first labelling other versions as fiction: 'Tío — murmuró la joven — no creáis lo que mi abuelo os ha dicho respecto a Don Enrique Enríquez de Rivera. Esa es una novela inventada por sus enemigos para desprestigiarle' [Uncle — the young woman murmured — do not believe what my grandfather has told you about Don Enrique Enríquez de Rivera. That's a novel made up by his enemies to discredit him] (Asensi 1883: 19). Likewise, when Lorenzo probes the veracity of her story, her passionate response gives her position away: 'No se portó nunca más que como un hombre honrado y un valiente — contestó Inés con alguna exaltación que alarmó a Lorenzo' [He never behaved as anything less than an honest and brave man — Ines replied with an exaltation that alarmed Lorenzo] (21). However the story Inés recounts sounds rather novelesque and, like that of her grandfather, owes much to subsequent myths created around the figure of El Encubierto. The young woman vouches for his royal ancestry and declares him to be the long-lost grandson of the Catholic Monarchs. The invocation of these monarchs, responsible for the reunification of Spain in popular imagination and thus the 'parents' of the nation, provides El Encubierto with an impeccable pedigree rather than the suspect lineage advanced by Antonio.

The dynastic pairing of Isabel I of Castile and Fernando II of Aragon, whose union brought the two major kingdoms together, occupies 'un lugar central en la genealogía imaginaria de España' [a central place in the imaginary genealogy of Spain] (Pérez Viejo 2013: 484). Boyd also concludes that, although they emphasized different aspects, both progressives and conservatives conceived of the reign of the Catholic Monarchs as a significant milestone in the consolidation of Spanish identity (1997:84). El Encubierto is thus inserted into this emblematic lineage. The version of Inés follows some earlier re-imaginings that alleged him to be the secret son of Juan of Aragon and Castile, offspring of the Catholic Monarchs and their only male heir. Married young, Crown Prince Juan had died in 1497 at the age of nineteen without any known descendants. His wife Margarita of Austria had been pregnant at the time of his untimely death but had given birth to a stillborn daughter, thus putting an end to that line, and the crown passed on to his younger sister Doña Juana. However some conspiracy theories would later maintain that Cardinal Don Pedro González de Mendoza, in collusion with the midwife, had claimed it was a stillborn girl rather than a healthy baby boy so that Felipe I the Fair, the husband of Doña Juana, could govern. Stripped of his royal identity, the surviving boy would have been given to a shepherdess in Gibraltar, who brought him up (García Cárcel 1981: 132–33). After the equally early passing of the alleged usurper Felipe I the Fair, which Inés interprets as divine punishment, his son Carlos I occupied the throne. This was the monarch whom the Valencian guilds later fought in the Revolt of the Brotherhoods, a clash that had been described earlier to Lorenzo as a national war. But according to Inés and other sympathizers of El Encubierto, Carlos I does not descend from the legitimate line. With this alternative genealogy, those who oppose Carlos I question his right to reign by delegitimizing his line, hailing instead El Encubierto as the returning king, a figure who will re-establish order and deliver justice.[4]

As for El Encubierto himself, we never get to hear his own version as he has been dead for some years by the time Lorenzo returns to his hometown. Yet his figure still exerts a strong influence on both his defenders and detractors, who keep his memory alive through the constant invocation of his name, together with their disagreements over his actions and legacy. Each one of these depictions is vividly rendered to the extent that they still affect the actions of the living. In this respect, Asensi's legend could be seen as echoing some of Zorrilla's work, specifically his historical drama *Traidor, inconfeso, mártir* [Traitor, Unconfessed and Martyr] (1849) on the figure of Sebastian I of Portugal, another popular variant of the returning king. The story centres on a baker who claims to be the Portuguese heir, dead in battle years ago, a fact that did not deter several pretenders claiming his identity over the years. Yet in Zorrilla's version, the protagonist of the play — with a contested pedigree like El Encubierto — remains similarly hidden from readers. Instead his importance is established through other characters who constantly allude to the mysterious figure, a technique that Asensi also employs to establish the centrality of the equally enigmatic El Encubierto. As a critic has observed on the dramatic build-up in *Traidor, inconfeso, mártir*: 'El resultado es que, a lo largo de estas tres escenas consecutivas, el viajero misterioso del que tanto se habla asume la función de personaje central sin hacer siquiera acto de presencia' [The outcome is that, through these three consecutive scenes, the mysterious traveller who is talked about so often becomes the central character without so much as appearing] (Ricardo

Senabre, in Zorrilla 1978: 36). However, unlike El Encubierto, the pretender in Zorrilla's tale does not only show up eventually, but also disperses any doubts about his royal ancestry in the very last scene. Asensi takes it one step further and leaves her tale without its central character, who never materializes, or a resolution to his controversial pedigree.

The centrality of the two characters is reflected in the titles of both works. Zorrilla's *Traidor, inconfeso, mártir* can be read as a potted biography that summarizes the life of the protagonist as well as the different roles he fulfils within the narrative arc for different people: to some he is a traitor but to others he is a martyr. In a similar vein, Asensi's 'El encubierto' refers to the eponymous shrouded one although this might perhaps have been pluralized to *los encubiertos*, or the shrouded ones, a term that would more accurately reflect the two competing portrayals presented to the reader throughout the story. A traitor to some and a martyr to others, Zorrilla's title could equally apply to the enigmatic figure who haunts the pages of the legend penned by Asensi.

This multiplicity echoes the real events on which the story is based and the literal profusion of *encubiertos*. Chronicles do not only offer us different takes on the family tree of El Encubierto, they also record the appearances of several individuals who claimed clandestine royal origins. The polysemy of Encubierto not only encompasses different versions projected on *one man* — opportunistic fraudster or legitimate heir — but also on *multiple men*, each one of them presenting his own version and ancestry. Cárcel christens this phenomenon 'encubiertismo', which he views as attempts to articulate different social concerns projected onto the figure of El Encubierto:

> Más que el Encubierto debe interesarnos el encubertismo, fenómeno social que desborda las fronteras cronológicas de la biografía del Encubierto dando paso al mito redentorista agrario socializante — si es válida la expresión — que engendraría sucesivamente múltiples nuevos encubiertos, cada uno de ellos detentando el mismo patronímico aglutinante. (García Cárcel 1981: 137–38)
>
> [More interesting than the Encubierto is Encuebiertism, the social phenomenon that stretches beyond the limits of the Encubierto's lifespan, giving way to a collective agrarian redemptive myth — if such an expression is valid — that will produce multiple new *encubiertos* in succession, each one with the same binding patronymic.]

There are at least four different recorded cases of *encubiertos*, with two reported in the capital of Valencia, and another two in nearby Xátiva. Asensi, though, seems to introduce an archetypal amalgamation of several past incarnations rather than attempt to faithfully reconstruct any past episode. The disputed pedigree of El Encubierto haunts her story, not only metaphorically but also literally, as an alleged apparition who returns each night to the room where Don Enrique was apprehended by his enemies. Although in disagreement about his origins, both Inés and Antonio vouch for the existence of this spectre. Intrigued by these apparitions, Don Lorenzo decides to sleep in this now cursed space in the hope he might disprove its supernatural dimension, his mind unaffected by past events, and thus less susceptible to projections. After a fitful night plagued by oneiric sequences of a wounded female figure in white, he wakes up to find that bloodstains in the room — vestiges of the grim fate of El Encubierto — are present but freshly scrubbed, as if somebody had attempted to remove them. Don Lorenzo does not mention these irregular occurrences to his hosts, but decides to gather more evidence in his self-assigned role of Doubting Thomas before passing judgment.

Asensi, however, hints at the involvement in these hauntings of the foster-sister of El Encubierto, driven to madness by her grief as she aimlessly wanders through the village decked in white (the colour of the supporters of the Valencian guilds).[5] Raised together with her charismatic adoptive brother from childhood, she had become infatuated by him and accompanied him in his campaigns — a loyal but lovelorn companion. Her tragic story had been introduced earlier by the young Inés as she painted her impression of the infamous Don Enrique. Faithful to this foreshadowing, Lorenzo wakes up the following night startled to discover the presence of a white-robed woman, oblivious to his presence as she attempts to remove the blood stains on the floor, in a ritual that also includes prostrating herself before the crucifix in the room, and the invocation of the spirit of the *germanías*. The ghostly figure then slips through the open window, leaving a now terrified Lorenzo unable to return to sleep.

Later that day, it is revealed that the man who betrayed the whereabouts of El Encubierto to the Royalist authorities had appeared hanging from a tree in an apparent suicide, on the very same day Don Enrique was arrested and executed years ago. The traitor was commonly known in the village as 'Judas', and sold El Encubierto for 400 ducats rather than the proverbial 30 pieces of silver. So intrinsically linked with this betrayal has he become in popular imagination that he now functions strictly as an archetype — Inés is unable to recall his real name. Similarly, the bereaved and equally nameless foster-sister, already with one foot in the grave, as hinted at by her ghostly white appearance and complete disconnection from the world of the living, fulfils her inevitable Ophelia-like fate by drowning in the river. However, the blood-stains that had been the object of her nightly exorcisms have now magically vanished, although it is hinted that the figure of the doomed Don Enrique might still haunt the community. When we leave Inés, she has convinced Lorenzo to accompany her and her mother to a commemorative mass on the anniversary of the death of El Encubierto, an act that further cements his status as a martyr. After this revelation the story ends almost abruptly, with no reflection on the events narrated, and no further clues that point towards the real identity of El Encubierto.

The readers are left with the versions presented by Antonio and the competing vision offered by Inés on the true roots of El Encubierto, both of which draw from an extensive pool of myths and archetypes that emerged round this historic episode. Ironically then, the two stories are actually what Inés and Antonio both dismiss as a 'novela inventada' [made-up novel], or at least tales assembled from past re-imaginings that reveal the reading habits of an author who must have consumed her fair share of historical fiction. Since Asensi does not explicitly side with any version, the legend almost feels like a compilation of the best-known fanciful legends surrounding El Encubierto, a feature that undermines the insistent impartiality and veracity Antonio and Inés claim to possess. Instead both stories lack originality and are regurgitated variants of versions with which Asensi's readers might already be familiar, particularly if they too had been exposed to their fair share of historical fiction.

An Unexpectedly Ambiguous Ending

The story comes to a halt after the irruption of the supernatural has been dispelled, although ironically, one suspects that verifiable facts would not affect the unwavering faith displayed by adherents of each camp. It could be said that the subversive streak lies precisely in Asensi's neutrality and unwillingness to commit to a single interpretation, even the official version championed by historians like Danvila y Collado who claim El Encubierto to be a fraud. Asensi opts neither for the version presented by the men in her story, nor for the contradictory one endorsed by the women, this impartiality almost dangerously implying that both versions are valid. Both will certainly remain so to their supporters in an ongoing disagreement that echoes the later clashes over the past that characterize nineteenth-century historiography. The potential of its unresolved ending and the uncertainty surrounding El Encubierto's pedigree linger. Whose ancestral line is it anyway?

That this latent ambiguity could be subversive, or at least disorienting, is supported by a later edition of the legend that appeared in *Victoria y otros cuentos* [Victoria and Other Tales]. A compilation of some of Asensi's stories, it was published in 1905 by Edgar S. Ingraham, professor of Romance languages at Ohio State University, aimed at Spanish language students. With this audience in mind, Ingraham added explanatory glosses that provided socio-historic context. Thus in a note on the genealogy of El Encubierto, the editor points out how 'the version given by Antonio, according to which he was an impostor, is the one generally accepted by historians' (Asensi 1905: 119). This paratext thus dispels any unsettling ambiguity raised by its inconclusive denouement and curtails any potential polysemy in the process. The women presented within this fiction are bereft of their discursive authority as the version espoused by the male camp is declared to be the legitimate one. Ingraham also provides a brief overview of the Revolt of the Brotherhoods that similarly fixes the narrative and limits the uncertainty triggered by the two competing visions presented in Asensi's story. To American readers, the clash between Carlos I and the Valencian guilds might be alien enough that it merits some necessary background. Yet Ingraham's explanatory footnotes ironically flatten the ambiguous depth present in the Asensi story. Spanish audiences on the other hand would have been familiar with an episode that became firmly ensconced in the emerging historical collective, and subject to a growing number of often competing interpretations.

As we have seen, some of these readings could be rather controversial, as they served to provide historical fodder to contemporary hot-button issues such as the

Cantonal rebellion in the 1870s that questioned more centralist conceptions of the state. By fashioning El Encubierto as a champion of regional rights and biological grandchild of the Catholic Monarchs, federalist sympathizers like Fernández Herreros were not only delegitimizing the hegemonic aspirations of Carlos I, but also the legitimacy of the current Spanish government against the seceding cantonal regions. This conflict triggered the resignation of Francesc Pi i Margall, leader of the Democratic Republican Federal Party, as president of the First Republic. A main promoter of the federalist model in Spain, Pi i Margall was also a keen patron of Asensi's work, and yet despite these connections and her decision to tackle El Encubierto, she remains depoliticized.[6] Her occupation of such neutral space led later critics to further remove her from public debates, so that her surprisingly ambiguous ending remains under the radar. It seems to neither support the federalist aspirations of her friend Pi i Margall, nor the centralist agenda supported presumably by the likes of her father. Instead of asserting one version as the true one, it can be read as a commentary on a political tribalism that still haunts the country today. Written only a few years after the end of the last Carlist war, the clash in 'El encubierto' over the legitimate heir cannot simply be dismissed as a historical re-enactment of a now residual Romanticism. The end of this conflict in 1876 even led Asensi to abandon her nonpartisan position and express her public support for the newly crowned Alfonso XII, whilst lamenting the human cost of the civil confrontation. The opening lines of 'A. S. M. el Rey D. Alfonso XII' read:

> ¡Cuatro años de lucha fraticida,
> cuatro años de tristes privaciones;
> Tanta sangre vertida
> Y tantos desgarrados corazones!
>   (Asensi 1876: 481)
>
> [Four years of fratricidal fights,
> four years of miserable hardship;
> So much blood spilled
> And so many hearts torn!]

In her panegyric Asensi lauds the king as the *rightful* leader of all Spaniards, and by implication rejects the Carlist pretender Carlos VII, whose claim that he was the usurped heir had started the war in 1872 (Canal 2000: 170–210). But it uncomfortably also mirrors the narrative of Alfonso XII himself before the restoration of the Bourbon dynasty with his crowning, regarded as the returning king by some whilst in exile during the brief republican interlude and failed reign of the imported hapless Amadeo I. Asensi's poem had been commissioned to appear in an *Álbum Poético* [Poetic Album] published by the *Gaceta de Madrid* [Madrid Gazette], a previous incarnation of the *Boletín Oficial del Estado* [Official State Bulletin], to commemorate the end of the armed conflict. In other words, we find the normally shy Asensi voicing her version of events and asserting the legitimacy of Alfonso in an official organ. Her story 'El encubierto' might not engage in politics so overtly, but as this chapter has hopefully shown, nor can it be isolated from its sociohistorical context.

Notes to Chapter 3

1. A *comunero* is a joint holder of a tenure of lands, although it is mostly a name associated with those landowners who rebelled against Carlos I. The episode of the *comuneros* had more of a national impact than that of the *germanías*. Immortalized by Antonio Gisbert, it received an institutional nod when the painting *Los comuneros de Castilla* [The *Comuneros* of Castile] won first prize at the 1860 Exposición Nacional. See Pérez (1997) for historical background and Berzal de la Rosa (2008) for a development of the myth.
2. The 'Cantonal Revolution' took place during the First Republic between July 1873 and January 1874, lead by republicans who wanted to install a federalist model from the bottom up rather than wait for Parliament to pass a new constitution along the lines championed by Francisco Pi i Margall, president at the time. See Fontana (2007) for an overview. The episode is also immortalized by the omnipresent Pérez Galdós in the fifth and last series of his *Episodios nacionales: de Cartago a Sagunto* [National Episodes: From Carthage to Sagunto] (1911).
3. Even Asensi makes an indirect allusion to the succession issue in her children's story *La princesa Elena* [The Princess Elena] wherein she defends the right of women to inherit the crown (Rosario Delgado 2012: 62), as expressed in the following description of the protagonist: 'La heredera del principado, porque en él podían las hembras ser sucesoras' [The female heir of the principality, because here women could be heirs] (Asensi 1897: 95).
4. Some versions go so far as to claim that the deceased prince Don Juan was the real Encubierto, instead of any alleged secret offspring (García Cárcel 1981: 134).
5. David T. Gies (1994: 345) points out how 'these disheveled women (usually dressed in white), symbols of social disorder or emotional chaos, are frequent in Spanish drama from the 1820s through the 1850s. They appear in Grimaldi's *La huérfana de Bruselas* [The Orphan from Brussels] (1825), García Gutiérrez's *El rey monje* [The Monk King] (1837), Gil y Zarate's *Carlos II el hechizado* [Carlos II the Bewitched] (1839), and Lozano de Vilchez's *María o la abnegación* [María or Abnegation] (1854)'.
6. A brief biography describes Asensi as 'solicitada su colaboración por hombres tan eminentes como el Sr. Pi y Margall' [her collaboration sought after by such eminent men as Mr. Pi y Margall] (Bastinos 1903: 197). Pi i Margall collaborated too with the Biblioteca Universal, and had his own copies of two of Asensi's works (one of them being *Leyendas y tradiciones*) bound together, now held by the Biblioteca Nacional de España.

CHAPTER 4

❖

Blanca de los Ríos: 'More than a Daughter, Wife, Niece'

While posterity remembers Julia de Asensi as primarily a children's author, the name of her contemporary Blanca de los Ríos remains linked with her labour as a Golden Age historian, a filter that overshadows a vast and varied output that spans nearly eight decades. Like Asensi, her stories contain characters of questionable pedigree — often women — who testify to the liberal legacy inherited by the author and her own disenfranchised status as a woman in the androcentric narratives of nineteenth-century historiography. Ríos herself contributed assiduously to the emerging national mythos throughout her long career, both as a literary historian, a writer of fiction and a tireless promoter of the so-called *americanismo* movement, the ongoing efforts to rekindle ties between Spain and its former South American colonies to counteract the Anglo-Saxon ascendancy. To this end, Ríos founded the influential periodical *Raza Española* [Spanish Race], a mouthpiece for her own nationalist doctrine. Even the name itself, *Raza Española*, testifies to this genealogical imagination.[1] Yet ironically, Ríos found herself relegated to a passive role and defined by her relationships with men despite her role in assembling the macro genealogies that made up the new nation-state. This demotion has been noted by Kathleen M. Glenn who remarks that:

She has often been identified in terms of male figures: her father, architect Demetrio de los Ríos; her husband Vicente Lampérez, also an architect; her uncle, literary historian José Amador de los Ríos; and the writer with whom her name is most frequently associated, Tirso. Ángela Ena Bordonada argues that she could be called "la mujer de la Generación del 98" [the woman of the Generation of 98] (32), but Blanca de los Ríos is more than a token appendage to the male Generation, more than a daughter, wife, niece. (Glenn 1999: 223)

Born in 1862, Ríos would die in 1956 at the age of 96 under the Franco dictatorship. Featured in the 1950s in *Noticiarios y Documentales* [News and Documentaries] — the official news vehicle of the regime — the only footage of her depicts the writer as a frail venerable nonagenarian in her home surrounded by old books and other keepsakes, a relic from the past.[2] It is an image explicitly articulated in a eulogy published briefly after her death, in which the journalist Melchor Fernández Almagro recalls the author as:

Menuda, hundida en su butacón, regazo ya de la Historia, doña Blanca, vivía, pervivía milagrosa y patéticamente, se sobrevivía, respirando la atmósfera de su tiempo, allí remansado, entre terciopelos y moldura dorados: camarín de ilustres sombras, de efigies debidas a lienzos y fotografías o presentidas por sugestión de ambiente. (Fernández Almagro 1956: 3)

[Small, sunk into her armchair, already in the lap of History, Doña Blanca existed, persisted, miraculously and poignantly, outliving herself, breathing in the atmosphere of her time, preserved there amongst velvet and gold mouldings: a chapel of illustrious shadows, of effigies evoked by paintings and photographs or simply suggested by the atmosphere.]

Upon her death, the regime remembered a woman who 'se caracterizó siempre por su catolicismo acendrado y su alto amor a España' [was always known for her true Catholicism and her deep love for Spain] as the voiceover for footage of her funeral describes her (Anon. 1956b). Hooper (2008: 4) recalls a similar rebranding of Ríos's contemporary and equally long-lived author Sofía Casanova, commemorated as a 'passive, sentimentalised icon of Francoist femininity' at the expense of her other achievements and intellectual pursuits. This is echoed by a biography of Ríos, the first and only that exhaustively follows her literary and journalistic trajectory, which describes the shift as 'la imagen de una abuela entrañable reacia a acatar los dictados inapelables de la naturaleza fue sustituyendo a la poderosa aureola de erudita historiadora' [the image of a beloved grandmother reluctant to obey the inescapable dictates of time gradually replaced the powerful figure of an erudite historian] (González López 2001: 334). In this way, Ríos's longevity could have contributed to her subsequent image as a stern matron detached from worldly matters.

The conservative leanings of Ríos are also recast to give the impression that they aligned neatly with those of the dictatorship, another enduring misrepresentation. Instead her sympathy for the regime should be described as acquiescence. Ríos remained a monarchist her whole life, under the first republic, during the restoration of the Bourbons, during the royally-approved autocracy of Primo Rivera, and even under Franco, when an allegiance to the now disenfranchised royal family would have been frowned upon. At the same time, she entertained diverse and sometimes disparate political ambitions, including her *americanista* agenda and an equally ardent wish to bolster the political standing of women, which could not always be reconciled on the same platform. Her strategic approach to furthering her causes meant Ríos often associated herself with conservative factions with whom she shared only a common nationalism in an increasingly polarized political landscape. This collaboration with the far right has painted her as more reactionary than she really was, or even simplified her views (González López 2001: 320). Her conservative outlook and collusion with two autocratic regimes — that of Primo Rivera and later Franco — may have discouraged initial revisionist scholars to whom the dictatorship was still a recent memory. In this way, the self-professed feminist Carmen de Burgos, who died a republican before the irruption of the Civil War, and is thus more in line with modern sensibilities, received initially more attention than her conservative peer. Yet Ríos continues to be the only woman buried in the Pantheon of Illustrious Men, a shrine established by the Association of

Writers and Artists, which inducted her, at least in death, to the hall of canonized writers such as Mariano José de Larra and José de Espronceda, an achievement not reflected in the negligible space she occupies in literary history manuals. It is only within the last three decades that critics have started to reevaluate the contributions of a woman who helped establish the male canon initiated by liberal historiography, but more importantly, attempted to expand it by including more female figures.

Before this recent reevaluation, if mentioned at all, Ríos appears in literary histories only as a literary historian, even during her own lifetime. The Hispanist James Fitzmaurice-Kelly mentions 'la erudita escritora' [the erudite historian] (1901: 292) in a footnote on Cervantes in his influential *Historia de la literatura española* [History of Spanish Literature], the only contemporary woman referred to other than the expected Emilia Pardo Bazán. The literary historian Francisco Blanco García, who had included Asensi in his 'larga y no gloriosa serie de escritoras más o menos consagradas a la imitación' [long and unremarkable number of women writers more or less devoted to imitation] (1899: 388), has kinder words for Ríos, who is mentioned in connection with her work on Don Juan, although once again as an aside at the bottom of the page. She is sometimes brought up in conjunction with Marcelino Menéndez y Pelayo, as in *Historia de la literatura española* by Juan Hurtado and Ángel González Palencia (1921: 1072) which lists Ríos as his disciple. As Glenn (1999: 223) observes, Ríos rarely appears unaccompanied and is often defined by her relationship to others, whether it is her admiration for Menéndez y Pelayo, her work on Tirso de Molina or Don Juan, or her friendship with Emilia Pardo Bazán. Even the latter, in an article about her friend in the *Nuevo Teatro Crítico* [New Critical Theatre], emphasized Rios's labour as a historian and her family connections: 'de casta le vendrá, pues es sobrina del eminente historiógrafo de nuestra letras, D. José Amador de los Rios' [it must be in the blood, as she is the niece of the illustrious historian of our literature, Don José Amador de los Ríos] (1891: 87).

Pardo Bazán's article, 'Blanca de los Ríos' (1891), has been analyzed by both Bieder (1992) and Scanlon (1986). Although they still focus primarily on its author Emilia Pardo Bazán, these pioneering efforts inaugurate a new period of increased interest in the figure of Ríos. However, Ángela Ena Bordonada had already in 1990 produced what could be considered the first contemporary study centred on an unchaperoned Ríos by including the chapter 'Las hijas de Don Juan' [Don Juan's Daughters] in her anthology *Novelas breves de escritoras españolas (1900–1936)* [Short Novels by Spanish Women Writers (1900–36)]. Her analysis of 'Las hijas de Don Juan' is the first of a number of studies that are still prising away the many discursive layers that compose this novella and which forms a tradition of its own.[3] Given the extent of Ríos's *œuvre*, different critics have approached her intellectual legacy from many different angles and have contributed to a more nuanced take on her intellectual activity.[4]

The Ríos Nostench: Curators of the Past

Like Asensi, Ríos grew up in a family firmly ensconced in the new liberal establishment, and was also the recipient of a polished education together with healthy doses of historicism from a young age. Born in Seville in 1859, she received the full name of María Blanca de la Asunción de los Reyes Dolores de los Ríos. Her godfather was her uncle José Amador de los Ríos, the prominent literary historian who in 1861 had started publishing the multivolume *Historia de la literatura española*. The father of Blanca was the architect Demetrio de los Ríos, who shared an interest in literature with his older brother Amador, leading him to try his hand at poetry. These compositions, read at literary gatherings but never published, reflect his preoccupation with the political reality and the active engagement of the Ríos family in its shaping. González López similarly remarks that 'la familia estaba comprometida con la realidad política, tanto por la faceta pública de su padre como por la intervención directa del tío Amador' [the family was engaged with political reality both through her father's public presence and the direct intervention of her uncle Amador] (2001: 15). Ríos' uncle was a member of the Conservative party in parliament, representing the province of Almería. Such public engagement might have coloured Ríos's own political stance. Later campaigns for the *americanista* cause as well as her devout admiration for Isabel the Catholic as a pillar of Spanish nationalism could have been partly encouraged from an early age by her father's recital of his own poems such as 'La isla de Cuba' [The Island of Cuba], an ode to the discovery of the Americas and the providential role played by the Castilian queen in the enterprise (González López 2001: 16).[5]

As inspiring as these readings would have been, the maternal influence in the early moulding of Blanca's historical imagination should not be neglected. It is particularly relevant in the case of an author who would later dedicate considerable energy to the reinsertion of women into history. This is most clearly expressed in the series of articles entitled *Mujeres de la historia* [Women in History], which she wrote for the magazine *Blanca y Negro* [Black and White] in 1915, now as an established historian. Each essay is dedicated to a woman whom Ríos considers to have actively shaped the fate of Spain. Herein Ríos pens such claims as: 'Porque entre nosotros fueron más y mejores estadistas las Reinas que los Reyes. Cada paso hacia la unificación y la grandeza tiene en nuestra historia un nombre de mujer' [Because through history Queens have been better statesmen than Kings. Each step towards unification and greatness in our history bears the name of a woman] (Ríos 1915b: 18). A similar assertion is found in 'La madre de San Fernando' [The Mother of Saint Fernando], devoted to the mother of King Fernando III of Castile, Berenguela of Castile and Leon. The maternal imprint is clear as Ríos conflates the queen mother with her own mother in an illuminating passage that deserves to be quoted at length. Reminiscing about her own childhood and past heroic deeds recounted by her mother, the writer fuses history and histories in what would later become a recurring motif:

> ¿Quién discierne lo vivido de lo ensoñado en el limbo auroral donde arranca nuestra vida? Yo sé que sobre aquel fondo de historia y de ensueño he visto

sentada en altísimo trono una gran Reina medieval, una sublime Reina-madre, que ahora me parece que tenía los mismos claros ojos profundos y el mismo rostro oval y místico de la santa mujer que me contaba aquellos heroicos gestos. ¡Madre! ¡Patria! ¿No sois una misma cosa? (Ríos 1915b: 14)

[Who can distinguish between the lived and the dreamed in the twilight zone where our life starts? I know that in this place where history meets fantasy I have seen a great medieval Queen sitting on a very high throne, a sublime Queen mother, who now seems to have had the same deep clear eyes and the same oval and mystical face of the saintly woman who told me these heroic tales. Mother! Homeland! Are you not but the same thing?]

The personification of the patria in the figure of the mother would similarly become a trademark trope in her work, and also figures prominently in nationalist discourses of the time, which permitted women to intervene in debates, particularly in those concerning regeneration. It takes us back to yet another of Pilar Sanjuan's exhortation to schoolchildren: 'acostúmbrese a designar a la patria con el nombre de segunda madre' [make it a habit to refer to the homeland as your second mother] (1864: 29). Not only did María Teresa Nostench regale her children with these stories, she also seems to have written a novel that most likely emboldened her daughter Blanca's own literary inspirations. However like her husband's poetic compositions, this was never published, which makes it harder to assess precisely how it might have inspired Blanca.[6] In addition to her mother, the budding author could look to her mother's friends, who included Fernán Caballero, for whom she would profess admiration throughout her career, and the also well-known Seville poet Antonia Díaz de Lamarque. In this mapping of early influences one should not forget that María Teresa Nostench was a respected painter, and that the pictorial tradition shared an interest in the folkloric detail cultivated by her friend Fernán Caballero in her description of local customs. Both women championed a traditional vision of Spain as a Catholic and monarchic monolith. María Teresa Nostench passed on this nostalgia for an idealized unspoiled Andalusia to her daughter, as well as a talent for drawing and an eye for colour. References to light, colour, texture and shade abound in Ríos's work, as well as numerous nods to canonical Spanish painters such as Goya, Velázquez, Murillo, El Greco or Valdés Leal. It could be said that the stories of Ríos often resemble the paintings of her mother, colourful and populated with national archetypes.

The formative years of the life of Blanca de los Ríos are also marked by a father concerned by the fragile political equilibrium of the country's first foray into constitutional monarchy, ending with the proclamation of the republic and putting a momentary halt to the political ambitions of the Ríos family. Amador de los Ríos was removed from his position as director of the Archaeological Museum of Madrid (the institution that would host some of the Egyptian artefacts collected by Tomás de Asensi, the father of Julia de Asensi). The same fate befell his son Rodrigo Amador Ríos, the cousin of Blanca, who worked as archivist for the museum, presumably appointed by his father so making the curation of the past seem almost like a family tradition. In the same spirit the father of Blanca attempted to preserve churches marked for demolition in his role as vice-president of the so-called Provincial Monument Commission, which succeeded in preserving some of Seville's sanctuaries (Montoto y Rautenstrauch 1929: 132–33). The Restoration would rehabilitate the legitimacy of the Bourbons but leave Blanca with childhood memories of a chaotic republican interlude that particularly afflicted Andalusia and forced her family to flee temporarily the turmoil. As a result, Ríos would always harbour a deep dislike for republicanism and would later evoke the chaos of those years in overtly political stories like 'Por la República' [For the Republic] (1901), in which a young man gripped by revolutionary fever joins the cantonal revolution with only a tenuous grasp of politics. Quizzed by his lover over the exact definition of the state model for which he is fighting, the would-be revolutionary defensively replies 'vosotras las mujeres no sabéis de estas cosas' [you women don't know about these things] (Ríos 1901: 104). The irony lies of course in the fact that Ríos knew a lot, with an erudition she had no qualms in displaying and which made her a respected literary historian and intellectual in her time.

Examples abound of Ríos's endeavours to encompass more women in ongoing reconstructions of the country's past. Married to Vicente Lampérez y Romea, an illustrious architect and archaeologist, one could say that just as her husband restored churches, Ríos was keen to restore the female presence in the cultural landscape. Her revisionist impulse knows no bounds, even claiming that women spearheaded the popular uprising against Napoleon's army on 2 May 1808 — considered the awakening of the nation — in 'Las madrileñas del dos de mayo' [The Women of Madrid on the Second of May], another essay forming part of *Las mujeres de la historia* mentioned earlier. Ríos reinserts women in the public space and at the heart of nation-building in 'Las patriotas de la Independencia en Cádiz' [The Patriotic Women of the Independence in Cadiz], the closing instalment of *Las mujeres de la historia* in which she claims that 'y en las Cortes, en la calle Ancha, en los corillos de puerta de calle, en las tertulias, y — aunque hoy sorprenda — en los periódicos también, se asociaba la mujer fervorosa, apasionada, impetuosamente a las contiendas políticas' [and women joined political debates with great fervour and passion, in the Courts, on Ancha street, in groups huddled by portals, in literary gatherings and — even if it might be surprising now — in newspapers too] (1915a: 12). *Las mujeres de la historia* itself builds on a revisionist tradition that includes Pilar Sinués, who in her *Mujeres ilustres: narraciones histórico-biográficas* [Illustrious Women: Historical-Biographical Narrations] (1884: 8) invites the reader to 'venid a mi galería de preladas, de guerreras, de poetisas, de santas, de artistas, de reinas, de admirables madres, de heroicas esposas y de ejemplares hijas' [come to my gallery of nuns, of warriors, of poets, of saints, of artists, of queens, of esteemed mothers, of heroic wives and of exemplary daughters]. Other notable examples include *Galería de mujeres ilustres* [Gallery of Illustrious Women] (1877) by Josefa Pujol de Collado, a series of articles that traces female feats back to antiquity published in the magazine *El eco de Europa* [The Echo of Europe]. Pujol herself is featured later in another *Galería de mujeres notables* [Gallery of Notable Women] (1883–84) that ran in *La Ilustración de la Mujer*. Pujol, Sinués and Ríos form part of a growing group of women who, despite their conservative leanings, are intent on including women in national genealogies. The number of these matrilineal galleries in the press reveal this drive to document the imprint of women throughout history, as remarked by Laura Vicente:

> De ahí que las 'galerías de mujeres célebres', que buscaban dignificar el talento femenino, fueran tan comunes en esta prensa. Encontramos una 'galería de mujeres notables' en *La Ilustración de la Mujer* y una 'galería de mujeres célebres' en *El Álbum del Bello Sexo*. (Vicente 2010: 14)

> [Hence that the 'galleries of prominent women', which aimed to dignify female talent, were prevalent in these publications. We find a 'gallery of notable women' in *The Illustrated Woman's Magazine* and a 'gallery of prominent women' in *The Album of the Fair Sex*.]

Vicente also notes that the genealogical imagination colours this impulse to recover the past: 'la "galería de mujeres notables", que iba siempre acompañada de un retrato en la primera página, indica la búsqueda de una genealogía' [the 'gallery of notable women', which was always accompanied by a portrait on the first page, indicates the search for a genealogy] (2010: 14).

Blanca de los Ríos, like Pujol, would also feature in some of these galleries, including the *Por ellas y para ellas* [By Them and for Them] section in *Mundo Gráfico* [The Illustrated World] (Galaín 1912: 7), and in *Feminal* [Feminine] (Anon. 1912: 7), a supplement published by *La Ilustració Catalana* [The Illustrated Catalan Magazine] dedicated to women.[7] It was an attempt to insert Ríos into the canon that did not last.

Ríos's own attempt to assemble female genealogies has been remarked by Denise Dupont in *Writing Teresa: The Saint from Avila at the fin-de-siglo* (2012), which examines how the saint became a national symbol and point of convergence for often contradictory discourses on gender, spirituality and the nation. Dupont includes the Santa Teresa put forward by Ríos, who conceives the mystic as a mother of tradition, even proclaiming her the indirect creator of *Don Quixote* — a Spanish archetype if ever there was one. Ríos figures amongst those who enthusiastically contributed to the image of the saint from Ávila as totem, a campaign that reached fever pitch with the four-hundredth anniversary of her birth in 1915. In her first study of Santa Teresa, *De la mística y de la novela contemporánea* [On Mysticism and the Contemporary Novel] (1909), Ríos traces the influences of *Don Quixote* back to Teresa of Jesus and Isabel the Catholic. Dupont observes how 'according to this theory, *Don Quixote* has two mothers, both of which take precedence over Cervantes as progenitor — an appropriate demotion for the author who referred to himself as stepfather, rather than father of his novel, in its prologue' (2012: 239).

The Ríos: A Literary Family

Before she rose to prominence for her Golden Age studies and hailed Saint Teresa as mother of all things Spanish, Ríos had begun her literary career with poetry. This is how Asensi had started too, with poetry as a traditional route for women with literary ambitions (Kirkpatrick 1989: 81). Some of these first lyrical endeavours were included in the collection *Corona fúnebre dedicada a la memoria de su Majestad la Reina Doña María Mercedes de Orléans* [Funeral Wreath in Memory of the Queen Doña María Mercedes of Orleans], put together to mark the early demise of the first wife of the recently crowned Alfonso XII. As González López (2001: 24) points out, the contribution of Ríos, which was added hastily to the final version, could be due to her family connections. The friendship between her father and Antoine Latour, secretary of the father of the deceased queen, or the acquaintance of her uncle Amador de los Ríos with the late Duke of Rivas would have certainly made things easier. It echoes the early stages of Asensi's career, who had also dedicated several poems to the restored Bourbon dynasty. Asensi's earliest commemorates the ascension of Alfonso XII to the throne in 1874, followed two years later by a poem to mark the end of the last Carlist conflict. As previously mentioned, this second work was published in *Álbum poético* by the *Gaceta de Madrid*, a previous incarnation of the *Boletín Oficial del Estado*. Asensi had also celebrated the engagement of the king to María Mercedes de Orléans, a marriage cut short by the unexpected death of the young queen, which Ríos in turn would mourn in her poem. Asensi and Ríos would eventually coincide in the pages of *El libro de la caridad* [The Charity Book], a lyrical anthology sponsored by the Crown with all proceeds going to alleviate the victims of the 1878 Murcia floods. Demetrio de los Ríos, the father of Blanca, also contributed a poem, as did established authors like Emilia Pardo Bazán and Julia de Asensi. It shows to what extent both Ríos and Asensi were part of the liberal establishment and reveals their active role in reiterating in their royal panegyrics the legitimacy of the constitutional monarchy.

Similarly, the budding research career of Ríos as a literary historian was aided by her illustrious pedigree and particularly her kinship with Amador de los Ríos. A calling card with a surname that linked her to uncle Amador, former Dean and Vice-Chancellor of the Central University of Madrid, would have helped her gain access to archives as well as the assistance of officials. As Julie des Jardins reminds us in her study of American female historians, archives and academies were mainly male spaces, illustrated by the experience of the historian Alice Earle visiting the New York Hall of Records. Des Jardins recounts how 'Earle felt lost in a bureaucratic sea of men and documents, and in the end no one would help her find the historical evidence she was looking for' (2003: 23–24). Aware of the aspiring scientific objectivism informing historiography, Blanca de los Ríos portrays herself as a representative of this approach:

> Desde que el moderno método científico exige, como base y nervio de la historia, 'el documento', ya no vale hacer fantasías 'sobre motivos' de tal o cual personaje [...] cuantos amamos estos estudios hemos de acudir a la fuente, al documento, al manuscrito, al adusto e imponente protocolo. (Ríos 1906b: 3)
>
> [Since modern scientific methods demand 'the document' as a foundation to history, one can no longer speculate on 'the motives' of this or that person [...] all of us who love these studies must turn to the source, to the manuscript, to a severe and imposing protocol.]

Ríos's research on Tirso de Molina would ultimately be acknowledged by the Real Academia de la Lengua [Royal Academy of Language], who in 1889 recognized the author for her efforts. She had failed to win the competition held by the academy, with the jury failing to find either of the two entries worthy. Instead she received a consolation prize that nevertheless carried a certain prestige. Such a gesture resonated at a time when the institution was once again under the spotlight for its refusal to admit women as members, as pointed out by journalists reporting on the event: 'se congratuló de que la Academia con aquel tributo, pudiese dar al bello sexo una muestra de consideración, ya que los reglamentos no autorizan a que tome parte en sus tareas' [the Academy was praised that with such a gesture it could show the fairer sex some consideration, given that the rules do not permit women to take part in the Academy's work] (Fernández Bremón 1889: 218). Ríos herself would enthusiastically campaign for her friend Emilia Pardo Bazán to join its ranks. Self-appointed guardian of the Spanish language and influential arbiter of taste, the academy was seen as a major milestone of legitimacy. Consequently 'la Real Academia se convirtió en uno de los retos por excelencia de las mujeres españolas que abogaban por el reconocimiento de sus derechos en el terreno artístico y literario' [The Royal Academy became one of the main milestones for Spanish women fighting for artistic and literary recognition] (González López 2001: 39). The academy conceded that the research undertaken by Ríos contributed significantly to the biography of Tirso de Molina, a recognition only amplified by its otherwise regressive stance on the participation of women in the cultural arena.

Tirso de Molina: Literary Genealogies and Genesis of the Nation

Ríos presented Tirso de Molina — also referred as the 'Mercedario' after the religious order to which he belonged — as a father of the Spanish nation. A passionate Ríos insisted that the Mercedario was on a par with other totemic figures such as Cervantes, but had been unjustly overlooked: 'disputárasele a Tirso todavía el lauro supremo de haber alcanzado a ser en el Teatro lo que Cervantes fue en la novela: el primer psicólogo de la raza' [Tirso's crown is still disputed for having achieved in theatre what Cervantes achieved with the novel: to be the first psychologist of a race] (1910: 26). In her campaign to vindicate Tirso, Ríos transcends figurative language, and goes beyond abstract pedigrees, to propose an actual noble heritage for Tirso. Such a literal implementation of the genealogical imagination deserves some further attention for what it reveals about the discursive logic of Ríos, which will become central to an understanding of her later literary output too.

In her award-winning research on Tirso's life, Ríos claimed to have located his birth certificate. Although later proved to be without foundation, Ríos's theory argued that the playwright was the illegitimate child of the Duke of Osuna (1928a: 35), perhaps in her attempt to compensate for his humble origins and provide him with a more illustrious pedigree that reflected his privileged position within Spanish letters.[8] It follows the well-trodden trope that a noble character must reflect a noble pedigree (Gilmartin 1998: 12). However, by proposing this origin for Tirso, the author comes perilously close to some of her own characters who assemble genealogies that fit their status better. This is the case with *Melita Palma* (1901) and *Madrid goyesco* (1907), analyzed in the following chapters. In *Madrid goyesco* Ríos satirizes Aurora Reinaldos, a relentless social climber who claims to be related to most of the noble households in Spain. There is no such straightforward condemnation of the protagonist in *Melita Palma*, an actress of the same name, who effortlessly adopts a noble persona after she falls for an aristocrat but encounters opposition from his mother. Yet Ríos herself employs the same legitimization strategy to connect her admired Tirso de Molina, the epitome of Spanishness in her eyes, to a more illustrious family than his origins would suggest. Well aware of how novelesque her proposed biography of Tirso may sound, Ríos observes that:

> Y en verdad que si la 'fantasía invencionera' de Tirso, para decirlo en frase suya, hubiérase dado a imaginar para sí mismo un origen legendario, romántico, egregio y propio para uno de los hazañosos y linajudos segundones, o para alguno de los más sabios bastardos estudiantes, orgullosos de la personal nobleza del entendimiento, que alientan en sus vivientes farsas de amor y de aventuras, su fértil e invencionera fantasía hubiera quedado corta ante la sorprendente realidad. (Ríos 1928a: 32)

> [And truly if Tirso's 'inventing fantasy', to use his own words, had decided to imagine for himself a legendary origin, romantic, illustrious and befitting one of his heroic aristocratic second sons, or for one of his wiser bastards, proudly possessing the nobility of empathy, all of whom breathe life into his stories of love and adventures, his fertile and inventing fantasy would not have lived up to the surprising reality.]

In this way one could say that family connections played an important role in Ríos's career, not only in getting her on the literary ladder but also in the blood links she established in her own research by producing a more noble family tree for Tirso de Molina. Also interesting is the reasoning that leads her to identify the playwright as an illegitimate child. There is a certain irony in advancing the literary legitimacy of Tirso by highlighting his illegitimacy. Ríos thus argues that the bastard or second son relegated to a smaller inheritance are both recurring figures in Tirso's theatrical production and are used by him as proxies to vent his own frustrations and sense of disenfranchisement (1906a: 46–47). However, there is no proof to support this claim. Instead, his status as a noble bastard is based purely on the psychoanalytical interpretation by Ríos, who writes of these 'segundones y bastardos, víctimas siempre de un mayorazgo déspota o de unos padres desconocidos' [second sons and bastards, victims of a despotic heir or of some unknown parents] (47). This is the conclusion reached by Margaret Wilson, who rejects Ríos's claim that Tirso is the illegitimate child of a nobleman, but nevertheless recognizes its narrative appeal:

> The evidence for this theory was at once seen to be somewhat flimsy, but it appealed by the element of romance which almost likened it to one of Tirso's own plots, and by the fact that it offered a plausible explanation, both for the general silence about Tirso's origins, and for the evident sympathy shown in his plays for bastards, younger sons, and other deprived for various reasons of the advantages of their birth. (Wilson 1969: 89)

Ríos's writings on Tirso propose him as a pillar upon which Spanish culture rests. Her reconstruction of Tirso's lineage relies also partly on her imagination as a guide, an approach approved of by her admired Marcelino Menéndez y Pelayo. Rather than endorsing an absolute objectivity, Menéndez y Pelayo emphasized the role of subjectivity as a guide in any historical reconstruction. Initially lacking the latter's clout, and perhaps wary of the link between women and instinct, Ríos highlights instead her empirical methodology reliant on primary sources. Eventually, as her own scholarly star rose, she became more confident in her exegetic abilities and her conception of history (González López 2001: 133).

Ríos would spread her views in public lectures held in such hallowed halls as the Ateneo de Madrid, a stamp of approval made concrete in later published lectures such as *Tirso de Molina: conferencia leída por su autora en el Ateneo de Madrid el día 23 de abril de 1906* [Tirso de Molina: Lecture Read by the Author in the Athenaeum of Madrid on the 23 April of 1906]. If Tirso de Molina was one of the fathers of the nation, then Ríos, by 'rediscovering' him, could be seen as his mother as she disseminated her version of Tirso, her creation. The alleged discovery of his illegitimate origins rests on Ríos's ability to decipher some words crossed through on his certificate of baptism: 'En suma, lo que aún puede verse de la nota no contradice en nada, y confirma en todo, *lo que leí en ella* cuando la luz no había obscurecido las tachaduras' [To summarize, what can still be gleaned does not contradict anything, and confirms everything, *that I read* when the light had not obscured the words crossed through] (Ríos 1928a: 35, my emphasis). The author boasts how 'así, penetrando por su vida en su obra, ascendiendo de su obra su alma, he ido reconstruyendo a todo Tirso' [in this way, peering into his life through his work, reaching his soul through his work, I have been reconstructing Tirso in his entirety] (1928a: 47).

Ríos's study of Tirso is also informed by gendered preoccupations, as seen in *Las mujeres de Tirso* [The Women in Tirso] (1910), read at the Ateneo and collected, like many other of her public lectures, in book form. Here Ríos presents Tirso as the most skilled portraitist of women, managing to capture nuances beyond the Madonna/whore binary. Lauding his depiction of the medieval monarch, Doña María de Téllez in *La prudencia en la mujer* [Prudence in Woman] (1622), Ríos uses this example to reconstruct a noble genealogy for all Spanish women, similar to that proposed for Tirso. Doña María de Téllez — popularly known as María de Molina — is conceived as a blueprint for the other women created by Tirso, described in a passage by Ríos which is worth quoting at length:

> Porque tan reales son, tan vivas están, que vemos en aquellas hembras de temple tan español y tan castizo las líneas genealógicas del árbol opulento de la raza; y los que nos preciamos de descender de madres virtuosas y amantes hasta el heroísmo, y vemos en la augusta Reina Doña María de Téllez, el noble étnico de la matrona española, y la raíz histórica de aquella egregia estirpe de mujeres de quienes nacieron nuestras madres. (Ríos 1910: 3–31)

> [Because they are so real, so alive, we see in these women of such impeccable Spanish temper the genealogical branches of the leafy tree of the race; and those of us who pride ourselves in descending from heroically virtuous and loving mothers see in the august Queen Doña María de Téllez the noble ethnic blueprint of the Spanish matron, and the historical roots of that illustrious lineage of women from whom our mothers descend.]

The sentence brims with ancestral imagery: 'líneas genealógicas', 'árbol opulento de la raza', 'madres virtuosas', 'noble étnico', 'matrona española', 'raíz histórica', 'estirpe de mujeres'. Throughout this oratory, Ríos inserts women into the nation's history, as she maps out a female family tree that descends from the 'raíz histórica' that is María de Molina. That Ríos picked this historical figure is no coincidence. The queen consort is best remembered for her role as a regent to both her son Ferdinand IV and then later her grandson Alfonso XI of Castile. Recovered during Romanticism, the story of her regency was revisited to provide historical continuity for the regency of María Cristina as her daughter Isabel II came of age.[9] Once again, it shows the deftness with which Ríos navigates the historical imagination. Ríos herself creates historical continuity by tracing one of the few women who feature in liberal historiography to Tirso and the Golden Age: beyond Romantic reimaginings but cut from the same nationalist cloth. Tirso even becomes the genesis for other Spanish totems such as Goya, as Ríos declares that 'la *Maja* goyesca tenía precedente excelso en la obra inmortal del Mercedario' [Goya's *Maja* had the most sublime historical precedent in the immortal work of the Mercedario] (1910: 51). Similarly, Ríos stretches and expands the female genealogy created by Tirso to encompass universal and biblical dimensions: 'Pero las mujeres de Tirso no son la raza desgajada de la especie, no: son las hijas de Eva, más bien, Eva naturalizada en España'[But the women of Tirso are not a race disconnected from the species, they are the daughters of Eve, or rather, Eve naturalized in Spain] (1910: 51).

Ríos also has no problem asserting her own scholarly significance, drawing attention to her work on Tirso that had in turn helped fill in gaps for other researchers, in particular how Marcelino Menéndez y Pelayo's studies on Lope de Vega are indebted to her own bibliographical efforts. Ríos lauds the work of Menéndez y Pelayo and bows to his erudition, whilst at the same time boldly claiming a stake for herself. In Dupont's words, 'thus, while she praises effusively and deferentially Menéndez y Pelayo's extensive work on Lope, Blanca de los Ríos implies that without the missing pieces of the Tirso puzzle, the study of Lope is incomplete — much like the literary history of men, without women' (2012: 232).

Don Juan's Daughters: Gender, Genealogy and History

Despite a growing interest in her output, the main locus of this contemporary attention remains her 1907 novella *Las hijas de Don Juan*, as noted by Wright (2007: 25) in one of the most recent studies of the story. In it, Ríos follows the tragic fates of Lita and Dora, daughters of a decadent Don Juan addicted to opium. In the same manner in which I took *Tres amigas* to provide an overview of Asensi's main concerns, I will conclude this introduction to Ríos with a closer look at *Las hijas de Don Juan*, as its gendered take on a Spanish foundational myth constitutes an ideal introduction to expanded readings in Chapters 5 and 6. The title of the story itself condenses the genealogical imagination that permeates both nineteenth-century cultural production and the prose of Ríos with its take on the ancestry of Don Juan, hailed as one of the founding myths of the nation together with other *castizo* totems like Don Quixote and Celestina. Yet instead of focusing on male descendants, we are presented with the daughters rather than the sons of the great seducer, a swap that testifies to the author's preoccupation with gender. It also fits nicely with Ríos's revisionist impulse. Glenn writes that 'this title of *Las hijas de don Juan* immediately alerts us to the fact that the daughters rather than the father are the central characters, and it intimates that paternal influence will be a significant factor in the ensuing story' (1999: 224), whilst Smith Rouselle (2014: 157) suggests that 'by presenting two daughters rather than sons in the story, de los Ríos highlights the significance of mother-daughter father-daughter relationships'.

At the same time, Ríos made no secret of her conservative leanings, reflected in the traditional role she allocated to women, and from which she so markedly departed. Although she devoted herself to scholarly pursuits and regularly lectured in public, Ríos championed the idea of the *ángel del hogar* [angel of the hearth], a devout woman with no ambitions outside the confines of her home.[10] In this respect, it should be noted, she did not deviate from other conservative female pioneers such as Fernán Caballero, Pilar de Sinués or Ángela Grassi, who also led unconventional lives whilst endorsing domestic compliance in their writings. The extent of her conservatism and implications of the characterization of the female characters, together with the denouement of *Las hijas de Don Juan*, have therefore been the subject of debate among the scholars who have studied the text. Although lacking a feminist agenda, the general consensus amongst recent studies had been that *Las hijas de Don Juan* could be viewed at least as gynocentric with its focus on the female descendants of the national myth. Critics like Wright argue that despite Ríos's own transgressive trajectory and personal achievements, the author ultimately recycles negative stereotypes about women (2007: 25). It is a view echoed by Hooper, who in an analysis of the female protagonist in the earlier novella *Sangre española* [Spanish Blood] (1899) observes that these clichés effectively write women out of the national project by casting them in a sacrificial role, without neglecting the equally complex gender discourse that informs the work (2007: 183). As the women in both stories embody the national spirit, the mother nation, they must perish rather than live with the shame of having been tainted by foreign influence.

This fate leads them into a narrative cul-de-sac, yet *Las hijas de Don Juan* presents multiple readings that has made it a text revisited by scholars interested in the gender dynamics behind *fin de siècle* nationalist discourse as seen through a woman's eyes. Consequently, in her dissection of the novella, and despite the hegemonic gender roles endorsed by the author, Johnson draws attention to what she calls the domestication of Don Juan. Johnson (1998: 225) sees the deliberate feminization of the myth by women writers like Ríos as an effort to carve out a niche for themselves in the face of the amoral womanizer Marquis of Bradomín, the modernist Don Juan created by Valle-Inclán and influenced by an aesthetic that once again excluded women, who are reduced to a mere artistic motif to be conquered. As the title of Glenn's essay, 'Demythification and Denunciation in Blanca de los Ríos' *Las hijas de Don Juan*', suggests, it too explores attempts to demote Don Juan from the modernist Parnassus and its solipsistic narcissism to a domestic reality closer to the experience of women and their preoccupations. In this more pedestrian incarnation, Don Juan is reduced to an alcoholic, married below his class and father to two daughters, who struggles to make ends meet in Restoration Madrid.[11]

Las hijas de Don Juan contains two recurring motifs that my own analysis of Ríos's work holds central to understanding her work. Firstly, the tension between the undeniably conservative agenda Ríos promoted and her equally conscious effort to insert women into national genealogies, both in her fiction and in her work as a literary historian: it leads to a textured complexity that in turn provokes a necessary debate among critics, one that Hooper succinctly summarizes as the 'imperative to acknowledge the inconsistencies, difficulties, and hidden sites of complicity in the work of our foremothers, rather than simply celebrating them as straightforward pioneers and sole occupiers of the moral high ground' (2007: 179).[12] Secondly, most critics draw attention to the genealogical imagery present in *Las hijas de Don Juan*, and the decision of Ríos to focus on the female progeny of Don Juan rather than just his conquests. The earliest study by Bordonada even suggests that it is a reply to *El hijo de Don Juan* (1892), a play written by the then wildly popular José de Echegaray, in turn inspired by Henrik Ibsen's *Ghosts* (1881), an intertextuality that Echegaray himself acknowledges in his introduction. Later scholars such as Glenn (1999: 224) question the legitimacy of the literary genealogy that directly connects these plays to Ríos's novella. However, these three works do have a common denominator, in that they all draw from the same stock and articulate moral legacy in the language of consanguinity, influenced in this by *fin de siècle* discourses on degeneration that conflate hereditary pathology with lax ethics. In other words, all three stories follow the biblical dictum that the sins of the father will be revisited upon the sons, or as Ríos reminds us, upon the daughters too. Thus 'both daughters ultimately find no escape from their father's sins other than death. Both daughters and their father are removed from the scene as tragic casualties on the road to a purer one' (Wright 2007: 39).

The decision to make Don Juan the father carries then a host of symbolic ramifications that insert *Las hijas de Don Juan* into the historical imagination of Spain during the Restoration, to which Ríos so heavily contributed.[13] In his analysis of the novella, Reyes Lázaro suggestively summarizes it as 'en suma, el relato pinta una nación de hijas nobles y defraudadas, con cuya situación vital probablemente se identificaba su autora en cuanto mujer de la élite cultural' [to summarize, the story depicts a nation of noble and disappointed daughters, whose situation the author identified with, being a woman from the cultural elite] (2000: 476). Despite her status at the time as an eminent Don Juan scholar, Ríos has been mostly neglected in later studies and anthologies (Glenn 1999: 224; Wright 2007: 25). The following two chapters focus on two even more neglected texts, *Melita Palma* and *Madrid goyesco*, that both carry the imprint of Ríos: gender, genealogy and history.

Notes to Chapter 4

1. David Marcilhacy (2010) has studied *americanismo*, including the contribution of Blanca de los Ríos. For an analysis of the family imagery in *americanismo* (although it does not explicitly mention Ríos) see the section 'La madre España y sus hijas hispanoamericanas: el esquema

familiar aplicado a los pueblos de la Raza' [Mother Spain and Her Latin American Daughters: The Family Model Applied to the People Belonging to the Race] (462–70). María Antonieta González López also covers the *americanista* labour of Ríos in her study (2001: 197–270).
2. Ironically the sound on the reel has been damaged, so that our only image of Ríos is that of a voiceless woman, 'Figuras literarias: en el hogar de Blanca de los Ríos' [Literary Figures: At Home with Blanca de los Ríos], 19 November 1951.
3. So far they include Johnson (1998), Vázquez Recio (1998), Glenn (1999), Lázaro (2000), Paredes Méndez (2007), Wright (2007), Ryan A. Davis (2012) and Smith Rouselle (2014). The story has also been used as a representative example in a recent study by Aresti of gender construction in the nineteenth century (2007: 630).
4. Some scholars have focused on her lyrical production, see Guerrero Cabrera & Villalba Muñoz (2007), Arteaga Soler (2006) and Keefe Ugalde (1997); others have devoted their energies to her *americanista* campaign, Marcilhacy (2010), to her short stories, Ezama Gil (2001), or all of the above in the only comprehensive biography on the author, Gónzalez López (2001). Hooper (2007) has produced a suggestive study on the gendered imperialism in her work.
5. Although her father's poems were not collected and have therefore been lost, this one appeared in *Tertulia literaria: colección de poesías selectas leídas en las reuniones semanales celebradas en la casa de don Juan José Bueno* [Literary Gathering: Collection of Selected Poetries Read in the Weekly Meetings Held in the Home of Don Juan José Bueno] (1861).
6. In *ABC*'s obituary of Ríos, her mother is described as a 'mujer que poseía extraordinarias dotes para la pintura y la poesía y que tuvo marcada influencia en la dedicación de doña Blanca a la labor literaria' [a woman who showed an extraordinary talent for painting and poetry and who significantly influenced Doña Blanca's dedication to writing] (Anon. 1956a: 31).
7. González López (2001: 364–67) has also compiled a comprehensive list of profiles and homages.
8. The fifth Duke of Osuna, Gaspar Téllez-Girón y Sandoval (1656–94) shared surnames with Tirso de Molina, whose real name was Gabriel Téllez. However this is where the coincidences end.
9. The best known of these Romantic reimaginings is the historical play *Doña María de Molina* [Doña María of Molina] written by Mariano Roca de Togores y Carrasco in 1837, that is during the regency of María Cristina. Received well by the public, the play would be repeatedly staged during the nineteenth century. The queen would also be a subject of historical paintings, depicted by, amongst others, Antonio Gisbert in his *María de Molina presenta a su hijo a las Cortes de Valladolid* [María of Molina Presents Her Son to the Courts of Valladolid] (1863). Commissioned by the state, Gisbert was explicitly asked to recreate the historical episode in a painting that still graces the walls of Spanish parliament. The image, also known as *Jura de Fernando IV en las Cortes de Valladolid* [The Oath of Fernando IV in the Courts of Valladolid] was reproduced in several publications throughout the 1800s, including *El Museo Literario* [The Literary Museum] (1863–64), *El Museo Universal* [The Universal Museum] (1864), *La Ilustración de España* [The Illustrated Spanish Magazine] (1886) and *La Ilustración Católica* [The Illustrated Catholic Magazine] (1886) (Pérez Viejo 2001: 100). The figure of Doña María was already feted as a role model in the *Periódico de las Damas* [The Ladies' Newspaper], founded in 1822 and the first publication aimed exclusively at the female market. In the extensive biography it published of her, we read that her feats and diplomacy 'la hizo digna del título Madre de la patria' [made her worthy of the title *Mother of the Country*] (Anon. 1822: 19).
10. Dupont suggests that rather than 'ángel del hogar' Ríos strived for the creation of another female model, the 'ángel del archivo'. Within conservative parameters, she argues, Ríos wishes to reconcile the idea of the feminine with erudition: 'para promocionar una imagen de la mujer investigadora consonante con el feminismo cultural' [to promote an image of the female scholar as consonant with cultural feminism] (2010b: 224–25).
11. Interestingly enough, this pedestrianization or domestication of national myths is not limited to women authors. A year after the publication of *Las hijas de Don Juan*, the writer Eduardo Marquina staged the play *Las hijas del Cid* [The Cid's Daughters] (1908), which similarly shifts attention to the daughters and casts the Cid in a parental role. In his excellent analysis of the

work, Dru Dougherty observes that, just like in the case of Ríos's story, 'the novelty of *Las hijas del Cid* was Marquina's decision to place the Cid's daughters at the center of the action and suggest how they might have viewed their betrothal to the cruel Infantes de Carrión [Princes of Carrión]' (2004: 71). So while I agree with Johnson that the domestication of these national totems has a gendered dimension, it can also be read as a dramatic device that taps into a shared cultural heritage and humanizes myths. It makes them more accessible and relatable to contemporary concerns. In the case of *Las hijas del Cid* one could interpret the daughters' refusal to accept their betrothals as the growing emancipation of women or as criticism of arranged marriage as an increasingly outdated custom.

12. Hooper also remarks on the tension inherent in the novella when she wonders at the end of her study on Casanova how other works such as *Las hijas de Don Juan* contest or perpetuate contemporary images of masculinity and femininity (2008: 173–74).

13. Her interest in the myth translated into a string of studies that turned Ríos into a preeminent Don Juan expert in her time. Her articles on the figure graced the pages of such publications as *La España Moderna* [Modern Spain], in which the essay 'Don Juan: en la literatura; en la música' [Don Juan in Literature and in Music] appeared in 1889.

CHAPTER 5

❖

Performing Pedigree in *Melita Palma*

This chapter examines the novella *Melita Palma* (1901), which is centred on the eponymous protagonist, an actress who pretends to have a noble pedigree after her relationship with an aristocrat meets opposition from his mother. A melodrama of impossible love on the surface, this study situates *Melita Palma* in the aftermath of the Disaster of 98, recasting it as a reflection of the roles available to women in the regeneration discourses. The publication date of *Melita Palma* is indicative of a specific historical context. Ríos's novella appeared at the threshold of a new reign, that of Alfonso XIII who would come of age in 1902. Until this point, his mother the Queen Regent María Cristina had filled the vacant throne after the early death of Alfonso XII from consumption when she was pregnant with the future king, a potentially melodramatic situation in itself. Largely playing a ceremonial role, the regency of María Cristina would witness the loss of the Philippines and Cuba in 1898, Spain's last significant colonies, an event that triggered much soul-searching and calls for national regeneration. It would colour the reign of Alfonso XIII (1902–31), a period that saw the country shift from classical liberalism to mass democracy. The historian Carlos Seco Serrano (2002: 3) calls the four years between the Disaster of '98 and 1902, when Alfonso XIII ascended the throne, 'el examen de conciencia de la Restauración, el replanteamiento de sus supuestos y directrices' [the soul-searching of the Restoration, the re-examining of its assumptions and policies]. The 'desastre' as it was quickly dubbed, led indeed to much soul-searching and calls for national regeneration, another key concept that becomes a battle cry for all political stances and affiliations. Everyone was now talking about 'regeneration' and the word's malleability contributed to its ubiquity in *fin de siècle* discourse (Villares & Moreno Luzón 2009: 301).

Yet regardless of the form it took, a preoccupation with recovering a lost virility informs these recipes for national regeneration. All political parties, too, highlighted the important role played by women as mothers guiding new generations in this national renewal (Blasco Herranz 2013: 173). It is a role that women themselves rhetorically exploited, as is evident in the declarations of the writer Concepción Gimeno de Flaquer, who in 1900 warned that one could not achieve 'la deseada regeneración de la patria mientras no contéis con la influencia femenina' [the desired regeneration of the homeland as long you exclude female influence] (Gimeno de Flaquer 1900: 265). Taken from her book *Evangelios de la mujer* [The Women's Gospel], Gimeno de Flaquer advocates for increased female participation in this genesis of the Spanish nation, whilst simultaneously highlighting her procreational role as in its biblical antecedent. Echoing her contemporaries, she invokes a female force that has yet to be diluted or corrupted, unlike its male counterpart, and which will give birth to and nurture a new generation. Women are construed in terms of this maternal instinct and didactic vocation. In *Carta a las mujeres de España* [Letter to the Women of Spain], María de la O Lejárraga addresses her compatriots as: '¡Mujeres de España, cread la España nueva e inmortal en el entendimiento de vuestros hijos, que ahora son como cera en vuestras manos!' [Women of Spain, create the new and immortal Spain for your children, so malleable in your hands now!] (Martínez Sierra 1916: 78). María de la O Lejárraga, who was later revealed as the author of many works originally published under her husband's name, Gregorio Martínez Sierra, encapsulates the discursive complexity present in the output of many of these women, often judged contradictory by today's definition of female emancipation.

Ríos is another complex case who shared María de la O Lejárraga's preoccupation with the fate of Spain, actively pushing for its regeneration through her *americanista* campaigns and other initiatives that sought to renew the cultural clout of Spain. *Melita Palma* can thus be read as a reflection on how women, embodied in a Melita haunted by her own precarious pedigree, can help restore a now-decaying noble household, with a clear parallel to the Spain of the Queen Mother María Cristina and the recently crowned Alfonso XIII.

In *Melita Palma,* Ríos narrates the story of the young actress Carmen or Carmela Palma, known affectionately as Melita, and the aristocrat Alfonso de Mendoza de Castilla y Aragón, who falls in love with her after attending a theatre performance. Called Poncho by his nearest, Alfonso is heir to the earldom of Villa-Enhiesta via his mother and the baronetcy of Castro-Infanzones via his father, and thus possesses an impeccable pedigree, being both a baron and a count. Melita, on the other hand, descends from a more humble lineage, the daughter of an impoverished couple, and she is forced to tour the provinces to earn a living. She ranks low in the world of theatre, an understudy who has just got her lucky break, replacing the actress who normally plays the supporting role of Cintia in Agustín Moreto's Golden Age love comedy *El desdén con el desdén* [Contempt with Contempt]. Faced with a new performer, a curious audience tries to place Melita and links her with the better-known Pepita Palma, with whom she appears to share a surname. The influential theatre critic Pepe Sútis quickly corrects this erroneous parentage, exclaiming '¡qué mal andáis de genealogía histriónica!' [how poor is your knowledge of thespian genealogy!] (Ríos 1901: 18), and proceeds to sketch out the true family tree of Pepita Palma who is unrelated to the unknown Melita.[1] Not only does Melita lack aristocratic credentials, she cannot claim parentage to theatre royalty either. However, this confusion over her true genealogy expressed by the theatre audience augurs the narrative fate of the young actress, destined to inhabit different personas offstage too. This multiplicity of identities will become a central theme in the story. Melita goes under different aliases depending on which character is addressing her, yet all these names share underlying connotations of blankness that envision Melita as a clean slate without history.

In her reading of *Melita Palma*, González López sees in this clean slate the embodiment of the people that will rescue Spain from its quixotic trance, represented here by her would-be lover and his mother, Alfonso Castro Infanzones and Isabel of Castile. Such reading fits with Ríos's well-documented preoccupation with national regeneration. González López concludes that:

> Castro Infanzones representa a una rancia aristocracia desprovista ya de función social. Melita, la potencialidad escondida en un pueblo bajo que atesora domésticas y sencillas virtudes. Isabel de Castilla de Mendoza el inmovilismo de una sociedad que tiene que desaparecer para hacer posible la nueva conjunción de valores. (González López 2001: 80)

> [Castro Infanzones represents a stagnant aristocracy now lacking a social function. Melita on the other hand represents the hidden potential of the common people with their modest and domestic set of values. Isabel of Castile of Mendoza, the stagnation of a society that has to disappear to make way for the new set of values.]

The unequal union between Melita and Castro Infanzones proves too much of a transgressive solution for Ríos, at least according to González López. Thus in the later story 'Romanticismo' [Romanticism], Ríos has the working-class protagonist sacrificing himself to save the fortune of his beloved, a ruined aristocrat. This end guarantees the continuation of the existing rigid social order.

I argue however that the denouement of *Melita Palma* is not that subversive, partly because the story finishes unresolved, without the confirmation of any nuptials, and partly because striving to be part of an established social order, as Melita does by posing as an aristocrat, is not particularly revolutionary either. Tightly packed with literary references that often refract against each other, *Melita Palma* the story can be viewed from multiple angles and, like Melita Palma the actress, can support many readings. Ríos spends very little time on the backstory of Melita and we rarely hear any of it recounted by the actress herself. Instead that role falls to her admirers and detractors, as in 'El encubierto', wherein the protagonist remains similarly silent on his origins although for different reasons. As the pretender figure of El Encubierto serves as a site for others to project their visions for the role of the monarch in the new liberal state, so the actress serves as a projection of visions for the roles that women could legitimately perform in a post-1898 Spain, particularly with regard to its regeneration. What part should they play in suggested recovery plans?

Before further textual analysis, we need to first dispel the belief that this novella is merely a pale copy of better and more representative works, often novels or short stories penned by authors associated with Realism. Secondly, we must recast the novella, a genre historically stigmatized for its commercial aspirations and mass appeal, as an equally valid platform on which to present concerns. After all, *Melita Palma* shares a semiotic polysemy with *Las hijas de Don Juan*, a text that has been interpreted by scholars as both a dismantling of androcentric myths such as that of Don Juan and an affirmation of sacrificial female archetypes, proven by the ultimate death of the female protagonists. While this intertextual richness continues to attract the attention of critics, the similarly ambiguous *Melita Palma* has yet to be the subject of a monograph. It is dismissed by González López as 'trasunto de *Juanita la Larga*' [a variation of *Juanita the Long One*] (2001: 60). By effectively labelling it as a lesser version of *Juanita la Larga* (1895), a novel by the canonized Juan Valera, González López contributes to the image of Ríos as a derivative writer. In her overview of the narrative of Ríos, González López concludes that Ríos 'no dudó en tomar prestados temas y argumentos de cuentos y novelas de sus mejores amigos o de sus más admirados escritores' [did not hesitate in borrowing themes and plots from the stories or novels of her best friends or from her most admired writers] (2001: 60). She then demonstrates this thematic affinity by linking some of the motifs that appear in the stories of Ríos to previous outings in the work of more prominent writers such as Benito Pérez Galdós, Juan Valera, Luis Coloma and Emilia Pardo Bazán. However, many of the themes pinpointed by González López as the creation of another particular author have extensive family trees themselves, with roots either in folklore or nineteenth-century literary lore. The themes of hubris, family rivalry or impossible love are basic building-blocks in the construction of any narrative tradition — Pérez Galdós or Pardo Bazán may have incorporated them successfully into their fiction and popularized certain variants, but this does not make them sole shareholders. Such a value system has led to misleading comparisons between *Juanita la Larga*, a Realist novel set in Andalusia with evocative descriptions of rural customs, and *Melita Palma*, a novella set in urban Madrid.

Similarly, Ezama Gil compares Ríos's work to her peer Pardo Bazán and finds it wanting although concedes that her mastery of the Spanish language is second to none (2001: 187). Such comparisons recall the conclusions reached by Diéz Ménguez who sees Asensi as a belated Romantic who emulates Zorrilla and Bécquer because she too writes legends and shares a thematic overlap. This categorization that identifies a particular source as the original establishes in the process a pyramid with canonical authors like Valera or Bécquer at the top and people like Ríos and Asensi at the bottom, relegated to the status of imperfect copy. This is a contextualization that, as we have seen, narrowed the analytical framework of Asensi's work.

In an article on the intellectual legacy of Ríos, part of the current revisionist wave, Dupont speaks of another kind of contextualization:

> La necesidad de contextualizar la obra de 'los grandes' junto con la de los autores menores — incluso se cuestiona esa distinción, porque hemos establecido que muchas veces la diferencia entre un autor mayor y uno menor se debe a una serie de casualidades, sobre todo en el caso de mujeres. (Dupont 2010a: 9)
>
> [The need to contextualize the work of the 'greats' together with that of minor authors — this distinction is now being questioned, as we have established that often the difference between a major and a minor author is due to a series of coincidences, particularly in the case of women.]

Similarly, Hooper volunteers for this task with her enlightening re-examination of the work of Casanova, and in her concluding remarks proposes *Melita Palma* amongst a series of texts that would broaden our horizons of the past with their often alternative take on gender, empire, race or nation as compared to the main narratives (2008: 173). *Melita Palma* certainly loses some texture if removed from its context and measured against parameters that misleadingly universalize certain experiences or literary manifestations at the expense of less 'legitimate' ones. As we have seen, the ambiguity of 'El encubierto' and its indebtedness to liberal historiography is further amplified against an analysis of the disseminating function of universal libraries. In the same way, *Melita Palma* benefits from a closer look at the means of production and the medium in which it appeared in order to better assess the aims and audience of Ríos. Without at least a partial reconstruction of the circumstances surrounding its publication it is easy to dismiss her fiction, in this case *Melita Palma*, as conventional.

This conception of Ríos as traditional and wary of innovation stems from the fact that she only penned one novel at the beginning of her career, *Margarita*, published in 1878 under the anagrammatic pseudonym of Carolina del Boss, and which González López dismisses as 'esta obra primeriza de una joven escritora se sitúa completamente al margen de las inquietudes ideológicas que condicionan decisivamente el género en ese período' [this first work of a young writer is set completely outside the ideological concerns that decisively shape the genre during this period] (2001: 23). With this review, the critic implies a complete lack of engagement by Ríos with the political reality of the time, in contrast to more committed — and canonized — authors who portray this changing reality in their fiction. Again, the ubiquitous Pérez Galdós had released his thesis novel *Doña Perfecta* [Mrs Perfect] (1876) two years earlier, wherein he distilled the ideological confrontation between a progressive and a conservative Spain. The novelistic debut of Ríos could not be more different, resembling a Romantic narrative with its exalted tone and ethereal heroine condemned to a tragic end. In fact, Ríos references Zorrilla's historical legend *La pasionaria* [The Passionflower] (1840–41) with a heroine who will similarly meet the sort of calamitous fate that characterizes the genre. The preface to *La pasionaria* mentions in turn *Margarita la tornera* [Margarita the Gatekeeper] (1840–41), another of Zorrilla's legends that shares the title with Ríos's novelistic debut *Margarita*, thus constructing the sort intertextual hall of mirrors that characterizes her later work.

It should be noted that this first and last foray by Ríos into novel-writing includes a foreword by Nicolás Díaz de Benjumea, editor of *La Ilustración de la Mujer* and known Cervantist. Like her peer Asensi, Ríos prefers to enter the literary forum chaperoned and with a work that, like *Tres amigas*, is closer to the length of a novella. In his introduction, Benjumea locates the roots of Realism in England, giving special emphasis to its many female practitioners who had lent the genre such a respectable pedigree in the Anglo-Saxon world, yet fails to mention any specific examples (Boss 1878: 6). This is a Realism that documents the customs of the middle classes and their interiors, an activity that Benjumea regards as an instinctive fit for women, the domestic realm being their natural remit. Although circumscribed by the narrow confines of domesticity, it shows Ríos's chaperon attempting to legitimize the production of women and constructing a genealogy for Realism that includes their work. This is the case even if, as we have seen, Ríos's narrative in *Margarita* follows Romantic mores rather than the placid Realism praised by

Benjumea. The choice not to emulate Galdosian precepts in the novel itself comes therefore not from a place of ideological illiteracy or isolation. Ríos was aware of the clout of Realism as Benjumea's introduction testifies. Something similar would happen with her subsequent novella production, which would likewise fall victim to a literary hierarchy that hails certain literary modes as more representative of a period at the expense of other 'lesser' ones.[2]

Minor Literary Pedigrees: Ríos and the Novella

Melita Palma was published in 1901 as the seventeenth volume of the prestigious Biblioteca Mignon [Mignon Library], its author the first woman to be included and one of only two, with Carmen de Burgos, who published *Alucinación* [Hallucination] in 1904.[3] The Biblioteca Mignon had been founded in 1899 by Bernardo Rodríguez Serra and may be considered one of the first collections dedicated to the novella. Established authors such as Juan Valera, Leopoldo Alas 'Clarín', Benito Pérez Galdós, Pedro Antonio de Alarcón and José María de Pereda all contributed with stories. It famously published *Jardín umbrío: historias de santos, de almas en pena, de duendes y ladrones* [Shaded Garden: Stories of Saints, of Lost Souls, of Spirits and Thieves] (1903) by Ramón del Valle-Inclán, considered a major exponent of *fin de siècle* decadentism. The catalogue of the Biblioteca Mignon constitutes a juncture of older writers like Pérez Galdós, associated with the Realist novel, and younger ones like Valle-Inclán, adherents to a newer Modernist aesthetic (Bordonada 2006: 17). It offers an eclectic yet comprehensive mosaic of the cultural landscape, of which Blanca de los Ríos was part, even if subsequent literary taxonomy has excluded her. Her presence among such a select group of authors testifies to the literary standing of Ríos herself, echoing the solitary presence of Asensi as the female exception in another *biblioteca*, the Biblioteca Universal.

Smaller and more affordable in form than the tomes of the Biblioteca Universal, those of the later Biblioteca Mignon represent a further step in the expansion of the literary market propelled by an equally growing readership. This is reflected in the price, with a leather-bound *Leyendas y tradiciones* still priced at 10 pesetas in 1883 compared to a flimsy paper-bound *Melita Palma* costing a mere 75 cents two decades later, in 1901. The inclusion of illustrations, starting with the one that adorns the cover, serves as a further nod to the commercial aspirations of the Biblioteca Mignon. Published between 1899 and 1910, it could be regarded as a transitional collection, not yet as streamlined as the later *El Cuento Semanal* [The Weekly Story] (Sáinz de Robles: 1975). The brainchild of Eduardo Zamacois, *El Cuento Semanal* was founded five years later, in 1907, in Madrid and soon catalyzed the genre. Despite its name, the success of *El Cuento Semanal* helped consolidate the popularity of the *novela corta* [novella], and would spawn other collections with varying degrees of longevity.[4] These include *Los Contemporáneos* [The Contemporaries], *La Novela Corta* [The Novella], *La Novela Semanal* [The Weekly Novel], *La Novela Contemporánea* [The Contemporary Novel], *El Libro Popular* [The Popular Book], *La Novela de Bolsillo* [The Pocket Novel], *La Novela para Todos* [The Novel of the People] and many others.⁵ Adjectives such as *contemporáneo*, *corta*, *semanal* and *popular* allude to the distinguishing characteristics of this format: modern, accessible and brief.

It would be precisely this commercial and democratic nature that would later taint its image. The novella certainly did not replace the Realist novel as the legitimate vehicle to debate the state of the nation, even if some of its most famous exponents like Pérez Galdós or Blasco Ibáñez cultivated it. Instead the novella suffered the same fate as other genres that fell foul of a gendered appraisal system suspicious of the female and the foreign. As Hooper remarks:

> The *novela corta* — with its roots in popular literature, its sentimental themes, and its large female readership — was, by its very nature, a hybrid genre and therefore perceived as potentially threatening (and of course inferior) to the 'true' Spanish novel. (Hooper 2008: 110)

Instead the baton of legitimacy was taken up by the introspective prose of writers like Unamuno or Azorín or the avant-garde experimentations of Valle-Inclán. The marginalization of the novella in dominant models of literary criticism is even more acute in the case of those produced by women, as they are buried under a double-gendered discourse. On the one hand they are perceived as practising a genre pegged as feminine, byword for sentimental, and on the other hand they embody it themselves as women.

The critical neglect of this genre of the novella has left a significant void in our knowledge of its impact and particularly how the *novela corta* may have helped women in their literary pursuits.⁶ In her examination of Sofia Casanova as a writer of novellas, Hooper defends Casanova against critics like Amparo Hurtado (1998: 153) who had labelled her output as conventional, the same label she gives to Ríos. The more conventionally progressive Burgos, on the other hand, is seen by the same critic as someone who broke the passive mould. This rather simplistic categorization divides women writers into 'good' and 'bad' feminists based on modern sensibilities that make no reference to much of the historical context, and which 'reinforce the conviction that existing models for reading *fin de siglo* literature simply do not function for these complex and often contradictory texts' (Hooper 2008: 113).

This dismissal of novellas as a genre unworthy of concern was just as true in the case of *Melita Palma*, which as we have seen, was not even published in a fully-fledged novella collection, but in the more exclusive Biblioteca Mignon.⁷ Many of its contributors, including Clarín, Benavente and Valle-Inclán, had already collaborated with the founder Bernardo Rodriguez Serra in his short-lived magazine *La Vida Literaria* [Literary Life], which in turn had started as a literary supplement to the established *Madrid Cómico* [Comical Madrid], an influential satirical publication. The initial promotion of the Biblioteca Mignon, with its mix of accessibility and cultural curation, reminds us of the mission statement of the Biblioteca Universal, illustrated by descriptions such as the one printed in *El Álbum Ibero-Americano*: 'Publica en elegantes tomitos, que solo cuestan 75 céntimos, las mejores obras de los más notables autores nacionales y extranjeros. Desenvolver la cultura literaria en España es la patriótica misión que se ha impuesto Rodríguez Serra' [It publishes in small elegant tomes, priced at only 75 cents, the best works of notable national and foreign authors. Rodríguez Serra has taken upon himself the patriotic mission of unpacking literary culture in Spain] (Latorre 1901: 82). Just as Asensi's *Leyendas y tradiciones* forms part of a collection presented as a selection of the best of national and foreign works, *Melita Palma* appeared as one of the early volumes of another *biblioteca* with canonical ambitions.

As women, Ríos and Asensi both cut solitary figures in these predominantly male compilations, a gender disparity that only serves to further highlight their tales of problematic pedigrees and precarious legitimacy. Asensi leaves the ancestry of El Encubierto unresolved, while the flair for imitation displayed by the female protagonist haunts the story of Ríos. It would be tempting to conclude that it is a premeditated move on the part of both Asensi and Ríos to criticize conceptions of cultural legitimacy that repeatedly marginalized women and conceived their input as derivative. However this interpretation would entail succumbing to an equally simplified narrative that dismisses 'El encubierto' as a pale echo of Zorrilla and *Melita Palma* as mere melodrama.

Performing Pedigree: The Many Melitas

As I mentioned in the introduction to this chapter, Melita goes under many names but a common denominator of female passiveness characterizes all of them. She initially fails to catch the attention of her future lover Poncho, who does not notice her until the theatre critic Pepe Sútis goads him into meeting her during a performance of *El desdén con el desdén*. It transpires that the mother of Melita, weakened by hunger and hardship, had fainted during the interval, the first of many climatic collapses that punctuates the story, and the one that leads to the first encounter between the two lovers. Sútis, a fervent admirer of Melita, instigates this meeting in the hope that Poncho will assist the ailing mother. The aristocrat is initially reluctant to meet a lowly actress but Sútis, a great storyteller, pulls at his heart strings and persuades him to meet the tragically noble Melita: 'y le contó ce por be la conmovedora historia de Melita Palma, la gallarda Cintia que tenían enfrente, *Rayo de luna*, como Sútis la llamaba' [and he told him in detail the moving story of Melita Palma, the brave Cintia standing in front of him, *Moon Beam* as Sútis called her] (Ríos 1901: 27). We readers do not hear the details of this story but are only informed that it is a sad one. Instead we are left to project our own lachrymose biography on Melita, thereby imposing an archetypal construct on her roles. So before Poncho has been introduced to Melita, he has already become acquainted with Sútis's poetic projection: 'Impresión que irresistiblemente experimentó también Alfonso cuando, interesado por el relato de Sútis, fijó sus gemelos en la gentil muchacha' [Alfonso, intrigued by Sútis's tale, was left with the same impression upon fixing his opera glasses on the graceful girl] (27). His view through the opera glasses is coloured by his friend's portrayal, one that contains three women: 'Melita', 'Cintia' and '*Rayo de luna*'.

The latter designation, clearly his preferred one, reveals the romanticized vision Sútis entertains, as echoing the ephemeral *rayo de luna* popularized by Gustavo Adolfo Bécquer. In one of his better-known legends called 'El rayo de luna' [The

Moon Beam] (1862), Bécquer had recounted the story of the knight Manrique, who evocatively shares his name with the famous medieval poet Jorge Manrique, and his fervent search for the ideal woman, only to realize it is all a projection and that he has mistakenly been chasing a moon beam. By christening Melita '*Rayo de luna*', Sútis, an unrepentant bohemian who peppers his speech with literary references, implies that Melita is an ideal to him rather than a woman. Her physical presence, as per his description, contributes to this Romantic intangibility: 'la impresión luminosa que en él hacían la diafanidad de sus pupilas azules, la blancura nacarada de su tez, el tibio resplandor de sus cabellos de oro ceniciento' [he was left with the luminous impression of her diaphanous blue irises, the pearly whiteness of her skin, the restrained radiance of her flaxen hair] (Ríos 1901: 27). This description could as well have come from the imagination of Bécquer's Manrique, a similarity emphasized by passages such as '¡Tan buena, tan espiritual, tan etérea que casi no es humana! Que es, en efecto, lo que dice Sútis, un rayo místico de luna' [So kind, so spiritual, so ethereal that she is almost not human! She is indeed, as Sútis says, a mystical moon beam] (Ríos 1901: 52).

A moon beam in the imagination of Sútis, to Poncho Melita becomes 'Cintia', 'llamándola con el dulce nombre que le daba en sus intimidades' [calling her by the sweet name he used in private] (Ríos 1901: 75), after a role she played when they first met. She even stays in costume during this first encounter, her attire more worthy of her noble character than her worn-down daily getup. It further emphasizes her role as romanticized projection. With this literary epithet, Poncho attempts to elevate his Cintia from the less salubrious connotations attached to the profession of actress at the time, often lovers to the wealthy, and thus not too far from a courtesan in the eyes of Poncho's disapproving mother (62). To reassure himself initially that Melita is not a kept woman, he tellingly repeats to himself a phrase originally uttered by Sútis, 'Cintia no es una comedianta, sino un celeste rayo de luna' [Cintia is not an actress but a celestial moon beam] (44), a comforting mantra that reveals a penchant for poetic projections shared by Sútis. Like a good bohemian, Sútis also resorts to mythological imagery when, praising her thespian flair, imagining Melita as a goddess of deceit: '¡Oh, Cintia incomparable; si yo fuera Júpiter, te proclamaría *Diosa de la Mentira*, porque nadie como tú sabe convertir en pura verdad la ficción!' [Oh incomparable Cintia; if I were Jupiter, I would proclaim you *Goddess of Lies*, because no one like you knows how to turn pure truth into fiction] (40). Ríos waves a semantic web around the names of Melita that highlights her function as a passive sign that fits into the stories of other characters rather than someone with her own biography and narrative agency. As Charnon-Deutsch concludes in her study of images of the feminine in the Spanish nineteenth-century press: 'A floating signifier, she may be attached to any concept that requires symbolic representation to produce emotional impact' (2000: 94).

Even Ríos herself remains undecided on how to refer to her own literary creation. While Sútis calls her '*Rayo de luna*' and Poncho favours 'Cintia', the omniscient narrator alternates between 'Melita', 'Carmen' and 'Carmela', all three variations of the same name, taken from the Latin root of 'poem', 'song' or 'charm', an etymological overlap that further cements the role of the central female character as a lyrical entity, a multifaceted malleable text, rather than a concrete person.

However, none of these incarnations passes the strict pedigree requirements of Isabel, Countess of Villa-Enhiesta and mother of Poncho. Both *Rayo de luna* and *Cintia* might have impeccable poetic lineage but they lack aristocratic credentials. To gain her acceptance, Melita must adopt yet another identity, that of the patrician Clara de Alvarado, a name which true to the predilection of Ríos for patronymic puns also carries certain qualities the author wishes to associate with the character. The chameleonic Melita, who decides to pose as a gentlewoman to gain the blessing of the matriarch, now bears the name of 'Clara', which could be translated as 'clear', a transparent effort to prove she has nothing to hide, whilst her surname 'Alvarado' points towards a long noble lineage traceable to the early years of the Reconquista, the emblematic historical period in which Christians 'reclaimed' Spain from the Moors (García Carraffa 1922). Additionally, and to further emphasize the purity of this persona, 'Alvarado' also means 'whitened place', from the Latin root for white, *albus*. Combined with 'Clara', this new alias accentuates her immaculateness to an almost comic degree, and like a River Jordan, erases all theatrical traces that have tainted her image. Melita becomes once more a blank canvas upon which aristocratic pretensions can now be projected.

Although most pronounced in the case of the multiple Melitas, Ríos's predilection for symbolic names is not reserved for the young actress alone. The story opens with a description of the disapproving matriarch, whom Ríos saddles with the grandiloquent matronymic Isabel of Castile of Mendoza and Aragon and proceeds to describe as a 'matrona histórica' [historic matron] (Ríos 1901: 10), a suitable title for someone whose name so explicitly alludes to Queen Isabel the Catholic. Although known affectionately as 'Poncho', her only child and heir is called Alfonso, another name redolent of royalty and with a long line of monarchs who have carried it, including the current reigning king Alfonso XIII. Modesto Lafuente extols the ancestral brilliance of a name carried almost unfailingly by illustrious men: '¡Qué galería regia tan brillante esta de los Alfonsos de Castilla!'[What a brilliant royal gallery is that of the Alfonsos of Castile]. This is followed by a long list of Alfonsos that lead Lafuente to conclude that 'casi todos fueron, o capitanes invictos, o ilustres legisladores, o conquistadores célebres, y algunos lo fueron todo' [nearly all of them were either unbeaten captains, illustrious lawmakers or famous conquerors, and some were all of them] (1852: 6–7).

However, this Alfonso shares more qualities with Don Quixote, a figure hailed by national mythology as emblematically *castizo* as any Alfonso. González López (2001: 212) calls this reliance on literary figures to explain national character a 'visión literaturizada de la realidad española' [the reality of Spain filtered through a literary lens], and one which characterizes the second half of the nineteenth century. Ríos writes of a metaphorical 'roto lanzón, la contrahecha adarga y el apócrifo yelmo de Mambrino' [broken lance, bent shield and the apocryphal helmet of Mambrino] (Ríos 1901: 11) to highlight the mystical knight persona of Alfonso reduced, like his Cervantine counterpart, to inhabit the more prosaic reality of Quixote.[8] His familiar name 'Poncho' resembles after all the similarly prosaic 'Sancho Panza'. His imagination ignited by Sútis, Poncho envisions Melita as a damsel in distress in need of his protection and asks himself: '¿Ni dónde empresa más digna de caballeros, y aún de príncipes que la de proteger al genio obscurecido y amparar a la doncellez desvalida?' [Is there an enterprise more worthy of knights, and even princes, than defending the overlooked genius and protecting the damsel in distress?] (35–36). It is a role that Melita easily fills, almost playing along or as if it were expected from her, implied by sentences such as 'después, cual si la muchacha adivinase la primera impresión del visitante' [afterwards, as if the girl had guessed the visitor's first impression] (30) and 'como si hubiese leído el pensamiento de Mendoza' [as if she had read Mendoza's mind] (37). However, without a solid pedigree to support the noble persona for whom her son has fallen, a scandalized Doña Isabel refuses to give her blessing to such a union:

> ¡Nunca hubiera creído que un hijo de aquel padre, un hijo de mis entrañas perdiese la dignidad y el decoro, hasta el punto de atreverse a dar su nombre — ¡un nombre como el suyo! — a una mujercilla de teatro que nada tiene que perder y que se deja mantener por sus amantes! (Ríos 1901: 62).
>
> [I never would have thought that a child from that father, a child of my own flesh would lose his dignity and decorum, to the point of daring to give his name — a name like his! — to a mere woman from the theatre that has nothing to lose and lets herself be kept by her lovers!]

Faced with such maternal opposition, Alfonso or 'Poncho' conducts his meetings with Melita or 'Cintia' clandestinely, and, forced to lie to his mother, finds himself playing more than one role. Eventually he tells the truth, a confession that triggers an attack that in true melodramatic fashion leaves his mother bedridden, concerned that her only son is tarnishing the family name and has intentions of diluting the lineage through marriage to an actress. Needing a nurse for the ailing countess, Melita convinces Poncho she can fill this role with the help of the family doctor, confidant to the lovers and sympathetic to their plight. She now enters the household of the countess as Clara de Alvarado, a young nun of noble family, who will look after the invalid. The doctor together with Sútis helps to erase all previous traces of Melita and claims that she has emigrated to the Americas. Clara de Alvarado soon proves popular with the countess, who believes that such modest distinction can only be inherited, leading to the earlier-mentioned conclusion that 'ya se le conoce cuna, porque esa distinción tan señoril no se aprende, se hereda' [one can tell she is of gentle birth, because that aristocratic distinction cannot be learnt, one inherits it] (84). To further highlight Melita's talent for performance, the countess lauds the devotion and candour with which Clara reads *The Imitation of Christ* (86). Clara performs the role with such conviction that her lover starts to doubt whether he knows the real person behind the mask, even though ironically he refers to her by the name of Cintia, the name of the character she plays on stage as an actress.

Even Melita herself blurs the lines between fact and fiction as she attempts to reconcile her many selves. In her own twisted logic she reaches the conclusion that her current incarnation of the noble Clara accurately reflects her own spotless spiritual pedigree and that her performance should therefore not be considered a deceit but actually a rehabilitation of the truth. In a way, this is what Ríos had done with Tirso de Molina, suggesting a noble origin that reflected the playwright's noble character. As an actress the countess could never accept Melita, but now that the latter has removed the negative assumptions that surround her profession by pretending to be someone else — the logic goes — she will be seen for who she really is. She reasons with a sceptical Alfonso: '¿Soy yo como ella me veía? No; luego la engañada era ella, luego no hay engaño alguno, en ésta que tú llamas ficción, y no es sino restablecimiento de la verdad' [Am I as she first judged me? No; so she was the one deceived, and there is no deception, and what you call fiction is merely a reestablishment of the truth] (101).

The countess overhears this conversation whispered behind a folding screen, another nod to the theatrical setting of the story, as the two lovers are depicted standing behind the scenes out of character before reprising their roles in front of the ailing matriarch. Soon afterwards the condition of the countess rapidly deteriorates whilst at the same time she shows a new-found interest in the family history of Clara, a clear sign that she has started to suspect the alleged pedigree of her pious nurse. On her deathbed, the countess forgives the deceit and blesses the union between the woman she calls Clara and her son. The story ends dramatically with the matriarch expiring to the dismay of Alfonso and 'Carmen', which is how the author refers to the young actress in her last mention of the character. One presumes that with all major obstacles cleared, Melita will now finally gain a noble pedigree that reflects her noble character, although it remains unclear whom Alfonso 'Poncho' Mendoza will marry. Will she remain Clara Alvarado? Will he still address her as Cintia in private? Has Melita Palma ceased to exist? And despite presumptions that she will become part of the noble household, her fate remains uncertain. Like 'El encubierto', *Melita Palma* ends rather abruptly, without any indication as to whether the protagonist marries her love interest and finally acquires the aristocratic credentials she already emulates with such ease. Will her noble spirit be vindicated with a noble pedigree? Unlike the situation in 'El encubierto', the humble origins of Melita are known from the start. Yet her legitimacy remains equally in limbo, as it is uncertain whether a marriage will materialize from the clandestine affair, and if so, whether this morganatic union will receive society's stamp of approval.

In this respect, the ending of the story defies genre conventions whilst at the same time conforming to the status quo. Melita does not turn out to be of noble birth, a solution that would have solved her plight in a manner befitting melodramatic conventions. The characterization of the countess, whom the author repeatedly refers to as a 'saint' shows that the conservative Ríos had no intention of dismantling the social order. Ultimately the triumph of Melita and her ability to pass as a noblewoman is countered by the death of the countess, who struggles until the end to come to terms with the plebeian pedigree of her prospective daughter-in-law. Similarly, while the ease with which she feigns a pedigree questions its quality, her transgression can also be framed within a stratified worldview in line with the orthodox political allegiances of the author. In his study on the figure of the impostor in Victorian society, Rohan McWilliam notes that:

> Whilst the impostor may appear to be a subversive figure, it should also be added that the impostors treated here were usually people who wanted to become aristocrats and thus endorsed the aristocratic principle, underwriting elitism. Impostors were ultimately conservative. (McWilliam 2010: 69–70)

Despite the emergence of the liberal state and the rise of the bourgeoisie, the aristocracy retained much cultural clout, as well as political influence and wealth. The mechanisms of legitimacy might have undergone substantial changes but a noble pedigree still carried considerable currency. Gilmartin (1998: 12) had earlier pointed out how the figure of the foundling who turns out to be of noble lineage, reflecting his or her noble character, pervades much of eighteenth- and nineteenth-century literature. In these stories the noble birth is revealed, leading to pedigree being retroactively reinstated, a strategy Ríos had herself used for Tirso de Molina to promote the playwright to a privileged position within the Spanish canon. In the absence of a coat of arms, a noble character offered the possibility of reflecting the concern of an ascendant middle class to strengthen their authority by inscribing themselves into an emerging national genealogy.

Pérez Galdós mocked the 'rags to riches' storyline in his *La desheredada* [The Disinherited Lady] (1881), which echoes both the title and content of *Los desheredados* [The Disinherited Ones] (1857), a serialized novel by the wildly successful Manuel Fernández y González (Ríos-Font 2004b: 58). Pérez Galdós's version follows the misadventures of Isidora Rufete, who becomes convinced she is the long-lost illegitimate offspring of the Marquess of Aransis. Also hailing from La Mancha, Isidora falls prey to Quixotic delusions about her true self, inspired by her father — whose death in a lunatic asylum opens the novel — and further nurtured by her uncle.

Like *La desheredada*, *Melita Palma* centres around a female character from a humble background who becomes convinced of her own idiosyncratic ancestry. '¡Yo he leído mi propia historia tantas veces!' [I have read my own story so many times!] (Pérez Galdós 2000: 171) remarks Isidora Rufete, in reference to the many rags-to-riches stories found in popular fiction. To further highlight her portrayal as a female Don Quixote, Pérez Galdós not only has her hailing from a village in La Mancha, but also finds a squire in the figure of her godfather Don José de Relimpio. Although not entirely convinced by her claim to the marquisate, Don José remains, like Sancho Panza, Isidora's ever-faithful companion. Her campaign for legitimacy starts during the reign of King Amadeo I who is also struggling to establish his credentials. Caught in the egalitarian whirlwind of the subsequent republic, Isidora places her hopes in the law to recognize her birth right, and ironically to maintain a social hierarchy republicans sought to dismantle. The republican experiment falls apart and so does Isidora's case. Declared a fraud by the judge, a disenchanted Isidora loses faith in the ability of society to protect her interests and capitulates — falling further into a life of prostitution and debt. Inaugurating the cycle of what Pérez Galdós himself called his 'contemporary novels', *La desheredada* casts a critical eye on the bourgeois revolution and fall of the First Republic through the frustrated attempts of the middle-class Isidora to assert her credentials whilst at the same time clinging to the concept of noble titles.

Melita Palma lives comfortably within this literary tradition that articulates the idea of legitimacy in terms of kinship. Although possessing a noble spirit and innate grace, Melita is only accepted by her prospective mother-in-law when she becomes the patrician Clara de Alvarado. Similarly, while the fate of Isidora runs parallel to key national episodes — like countless creations of Pérez Galdós — it is similarly significant that Ríos penned *Melita Palma* at the historical crossroads between the regency of María Cristina and the coronation of Alfonso XIII. The influences and questions posed in Ríos's novella are therefore 'canonical', as they thematically overlap with the work of Pérez Galdós and other writers considered more 'representative' of the period.

Melita Palma not only reflects the preoccupations of a Spanish society in transition, but should be placed within a wider European context. In a recent study on the concept of illegitimacy in Georgian and Victorian Britain, the authors observe that the popularity of this trope reflects a 'widespread preoccupation with the idea of legitimacy in the broadest sense, its enactment, its ideological underpinning and its cultural fragility, spanned a wide range of social and legal practices, cultural forms and institutions' (Finn, Lobban & Bourne Taylor 2010: 3). *Melita Palma* is firmly enmeshed in the discursive background, yet as we have seen, the narrative fate of the protagonist remains unresolved, the story bereft of an epilogue that would bring closure. It lacks the tragic Naturalism of *La desheredada*, and above all the social commentary that deals more explicitly with the stratified society of the period. Instead, the interest lies in the agency of Melita in shaping her own story and the roles available to women to assert their legitimacy. Melita has many names and performs many parts to reach her objectives, first as a means of subsistence, and then to be close to the man she loves. Her theatrical break comes courtesy of Sútis, who wields his influence as critic for Melita, his *Rayo de luna*, to take over the role of Cintia ahead of another understudy. Infatuated with this image as the embodiment of poetic purity as passed on by his friend, Alfonso 'Poncho' Mendoza gives her the role, as he projects his own fantasy on the actress. She obsequiously fulfils this archetype, seeming to anticipate his every move to accommodate his vision of 'blanca azucena del pudor femenino' [white lily of female modesty] (Ríos 1901b: 34). However, when the mother forbids the relationship, the idea to pose as the noble Clara de Alvarado comes from Melita herself, persuading Alfonso that it is just a pious fiction that enables her to nurse his ailing mother and for them to be together. Her repertoire seems to be limited to female figures conceived by men and who share the common denominator of purity or blankness, as her aliases testify; yet Melita plays along, and in the case of her Clara incarnation actively contributes to the narrative. Very little is known about the past of the heroine, the story more invested in present projections instead. Melita's knowing self-awareness of her roles, together with the unresolved ending lends this supposedly straight melodrama unexpected layers of nuance.

The intricate web of names and allusions that Ríos weaves could be interpreted both as a consolidation of the angelic archetype or as a playful intertextuality that criticizes the reduction of women to poetic signs or passive metaphors. Like its protagonist Melita, it lends itself to several interpretations and similarly reveals a varied array of ways in which women could participate in shaping the intellectual landscape of the Restoration. The malleable identity of Melita can be read from a gendered angle and in relation to the roles available to women. The aristocratic persona portrayed by Melita forms part of a gallery of stock characters coloured by her thespian background or taken from books. Melita does not merely perform on stage: she goes under several names in private, prompted by the image projected onto her by different characters rather than a conscious duplicity on her behalf. More than a concrete woman, she often functions as a poetic sign that comprises all these projections. Rather than writing her own story, the young actress finds herself having to accommodate herself to roles for women created by men yet at the same time be berated for this dexterity. Defending herself against her lover's suspicions of an uncanny talent for pretence in one of the few passages that record the direct thoughts of Melita, she exclaims: 'he venido a esta casa donde se me despreciaba, negándome a mí misma, borrándome, falsificando mi personalidad' [I have come to this house where I was spurned, and I have denied my true self, erasing it, falsifying my personality] (Ríos 1901b: 90).

This lack of agency and inability to author her own narrative, together with accusations of mimicry, are partly articulated in *Melita Palma* in genealogical terms, expressed in the lack of pedigree that initially thwarts her aspirations of love. Yet her unsettling ability to become another person, or at least to perform as one, and thus compensate for any shortcomings of breeding also risks her incurring the mistrust of her lover. The path to legitimacy is thus blocked by many hurdles that Melita must negotiate and mirrors some of the battles waged by women writers in their quest for self-definition and inscription into genealogies that sustained the new national narratives. Chief amongst them is the identification of women with pretence, following the gendered logic characteristic of the period, a label that Melita exploits to her advantage, but which can also be a source of frustration. This strategic interaction with gendered expectations mirrors the equally complex relationship most women had with their allocated roles within dominant discourses. Melita struggles to become a legitimate part of a household headed by a matriarch named Doña Isabel of Castile Mendoza and Aragon, with an heir named Alfonso who has inherited the mysticism of his mother, and which has left him ill-equipped to deal with the more prosaic modern world. It is hard not to see in this household, which has seen better days, a condensed version of Spain itself.

This recontextualization has thus aimed to restore layers. *Melita Palma* contains all the ingredients of a maudlin melodrama with copious tears and swooning heroines, but is also a text concerned with its own legitimacy. One interpretation does not preclude the other. Combined instead, they challenge conventional readings of Ríos and other turn-of-the-century women. It is a melodrama published alongside canonical Modernist texts such as Valle-Inclán's *Jardín umbrío*. The many classical references used by Ríos sit well with the cultural sophistication pursued by the Biblioteca Mignon. The playful intertextuality found in *Melita Palma* forms as much part of the text as its melodramatic plot. Filled with references to now consecrated Golden Age plays, Romantic archetypes, mythological muses and emblematic figures like Isabel the Catholic, Ríos forms a dense tapestry woven from the threads of liberal historiography to signal her grasp of the medium. Partly an attempt to live up to her own ancestry — her uncle and godfather being Amador de los Ríos — it also tries to ward off the spirit of discursive illegitimacy that haunts women most acutely. It was not an unfounded fear. As shown, subsequent criticism has stripped *Melita Palma* of any status it might have enjoyed, despite its immersion in this new culture of legitimacy.

Notes to Chapter 5

1. This is probably a reference to the real life actress Josefa 'Pepita' Palma (1830?–97), known for her sentimental roles in romantic dramas (Sepúlveda 1888: 189).
2. Similarly, her later interest in the Russian novel, represented by the spiritual introspection of Leo Tolstoy and Fyodor Dostoevsky, is dutifully observed by González López, but who remarks that 'los aspectos formales de todas las estas novelas le pasaron totalmente desapercibidos' [the formal aspects of these novels were totally lost on her] (2001: 42). With this statement the critic almost berates Ríos for not following this literary fashion, instead of it being a deliberate choice on the part of the author.
3. Technically the honour should go to María de la O Lejárraga who co-wrote many works with her husband Gregorio Martínez Sierra, including the short novel *Almas ausentes* [Absent Souls], published in 1900 as volume 14; however, it was only her husband who was publicly credited for them.
4. The term *novela corta* was sometimes used interchangeably with *cuento* or *relato* [tale] and other terms depending on context. For a brief overview, see Ezama Gil (1993).
5. For a more detailed list see Sánchez Alvarez-Insúa 1996.
6. Eugenio Suárez Galbán had already published in 1982 a brief essay on two rescued *novelas cortas* by Carmen de Burgos. However it was not until the 1990s when the bibliographical vacuum started to be filled by anthologies like Bordonada's pioneering *Novelas breves de escritoras españolas (1900–1936)* (1990) which contains the first study of *Las hijas de Don Juan*. A year earlier, Concepción Núñez Rey had recovered some of the novellas penned by Burgos in *La flor de la playa: y otras novelas cortas* [The Beach Flower and Other Novellas] (1989). While critics such as Hurtado (1998) and Pascual Martínez (2000) focused on the whole period, others studied the contributions of individual authors, as is the case with Rita Catrina Imboden (2001) on Burgos, Biggane (2000) on Pardo Bazán, or Hooper (2008), who devotes part of her survey on Casanova to her novella writing.
7. The unexpected death of Bernardo Rodriguez Serra led to his widow taking over, and constitutes another subtle example of how women contributed to the cultural landscape. Simón Palmer (2010) throws some light on the widow of Rodríguez Serra when tracing female networks of support.
8. The 'apocryphal helmet of Mambrino' is a reference to Don Quixote — in the novel Don Quixote believes a barber's basin to be the helmet of the legendary Moorish king Mambrino, who was a familiar figure in the romances of chivalry that Cervantes mocks.

CHAPTER 6

Women and National Mythology in *Madrid goyesco*

Like *Melita Palma*, *Madrid goyesco* (1907) fits into the melodramatic mould and also narrates the story of two star-crossed lovers from different social classes, the evocatively-named Maravillas Reinaldos, daughter of an actor, and Pepito León of Castile, youngest son of the Duke of Sansueña.[1] As for the genealogical imagination that suffuses Ríos's output, *Madrid goyesco* like *Melita Palma* articulates legitimacy in genealogical terms and contains counterfeit pedigrees concocted by women to advance their social standing. Both stories complicate the dichotic dyad of oppressor versus oppressed in that women attempt to transgress their patriarchal portrayals whilst at the same time consciously contributing to them. The protagonist in *Melita Palma* knowingly accommodates herself to male projections whilst actively playing a part in them. Melita is thus Cintia, *Rayo de luna* and above all her aristocratic alter ego Clara de Alvarado, a persona she actively constructs to remain close to her lover and gain parental approval. Her counterpart in *Madrid goyesco*, Maravillas Reinaldos, also falls for an aristocrat yet refrains from claiming a noble pedigree. This is left to her ambitious aunt Aurora Reinaldos, a pawnbroker with a flair for theatre and a vivid imagination who dreams up an august ancestry. Equipped with a questionable coat of arms, Doña Aurora hopes to join the ranks of genuine aristocracy through the marriage of her niece, and to further these ends she devotes her energies to grooming Maravillas as the physical embodiment of the Spanish woman, an ideal that will arouse the male imagination and thus provide them both with social recognition. The aunt highlights the resemblance of her niece to a *maja*, originally a member of the lower class in Madrid, whose distinct dress style would later be fetishized as an unadulterated manifestation of Spanish taste in national mythology. In fact, Doña Aurora deliberately fashions her niece as a *maja* with the customary mantilla veil. The symbolic ramifications of this sartorial strategy constitute a central theme in this chapter. While Melita fashioned herself knowingly, Doña Aurora shows no qualms in casting other women in similarly patriarchally-approved roles. The novella exemplifies how women were complicit in maintaining the status quo whilst simultaneously slowly eroding the privileges of patriarchy.

With Doña Aurora, Ríos introduces an economically independent woman whose main weapons consist of a fertile imagination and an ability to tap skilfully into the historical imagination that underpins her ancestral claims; in other words, a woman much like herself: resourceful, independent yet happy to support traditional roles that might be in tune with the economic realities faced by most women. As Charnon-Deutsch reminds us:

> Any critique of domestic fiction, consequently, has to recognize that even the most dogmatic and conservative novels are imbued with a deep sense of urgency about what it means to be and survive as a woman in a society where neglect and poverty seem to be the norm. (Charnon-Deutsch 2004: 465).

Together with *Melita Palma*, *Madrid goyesco* figures amongst examples suggested by Hooper for the re-examining of conventional narratives (2008: 173). The baton is taken up by Carmen Arranz, who labels Doña Aurora an agent of modernity and the story a recipe for national regeneration wherein 'consciente de la necesidad de actualización de España, recoge un modelo femenino más apto para el mundo de principios de siglo XX. Aunque el texto puede dar lugar a varias interpretaciones, las mujeres se convierten en seres modernos' [aware of the need to modernize Spain, it depicts a female model more suited to the world of the early twentieth century. Although the text can be interpreted in multiple ways, women become modern beings] (2010: 67–68). It is an explicit attempt to go beyond González López's remark that 'la satisfacción por la pervivencia de unos valores, presuntamente tradicionales, predomina sobre el pesimismo ante lo caduco e inconsistente de los mismos. Se acepta con complacencia la imagen romántica de la España oscura y supersticiosa, mística y frívola' [the contentment with the survival of certain values, allegedly traditional, prevails over the pessimism caused by the outdatedness and inconsistency of these same values. The romantic image of a dark, superstitious, mystical and frivolous Spain is accepted with complacency] (2001: 91). Whilst acknowledging the portrayal of Doña Aurora as a relic of a pre-capitalist *Madrid goyesco*, Arranz foregrounds the deftness with which Ríos's character navigates the modern market economy, even investing in bonds. Yet despite these complex gender dynamics, Arranz is the only scholar to have dedicated an extended study to *Madrid goyesco*. The present chapter builds on this complexity recovered by Arranz and argues that the text constitutes a valuable female addition to the gendered dimensions of national iconography and the historical imagination — still dominated by male authors — precisely because it is not a straightforward subversion of patriarchy.

As in many of her novellas, Ríos packs the references densely. Some seem to criticize narratives put forward by her male counterparts whilst others support the status quo. The precarious economic situation of women is emphasized, a dependency that leads to pragmatic compromise rather than abstract idealism. This is seen in the intertextual dialogue with which Ríos engages in José Echegaray's popular play *O locura o santidad* [Folly or Saintliness] (1877), about a male protagonist who would rather sacrifice the financial stability of his daughter than lie about his pedigree. An embellishment of the truth is Doña Aurora's preferred strategy. Maravillas, the modern *maja*, lives with her aunt Doña Aurora after losing both her parents at an early age. Her father had been an actor who, filling the Quixote archetype, died in the throes of madness convinced he was the characters he played. In particular, he believed himself to be his most reprised character — Don Lorenzo from Echegaray's *O locura o santidad*. This reference, ignored or overseen by other critics, adds another layer to *Madrid goyesco*, and can be interpreted as a tragicomic foreshadowing of the family drama about to unfold. It can also be read as commentary on the precarious economic stability faced by many women, contingent on a good marriage.

The play by Echegaray, a perfect example of legitimacy articulated in genealogical terms, narrates the dilemma that Don Lorenzo, a wealthy patriarch, faces upon discovering that he was adopted and is the illegitimate child of his nursemaid. He decides not only to reveal the truth but also renounce a fortune and title he now feels he has inherited under false pretences. Such an action would jeopardize the engagement of his daughter to an aristocrat, yet he feels compelled to tell the truth, even at the expense of his own child's happiness and his own economic ruin, The nursemaid, concerned that her sacrifice has been in vain if her biological son gives up his status, retracts her confession of which Don Lorenzo was the only recipient. Increasingly regarded as a madman, Don Lorenzo ends up confined to an asylum, lunacy a preferred state to illegitimacy.

In *Madrid goyesco*, Ríos narrates an almost opposite outcome. The father of Maravillas dies an impoverished actor, leaving behind his daughter. Like her brother, Doña Aurora has inherited a similar theatrical flair and fecund imagination that she uses to secure an advantageous match for her niece. Whilst the protagonist of *O locura o santidad*, honest to a fault, follows his conscience regardless of the impact on his progeny, the relentlessly pragmatic Doña Aurora forges the most fantastical ancestry to ensure the financial stability of her and her niece. Whilst both Don Lorenzo and the nameless father of Maravillas follow the redemptive idealism of Don Quixote, Doña Aurora fits the picaresque mould of another Spanish archetype, that of Celestina. Like her literary counterpart, Doña Aurora excels at storytelling, relying on her wits to climb the social ladder, and sees her beautiful young niece as her greatest asset. It is also a rendition of the national myth of the economic realities of women and their reliance on marriage as a source of security. As Belén Puente Pereda summarizes it in her thesis on *El Cuento Semanal*: 'la trama presentada da pie para mostrar las dificultades que una mujer tiene para sobrevivir cuando no está casada' [the story depicted shows the difficulties faced by a woman when she is not married] (2007: 168). In her study of the different ways female and male writers shape the national mythos, Johnson remarks that 'it is surprising how few of the male novelists' protagonists need to work for a living' (2003: 172). This contrasts with the precarious existence of Melita Palma and the workaholic Doña Aurora, constantly striving for stability. Writing about Carmen de Burgos, María Pilar Rodríguez also reflects on the relevance of marriage even for such a progressive writer, as the institution still afforded a certain degree of legal and economic protection. Rather than abolish it, many *fin de siècle* writers sought instead to improve or redefine marital status for women (1998: 390–91).

Ríos, whilst unambiguously condemning the morally-ambiguous aunt, clearly admires her resourcefulness and prodigious imagination, which surpasses that of her brother. Above all Ríos reserves special praise for her narrative agency: 'érase autora y actriz en una pieza' [she was at once the playwright and the actress] (1907b: 3). Yet her decision to mould her niece to the image of the *maja* to enhance her attraction and legitimacy as a Spanish icon ultimately traps them both in a narrative of female passivity or victimhood, recycling old roles rather than creating new ones.

Forgotten nowadays, *Madrid goyesco* enjoyed great success upon its publication and was the second of two novellas Ríos wrote for *El Cuento Semanal*. As we have seen, Ríos cultivated the novella with great success, a fame that might help explain the appearance of *Las hijas de Don Juan* earlier the same year, the inaugural year of *El Cuento Semanal*. It was *Madrid goyesco* however that would receive a higher number of critical accolades despite the scholarly attention later lavished on *Las hijas de Don Juan*. Both were included in the fifth volume of her complete works, tellingly titled *Madrid goyesco* after its opening tale, with *Las hijas de Don Juan* closing the volume. In a review of the volume for the literary supplement *Los Lunes de El Imparcial* [The Impartial on Mondays], Eduardo Gómez de Baquero concluded that 'merece, en verdad, 'Madrid goyesco' el puesto de honor que ocupa en el libro, pues aventaja a las otras novelitas' [Goyaesque Madrid truly deserves the place of honour it occupies in the book, as it is a cut above the other novellas] (1912: 4) An influential literary critic, Gómez de Baquero praised how some of its pages 'resucitan modernizada el alma de la antigua novela picaresca' [resurrect in modern form the soul of the old picaresque novel], a genre hailed as emblematically *castizo* in the literary genealogies of the nation. Yet at the same time he comments that 'hay asunto y materiales para el pleno desarrollo de una novela a la moderna' [there is material for the full development of a modern novel] (4). By 'modern', Gómez de Baquero refers to the Realist novel cultivated by Pérez Galdós and others, to which *Madrid goyesco* fails to conform mainly due to its melodramatic ending. In other words, the story veers towards the melodrama and thus less 'serious literature'. This is by now a familiar way to delegitimize female production, which became so natural that even González López reduces the story nearly a century later to a less accomplished attempt at a Realist novel. Aurora Reinaldos is seen as a copy of the Galdosian character Doña Lupe, while Pepito León of Castile is a variation of the doleful aristocrat popularized by Luis Coloma (González López 2001: 90).

Maravillas the *maja*

The story follows the young Maravillas Reinaldos, 'sugestiva reencarnación de la Maja goyesca' [suggestive reincarnation of the Goyaesque *maja*] (Ríos 1907b: 2), who lives with her scheming aunt Aurora Reinaldos. Ríos was not the only writer to cultivate the allegorical aura of the *maja*, who belongs to a long tradition that can be traced back to the time of Goya and the Spanish War of Independence, later construed as a watershed moment for the configuration of Spanish nationhood. In his novel *La maja desnuda* [The Naked *Maja*] (1906) Vicente Blasco Ibáñez presents Goya as a pivotal figure who 'había asistido a la resurrección del alma popular' [had witnessed the resurrection of the popular soul] (1998: 186), in passages similar to those penned by Ríos in *Madrid goyesco*. This highly romanticized conception of old

Madrid, with the bohemian figures of the *majo* and *maja* that had fascinated Goya at its epicentre, is broadly defined as *majismo*. Yet there are differences between early twentieth-century *majismo* seen in the work of Ríos or Blasco Ibáñez and its associations in the early nineteenth century. Although retrospectively romanticized, Goya himself had a complex relationship with the figures of the *maja* and *majo*, sometimes depicted as transgressive sexual figures who threatened public morality and hierarchal order. As the century progressed, the trope would shed some of its more subversive baggage to become a sanitized national symbol. In eighteenth-century Madrid *majos* were originally 'working-class dandies, male artisans and female fruit and flower vendors from certain "popular" quarters of Madrid and the Andalusian cities' (Noyes 1998: 199). Yet their characteristic dress started to cross class divides as members of the higher echelons of society were attracted by its performative potential. As Noyes posits, it enabled members of the nobility to indicate resistance to the French cultural influx by donning such Spanish attire. The *majo* costume signalled indigenous in contrast to adopted foreign fashion, a visual shorthand for cultural differentiation. More worryingly it also permitted them to mingle with the lower classes, to the disapproval of reformers and guardians of the social order.[2] Thus the typical components of the attire, a mantilla for women and a wide brimmed hat and cape for men, allowed wearers to partly conceal their identity, and as critics pointed out, were useful for sexual escapades and other licentious behaviour. Authorities even tried to ban the broad hat and cape combination in 1766 but were met with popular opposition (Noyes 1998: 206). The blurring of social classes remained a major source of concern, seen as a threat to social order in which one could no longer distinguish between those with pedigree and those without it. As Noyes points out: 'the deepest corruption of majismo is to treat the self not as an essence but as a performance' (1998: 212). The irony lies in that *majismo* would ultimately be hailed as an essence, and it is this immutability that characterizes the trope in the later nineteenth century.[3]

Noyes tracks the transformation of the *majo* persona from transgressive philanderer to synecdoche of Spain:

> The emergence of the popular classes of Madrid as heroes of the War of Independence strengthened the myth of the majo as sole maintainer of the uncorrupted national spirit — warlike, Catholic, patriarchal, not a product of the 18th century but a survivor of the Reconquest [...]. Taken out of history into the emblematic, they were soon shaped into consumer goods to lure foreigners and soothe the masses, and also into ideological weapons against Spain's own cultural peripheries and a variety of modernizing movements. (Noyes 1998: 214).

Such nostalgic reimagining of a fixed past is found in *Madrid goyesco*, written by the conservative Ríos and redolent with the fervent patriotism that characterizes her prose. Penned in the aftermath of the Disaster of 98, it fuses *majismo* with discourses of regeneration in the figure of Maravillas, who becomes a repository of the national spirit and potentially its redemption.[4] In her analysis of the ubiquity of the *maja* figure during this period, Zubiaurre-Wagner identifies the now familiar recipe that 'in dark times depleted of manhood, female "power" resurfaces with renewed vigor and a very specific mission to represent allegorically the nation and firmly stand for tradition' (2012: 268).

In *Madrid goyesco* the *maja* Maravillas grows up in a household that symbolizes this now decadent Spain:

> En aquella fantasmagórica atmósfera, que venía a ser penumbra entre la vida y el ensueño, crióse Maravillas Reinaldos, la sobrina de doña Aurora, sugestiva reencarnación de la Maja goyesca, bajo la apariencia de burguesita madrileña, casi europeizada de trajes y costumbres, españolísima de alma, chula de sangre y de briosos arrestos, en cuyos dormidos ojos de venturina puntilleados de oro ardía el concentrado fuego del alma castellana, que así puede ser pasión que mata como misticismo que se inmola. (Ríos 1907b: 2)

> [In this phantasmagorical atmosphere, in the twilight between reality and dream, Maravillas Reinaldos grew up, niece of Doña Aurora, suggestive reincarnation of the Goyaesque *maja*, under the guise of a Madrid bourgeois, her attire and customs almost Europeanized, with an impossibly Spanish soul, spirited and with Madrid running through her veins, in her brown eyes spotted with gold burned the concentrated fire of the Castilian soul, which can either be passion that kills or sacrificial mysticism.]

The passage reads as a checklist of Spanish stereotypes. Maravillas has been brought up in a superstitious atmosphere, with an atavistic soul unaffected by the modernity of her clothes and customs, and marked by the mysticism that Ríos herself had helped turn into a hallmark of Spanishness with her enthusiasm for Saint Teresa. It is a traditional vision of the national myth that Ríos celebrates and simultaneously rejects. The problem is that Maravillas, who embodies the motherland, lacks the maternal influence to channel this legacy in a constructive manner. Missing the tempering influence of a mother, Maravillas falls prey to mystic excesses: 'por el místico huerto cerrado de su alma fluían puras y generosas las aguas de la cristiana fe; pero estas agua nadie las encauzaba' [through the mystical garden of her soul the river of Christian faith ran pure and generous, but with no one to channel these waters] (1907b: 5). Maravillas would have benefitted from an education but left instead to her own devices she develops a love for the 'folletines patibularios y novelones truculentos' [horrid serialized novels and gruesome melodramas] (5), facilitated by a neighbour. This only exacerbates her passionate propensities, instead of curbing them and making her a more productive member of society. As Andreu Miralles observes, this restraining and educating role became increasingly more relegated to the mother:

> La mujer, como núcleo del hogar, tenía la obligación de transmitir a los hijos los valores, las costumbres nacionales, de infundirles su *carácter* peculiar. Hacer dejadez de ello, interrumpir la cadena histórica que unía el pasado y el futuro de la nación, era una amenaza para esta. (Andreu Miralles 2011: 103)

> [The woman, as the heart of the home, was obliged to transmit to the children values and national costumes, to instil their special character. To neglect this, to interrupt the historical bond that linked the past with the present of the nation, was a threat to its existence.]

By lamenting the lack of a steering influence on Maravillas, acting here as Spain,

Ríos emphasizes the tempering role of women in the ongoing project of nation-building. Similarly, and although not an orphan, the object of Maravillas's affections also suffers from maternal neglect. Pepito León of Castile, the youngest son of the Duke of Sansueña, has been brought up by a series of governesses but craves the attention of his distant foreign-born mother. The widowed duchess is more interested in frittering away her inheritance than inculcating in her sons a sense of duty and patriotism. Pepito's only source of affection comes from his grandfather, a bastion of liberal nationalism 'que se batió en África junto a Prim' [who fought in Africa with Prim] (Ríos 1907b: 7) and who dies when Pepito is a child, taking with him Pepito's sense of belonging. His older brother, heir to the title, shows no interest in picking up the baton, preferring to spend his time in Paris with his profligate foreign wife. Pepito is born into this atmosphere of disenchantment, a decadence he symbolizes through his strong resemblance to a Velázquez portrait. It complements the resemblance of Maravillas to a Goya painting. Both painters occupy a pivotal position in this national narrative of decadence, summed up by Blasco Ibáñez in *La maja desnuda* as 'los dos grandes pintores habían coincidido en su existencia con la ruina moral de dos dinastías' [the two great painters had coincided during their lifetime with the moral ruin of two dynasties] (1998: 184). While Maravillas stands for the feckless pre-Restoration Bourbons, Pepito embodies the equally emblematic Spanish Habsburgs, the reigning dynasty who inaugurated the twilight days of the Spanish empire. Ríos paints her hapless hero in these evocative terms: 'Tenía Pepito aquella finísima silueta y aquella aristocrática delgadez cimbreante, acerada, y nerviosa de ese tipo exótico-madrileño que Velázquez inmortalizó en sus Austrias, singularmente en el infante don Carlos — "el del guante"' [Pepito had the delicate silhouette and that slim build, swaying, steely and restless of that exotic Madrid type that Veláquez immortalized in his Habsburgs, particularly in Don Carlos — 'the one with the glove'] (Ríos 1907b: 6). It echoes the following description by Blasco Ibáñez, inspired by similar *fin de siècle* discourses of degeneration: 'los Austrias, nerviosos, inquietos por una fiebre de locura, sin saber adónde ir, cabalgando sobre teatrales corceles, en obscuros paisajes, cerrados por las nevadas crestas del Guadarrama, tristes, frías y cristalizadas como el alma nacional' [the Habsburgs, nervous, restless with a feverish madness, without knowing where to go, riding on dramatic steeds through dark landscapes surrounded by the snowy peaks of the Guadarrama, sad, cold and frozen like the national soul] (1998: 184). My emphasis on these parallels between Blasco Ibáñez, an avowed republican, and Ríos, a staunch royalist, are intended to highlight the reach of a historical imagination that often crossed ideological barriers. Both Blasco Ibáñez and Ríos subscribed to this prelapsarian conception of the past but dreamed of different futures.

It was a posture adopted by many turn-of-the-century intellectuals, regardless of political orientation, fetishizing a Quixotic transcendental idealism that distinguishes the country. Ríos shares many of the motifs cultivated by her better-known male peers. In an analysis of Ignacio Zuloaga's painting *El enano Gregorio el botero, vendedor de cuero* [The Artisan Dwarf Gregorio, Seller of Leather], completed the same year as *Madrid goyesco*, the philosopher José Ortega y Gasset identifies it as another Spanish archetype, symbol of a race that has remained impervious to European modernization. The portrait, with clear influences from Velázquez and Goya, embodies 'la pervivencia de un pueblo más allá de la cultura' [the survival of a people beyond culture], concludes Ortega, summarizing it as 'la voluntad de la incultura' [the will of ignorance] (quoted in Fox 1997: 170). Although at different ends of the political spectrum, Ortega y Gasset's and Ríos's conceptions of Spain share several points of intersection, chief amongst them an essentialist view that conceives the nation as an eternal metaphysical entity rather than the result of ongoing historical shifts — a viewpoint shared by many *fin de siècle* intellectuals (Baker 2000: 155).

The assimilation of this new national iconography can be seen in the illustrations that accompany *Madrid goyesco* in its original format when it was first published in *El Cuento Semanal*. Just as the characterization of Maravillas had its visual counterpart in a stylized *maja*, Pepito is depicted with the Velázquez portrait of the prince Don Carlos behind him, in a rather literal foreshadowing of the tragic fate that awaits his doppelgänger. Immortalized by Velázquez, his portrait hung on the walls of the Prado Museum, where it would have been admired by Ríos and her readers in the recently inaugurated Velázquez room to mark the 1899 tercentenary of his birth. The 1890s had witnessed a flurry of publications on the painter, as scholars, artists, curators and administrators busied themselves constructing and institutionalizing his figure as a Spanish landmark. In a Spain still smarting from defeat against the United States and subsequent loss of territory, Alisa Luxenberg notes how 'nearly every Spanish scholar and critic of Velázquez brought the image of the disaster into their writings' (1999: 141).[5] Ríos is no exception with her invocation of the hapless Hapsburg. Like Pepito, the prince Don Carlos was second in line after his brother (the future Felipe IV), and died at the young age of twenty-five. Given the fondness of the author for intertextuality, plot logic dictates that Pepito's existence will be equally short-lived. The choice of the Infante Don Carlos similarly raises other suggestive historical corollaries that fit into the narrative of decadence, amongst them his brother Felipe IV producing the last of the Habsburgs. Mentally feeble and physically frail, Carlos II came to represent the excesses of endogamy, a product of what a recent biographer calls 'la endiosada y demencial política matrimonial que [los Austrias] practicaron una y otra vez sucediéndose sin interrupción los matrimonios consanguíneos' [the conceited and demented marriage policy that they [the Habsburgs] followed repeatedly, with family members marrying each other without any gaps] (Poyato 1996: 21). His death marked the end of the Habsburg line in Spain, an event that would acquire considerable symbolic weight in the exegesis of *fin de siècle* degeneration. Thus, in an article analyzing the recent loss of Cuba, we are presented with a genealogy of decadence throughout the nation's history that reserves a special mention for 'el decrépito Carlos II' [the decrepit Carlos II] who caused 'un grado de postración y desfallecimiento inauditos en la crisis suprema de la potencia que ejerciera un siglo antes la hegemonía entre las naciones europeas' [unheard of levels of prostration and weakness in the largest crisis of a power that had a century earlier enjoyed hegemony amongst European nations] (Alzola 1898: 563–64).

The early passing of both the Duke of Sansueña, the father of Pepito, and that of Felipe III, progenitor of the prince Don Carlos, is another coincidence. That Pepito belongs to the house of Sansueña, so phonetically analogous to 'sin sueño' [without dreams], could be read as another humorous nod to the moribund Habsburgs. Such similarities do not necessarily mean Ríos believed that the Bourbon dynasty would suffer a similar end or that Spain was doomed as a geopolitical body. As we have seen, the fervent political activity of Ríos suggests the contrary, that she was very much invested in finding solutions to the fading imperial star of Spain and resulting insecurity. In some respects these multiple intertextual loose ends serve merely to establish a complicit relationship with readers of novellas through a shared cultural framework.

It is clear however that Doña Aurora does not believe the Sansueñas have a future. As a pawnbroker and the family's main creditor, she is familiar with the dire state of their finances. In fact Pepito meets Maravillas when he visits the household to part with some of the Sansueña's patrimony. Despite Pepito's obvious insolvency, Doña Aurora still engineers this initial encounter between Pepito and her niece, lured by the social prestige of his pedigree. The ambitious aunt views any potential relationship purely as a transaction to accrue social capital: 'un noviazgo casi ducal, para hacer boca, no es mal estreno. Los noviazgos son como las subastas, el caso es hacer corro y que haya puja; entre tanto, yo sabré si la Casa de Sansueña está bien muerta y bien enterrada' [an almost ducal courtship, to get tongues wagging, is not a bad start, courtships are like auctions, the case is to spread the word to get bids; in the meantime, I will find out if the House of Sansueña is truly dead and buried] (1907b: 9).

The financial health of the Sansueñas is not hard to gauge. Not only possessed of business acumen, Doña Aurora has built an extensive clientele, many of them aristocrats like Pepito, that also pawns family heirlooms, paintings and other historical artefacts to bankroll lavish lifestyles. Yet Doña Aurora does not consider herself a usurer and once again resorts to her own dubious claims to pedigree to legitimize her actions, casting herself as a Samaritan helping out her peers: '¿Qué cosa más natural sino que ella — ¡toda una Reinaldos de Matamoros! — acudiese en auxilio de aquellas señoras que la trataban casi de tú por tú?' [What could be more natural than she — a Reinaldo of Matamoros — coming to the aid of those ladies who treated her almost as an equal] (1907b: 3). Rather than being reduced to trafficking antiques — as many of these objects are — she sees herself as preserving the national patrimony and keeping it away from other lenders with less august ancestries who would turn it into an exercise of crass bourgeois commercialism. She even claims to protect this heritage from foreign buyers who snap up many of these priceless artefacts or, as Doña Aurora patrioticamente denounces it, 'ponen, en fin, en poder de extranjeros toda la Historia de España' [at the end of the day they put in the hands of foreigners the entire History of Spain] (1907b: 3). However, this veneration of the past and her self-ascribed patriotic philanthropy has its limits. Pepito and Maravillas fall for each other, while the aunt grows less enthusiastic about the relationship as the extent of the debts that plague the Sansueñas becomes increasingly apparent to her. Instead she sets her sights on the raffish Paco Alijares, soon to inherit the title of marquis and accompanying estate. A union with Maravillas would provide prestige and an economic stability that would lighten the load from Aurora's shoulders as breadwinner in an uncertain profession. It is no coincidence that *alijar* means 'to lighten' or 'unload'.

Hoping to direct the gaze of the marquis-in-waiting towards Maravillas, she unashamedly markets her niece as an alluring *maja*. Pepito brings Paco to the Reinaldos household on one of his visits which provides Aurora the opportunity to showcase her niece. Pretending to resolve which style of mantilla flatters the most, the lace or the tassels, she instructs Maravillas to model both with the complicit backing of the men: 'Que se vea, que se vea! — gritó el grupo masculino, dejándose engañar a conciencia' [Let's see her! Let's see her! shouted the group of men, letting themselves be purposefully deceived] (1907b: 10).[6] It turns Maravillas into a signifier of desire, the poetic representation of the patria: 'El acero de la mirada de Alijares despedía llamitas azules; los celestes ojos de Sansueña centelleaban de ira y de amor' [the steely gaze of Alijares set off blue sparks, the celestial eyes of Sansueña burned with ire and love] (1907b: 10). Tailored to the male gaze, the fashioning of Maravillas is initiated by a woman and is contributed to by other women, the neighbour Encarna who spontaneously brings red carnations to enhance the effect and Maravillas herself who dons the veils 'entre bochorno y vanidad' [between embarrassment and vanity] (1907b: 10).

The choice of the mantilla is no accident, and as an emblematically Spanish piece of clothing, carries a certain significance. Although the lace mantilla had been in existence for centuries, particularly favoured by the popular classes, it was in the eighteenth century that it suddenly gained esteem among the aristocracy. Yet it was the nineteenth century that witnessed what Zubiaurre-Wagner calls 'the definite consecration of the mantilla as head adornment par excellence of the Spanish woman' (2012: 259). It adorned the head of Isabel II, who had a penchant for the lace version and promoted its use. Later, it became a political weapon, paraded on the streets of Madrid by defiant aristocrats to show their discontent with the foreign Amadeo de Saboya. Eschewing the French custom that dictated a hat, the mantilla became a symbol of Spanishness to challenge a perceived French influence, echoing the adoption of *majo* costume a century earlier by Goya's contemporaries. It became known as the 'conspiracy of the mantillas' and helped cement the garment as an emblematic national symbol. As Dr Augusto Miquis — a recurrent character in the Galdosian universe — explains in *La desheredada*: 'Esto de las mantillas blancas es una manifestación, una protesta contra el Rey extranjero' [these white mantillas are a demonstration, a protest against the foreign king] (Pérez Galdós 2000: 135)

Predictably then, those present at the modelling of mantillas by Maravillas agree that the lace one suits her better, as she herself becomes the embodiment of the Spanish spirit.[7] Her transformation into a talisman is partly due to the allure of this lace because 'peinetas and mantillas are the weapons of patriotic women; they also shield women and the Spanish nation from the pernicious influence of (foreign-born) modernity' (Zubiaurre-Wagner 2012: 268).

Maravillas may have been fashioned into a powerful symbol, but her embodiment of Spain offers little room for manoeuvre. Like Spain, her fate must also follow that of the nation currently locked in a narrative of decadence. Like Pepito's resemblance to the infelicitous Habsburgs, her incarnation of Spain does not bode well. The sight of Maravillas, a patriotic vision decked out in her mantilla, leads another male character to deliver an impromptu eulogy. This orator is Sútis, a recurrent figure through whom, like a ventriloquist, Ríos once more articulates the images projected on Maravillas. Whereas Melita Palma fulfilled the female archetype of the poetic sign, her counterpart Maravillas Reinaldos is envisioned as the embodiment of Spain. An exalted Sútis exclaims:

> ¡Oh, España mater, representada en esa maja — Venus, en esa maja romántica que es Maravillas en persona! ¡Oh, emblema de la gran Madre, criatura pasional y neurótica, engendrada por el delirio, crecida en aura de quimera y sortilegio; tú estás predestinada a la catástrofe, eres la novia del desastre, la prometida del cataclismo, eres España! (Ríos 1907b: 11)

> [Oh, mother Spain, represented in this *maja* — Venus, in that romantic *maja* that is Maravillas in person! Oh emblem of the great Mother, neurotic and passionate creature, engendered by madness, reared in an atmosphere of illusions and spells; you are pre-destined to catastrophe, you are disaster's intended, cataclysm's betrothed, you are Spain!]

This identification of the motherland with the figure of a woman enabled women to participate in debates but also limited their interventions to a constrained repertoire. Herein lies the problem, namely that instead of being an active participant, Maravillas functions merely as a passive repository to which change happens, rather than being an agent of change. It is a complex dynamic by which Doña Aurora attempts to assert her legitimacy and advance herself economically by effectively casting her niece as a passive pawn. Such feminine iconography of the nation is further bolstered by illustrations of Maravillas as an archetypal *maja* within the pages of the novella itself. It constitutes a clear example of what Landes describes in a recent volume on the imagery of the French Revolution as 'how visual imaginings may be part of the process by which a citizen learns to love an abstract object [the nation] with something like the individual lover's intimacy and passion' (2001: 2).

Every male character is enthralled by Maravillas, and the different forms this fascination takes showcase different aspects of patriotic desire. The Don Juan-esque Paco Alijares covets her as a sexual conquest, while she galvanizes the imagination of the writer Sútis to produce the sort of essentialist eulogies favoured by Unamuno and other writers associated with the Generation of 98. To Pepito Sansueña, who represents the decadence of Spain, the love of Maravillas promises redemption and potential regeneration similar to the relationship between the patrician Poncho and plebeian Melita. However, Doña Aurora crushes the hopes of a romantic atonement and forbids her niece from seeing the impoverished Pepito, hoping instead for an engagement with the future Marquis of Alijares. Unable to contact Maravillas and believing himself to be spurned, the lovelorn Pepito takes to drink and grows increasingly resentful. It sets the scene for the inevitable tragic end foreshadowed by the totems they embody. Pepito spots Maravillas and Paco Alijares out together and to make matters worse recognizes the Maravillas's dress, a gift from her aunt and which had once belonged to his mother, the Duchess of Sansueña. Whereas the mantilla transformed Maravillas into an allegorical motherland, his mother's dress reminds Pepito of the real maternal neglect he has suffered: 'el desamor materno y la perfidia amorosa se fundían' [maternal indifference and amorous treachery merged] (Ríos 1907b: 17). This filial devotion fuses with romantic love in the figure of Maravillas, a combination that encapsulates the patriotic fervour promoted by nationalism. Blinded by fury, Pepito first aims his gun at the young woman but then points it towards himself horrified at the prospect of committing matricide by killing Maravillas 'al ser hecho de sus dos seres idolatrados' [as was composed of his two idolized beings] (17). Symbolically, his suicide marks the implosion of the decadence he represents and drives a heartbroken Maravillas to join a convent.

The priest Lázaro Murga, who also considers himself a father in the paternal sense, tries to dissuade her from embracing such a drastic solution. He suggests a more prosaic yet pragmatic role for Maravillas that will free her from the narrative of doom that surrounds her. Father Murga implores Maravillas to abandon her status as a signifier and become instead a tangible woman, or at least to occupy a role more in line with his project of regeneration: 'que dejes de ser la novia del cataclismo, imagen de la gran Maja trágica' [that you cease to be cataclysm's betrothed, image of the great tragic *Maja*] (1907b: 19).

It is no coincidence that these words are uttered by a man named Lázaro, engaged in the mission of raising up a moribund Spain enthralled by her own quixotic legend. That this task befalls a representative of the church fits reflects the author's own conservative vision of the role played by Catholicism, both as a key component of Spanish identity and a driving force along its path to regeneration. Ríos shared this idea of Catholic regeneration with Marcelino Menéndez y Pelayo, so admired by her, both considering faith the driving force and national glue that held the people together and provided them with a transcendental mission.[8] This strand of nationalism was already established in Spain, finding a suitable match in Menéndez y Pelayo, a man who 'busca ardorosamente la restauración de la cultura española que corresponde al genio nacional, esencialmente católico' [fervently searched for the restoration of Spanish culture that corresponds with the national character, essentially a Catholic one] (Morales Moya 2013: 502).

Father Murga urges Maravillas to contribute more constructively to the national project as wife and mother, traditional roles endorsed by the Church, but also to support her aunt financially. Maravillas remains unconvinced and so does the cleric despite his own sermon. In a moment of introspection he admits his own emotional investment and capitulates to this Romantic vision of Spain as the antithesis of mundane modernity: 'Él también pertenecía en cuerpo y alma a la leyenda. ¡Y quería poner en prosa llana, en prosa vil, el alma lírica de Maravillas!' [He also belonged body and soul to the legend. And he had wanted to turn into prosaic prose, into vile prose, the poetic soul of Maravillas!] (Ríos 1907b: 19–20). The closing reflexions seem to support the conclusion reached by González López, that Ríos defensively celebrates these excesses and turns vice into virtue. Spain might be losing its geopolitical clout, becoming a follower of trends rather than an originator, but its spirit remains unspoiled by foreign influences, an atavistic conception of the nation that ironically owes much to French Romantics such as Prosper Mérimée and his indomitable Carmen. Maravillas thus remains immune to rational interventions, associated with a Protestant utilitarianism alien to Mediterranean mysticism.

Doña Aurora and Female Narrative Agency

Modern readers might find it problematic that Ríos, a successful female author and influential public speaker, should embrace a discourse that portrays women as passive avatars — the 'ancestral bodies' of O'Toole (1997: 122) — rather than as agents of change. Again it overlaps with the ambiguity of *Melita Palma*, wherein Ríos seems both to parody the conception of women as poetic projections but also to embrace this role.

On the one hand the representation of Maravillas as a *maja* conforms to traditional narratives, but on the other we find the ambitious Doña Aurora, discontent with her social standing. Through a dubious coat of arms, she grafts both of them onto the family trees of all the major aristocratic families in a bid to ascend through the ranks, and in the process give them equal footing in the genealogy of the nation by linking her name to the likes of El Cid. Ríos mocks the picaresque schemes of Doña Aurora and her overheated historical imagination, starting with the description of the ambitious, and entirely fictious, coat of arms. Aware of the traditional importance of a polished pedigree, she constructs an impressive ancestry depicted in the overblown heraldic device that adorns the entrance to the house:

> Lo primero con que se topaba en la vivienda de doña Aurora, era el estupendo y policromo blasón de los Reinaldos de Matamoros, enlazado con el de los Afanes de Toledo; un verdadero derroche de color y fauna heráldica: águilas, leones, lobos y zorras volantes, tenantes, rampantes y fuyentes en campos de sinople, de gules, de oro y de azur. ¡Una barbaridad de nobleza! (Ríos 1907b: 2)
>
> [The first thing one stumbled upon in the house of Doña Aurora was the marvellous and polychromatic coat of arms of the Reinaldos of Matamoros, linked with that of the Afanes of Toledo; a profusion of colour and heraldic fauna: eagles, lions, wolves and flying foxes, angels, claws and fountains in fields of green, red, gold and blue! An aristocratic barbarity!]

Both her own surnames 'Reinaldos de Matamoros' and those of her late husband 'Afanes de Toledo' exude historical significance. The royal overtones of 'Reinaldos', which sound like a distorted version of 'reigning', are clear, whilst 'Matamoros' or 'Moor-slayer' evokes the so-called Reconquest, hailed as a founding event in the establishment of the geopolitical borders of the modern nation. 'Matamoros' is also the sobriquet given to Santiago, patron saint of Spain, who according to legend helped defeat the Muslims in battle. Likewise, Toledo, known as the 'Imperial City' after hosting the court of Carlos V, had come to occupy a central place in the cartography of nationalism as one of its spiritual focal points. That the author is playfully mocking Aurora's pretensions to grandeur can be gleaned in the complete surname 'Afanes de Toledo', that is, 'desire or yearning for Toledo'. Aurora's longing to be part of the establishment is articulated in her insertion into the national genealogies that emerged in the nineteenth century.[9]

The combination of 'Reinaldos de Matamoros' and 'Afanes de Toledo' results in such a symbolic supernova that one starts to wonder if the name itself is perhaps part of Aurora's overactive historical imagination, in the same way that her prized coat of arms might not be entirely legitimate. Thus, while this ambitious social climber uses the support of the age-old hierarchal distinctions that still privilege nobility, her constant references to totemic figures and landmarks of the historical imagination reveal a familiarity with more contemporary mechanisms of legitimization. To further highlight Aurora's awareness of the power wielded by historiography, Ríos writes that 'considerándose un César Cantù, desdeñaba la menuda depuración de los hechos y seguía haciendo Historia' [believing herself to be a Cesare Cantù, she looked down on the careful distillation of facts as she carried on writing History] (1907b: 2). The readers of *Madrid goyesco* would have known the Italian historian Cesare Cantù for his ambitious *Storia universale*, published in seventy-two volumes between 1838 and 1846 to great acclaim and translated into several languages, including Spanish. Strongly informed by Cantù's own political agenda and prejudices, it is considered of little critical value nowadays, although it is still of interest for the sheer magnitude of material its author collected, and has formed the basis of later studies. This prodigious output and unashamed bias even became the object of criticism during Cantù's lifetime, when the young discipline of historiography had still to define its parameters clearly. It prompted a contemporary critic who sympathized with Cantù to write in a eulogy: 'But first let us dispose of a slur thrown on the number of his histories. Fertility of mind is, however, rather a merit, if it does not degenerate into carelessness, of which he cannot be accused' (Finch 1886: 527). By comparing Cesare Cantù to Doña Aurora, an unashamedly enthusiastic historian on a smaller scale, similarly unencumbered by facts, Ríos displays her familiarity with historiographical debates whilst mocking and admiring her in equal measure. Yet this strategy uncomfortably mirrors her own ongoing efforts to promote Tirso de Molina by linking him to the Duke of Osuna. Ríos might scoff at Doña Aurora's hankering for distinction, but the more she pokes fun at characters with an overactive imagination and a penchant for storytelling, the more noticeable the precarious position of Doña Aurora as a spinner of yarns becomes. In Maravillas Reinaldos, Ríos recycles the image of women as passive repositories of the national spirit, but the writer herself is actively engaged in creating her own history, and her approach is closer to that of Doña Aurora. Like her literary creation, Ríos also made a living out of reshaping the past and telling stories.

Even the role of Maravillas Reinaldos, prescribed by male imagination, is sometimes performed with such self-awareness that it questions the passivity of the young woman. It befalls Sútis in both stories to present Melita and Maravillas as motifs that come with certain expectations, rather than being allowed to function as individuals free to forge their own destinies. Maravillas ends up in a convent, which together with marriage and death constitutes the restricted set of options offered to women. Any dreams of ascending the social ladder Doña Aurora might have harboured come crashing down when her main asset Maravillas fulfils the inevitable fate of the incarnation of a decadent Spain. Despite her enthusiastic appropriation of hegemonic discourses, Doña Aurora fails either to assert her own legitimacy or to gain economic stability.

It would certainly require much enthusiastic pruning to read *Madrid goyesco* as a straightforward subversion of the limited participation or roles available to women. At the same time, *Madrid goyesco*, like *Melita Palma*, lays bare the mechanics of this gendered discourse which, even if endorsed by the conservative Ríos, is mapped with a dexterity that perilously edges on a destabilizing irony. The explicit articulation of Melita as an actress adept at performance, the description of Doña Aurora as a performer and script writer, the rhetoric of Sútis filled with every single trope and metaphor to the point of saturation — they all contribute to this satirical effect, whether it is deliberate or not. In an effort to assert her own authorial legitimacy by displaying her cultural mastery, Ríos runs the risk of breaking the illusion by so enthusiastically drawing attention to the inner workings of the machine. Hooper reaches a similar conclusion in her analysis of *Sangre española* [Spanish Blood] (1899), an earlier novella by Ríos that also espouses a conservative gender agenda. *Sangre española*, she observes, can be read 'as an explicit demonstration of the dangers of unthinkingly appropriating the master's tools (to borrow Audre Lorde's vivid metaphor), for even when you are only trying to help prop up the master's house, there is a terrible danger that the whole construction might simply come crashing down on top of you' (2007: 183).

Notes to Chapter 6

1. *Madrid goyesco* was originally published as issue 68 of *El Cuento Semanal*, which came out in 1907, not 1908 as is often erroneously stated.
2. Xavier Andreu Miralles highlights too the transgressive potential of *majismo* rather than a nationalist stance against French cultural dominance. The fashion of dressing as popular types was not just limited to Spanish aristocracy but constituted a European-wide trend (2010: 43–44).
3. Although I have not given an exhaustive overview of the origins and transformation of the *maja* figure, it is worth noting the role played by Romanticism in the fetishization of a certain Spanish racial type, aided by foreign travellers in search of the exotic. Prosper Mérimée's 1845 novella *Carmen* epitomizes this image as an eroticized other, an indomitable spirit immune to European influences, what James Fernández calls an enduring 'metonymic misrepresentation' (quoted in Noyes 1998: 214).
4. González López (2001: 90–91) sees *Madrid goyesco* as an expression and celebration of *casticismo*, a term that overlaps with *majismo*, particularly in a joint fetishization of popular types, yet is not a synonym. *Casticismo* in turn sounds similar to *castizo*. Despite descending from the same stem, *castizo* and *casticismo* occupy ideologically opposite poles, the latter associated with a more conservative or even regressive view of Spain. The terms are famously defined in Miguel de Unamuno's *En torno al casticismo* [About Casticism] (1895), in which he positions himself against a *casticismo* that in his eyes recycles hackneyed clichés, whereas *castizo* is seen as an ethereal, intangible quality possessed by writers whom Unamuno coincidentally admires. These semantic

struggles reveal mostly ideological posturing between different parties over what constitutes Spain, and above all, how the future of Spain should look.
5. In fact, Velázquez became a popular platform for discussion of the future of the nation. Again Luxenberg observes that 'the reinterpretation of Velázquez paralleled the political-cultural debate over how to achieve regeneration in Spain. The prominent options were Europeanization, opening up Velázquez to European scholars and audiences who would interpret the artist from a wider European history, or *casticismo*, keeping him in a Spanish context to understand more fully his essential Spanishness' (1999: 129).
6. Ironically, the mantilla had been attractive to many of its earlier aristocratic adopters precisely because it veiled the face, as pointed out by Noyes (1998: 208).
7. The mantilla makes a symbolic appearance in another short novel by Ríos, *La niña de Sanabria* [The Girl from Sanabria] (1907c), in which the female protagonist dons the mantilla to present herself similarly as the embodiment of the motherland and takes to the streets in protest.
8. In this context it is also worth mentioning Ángel Ganivet, whose work *Idearium español: el porvenir de España* [Spanish Idearium: The Future of Spain] (1896) played an important role in shaping the recipe for regeneration of national Catholic discourse. To Ganivet, the solution to Spain's decadence was to be found in a devotion to tradition and the accompanying distillation of the national essence. Boyd provides an excellent overview of Ganivet's main tenets (1997: 180–82).
9. In Ríos's penchant for signposting satire through surnames, a custom shared by her contemporaries, González López singles out the bombastic titles of Doña Aurora and the duchess in *Melita Palma* (1901b: 100). The difference lies of course in the fact that whilst the former desperately wants to belong to the nobility, the duchess does so but, out of touch with modernity, proceeds to furnish her son with an equally quixotic imagination.

CHAPTER 7

Carmen de Burgos: Talking with the Descendants

Compared to her contemporaries Blanca de los Ríos and Julia de Asensi in particular, Carmen de Burgos is by far the least neglected of my chosen authors. Known for her outspoken persona and progressive stance, she also seems far removed from the cautious Asensi or the conservative Ríos. Burgos famously died in 1932 at the Radical Socialist Circle's weekly gathering whilst debating the merits of sex education. The progressive newspaper *El Sol* [The Sun] records her last words as 'Muero contenta, porque muero republicana ¡Viva la República! Les ruego a ustedes que digan conmigo ¡Viva la República!' [I die happy, because I die a republican: Long live the Republic! I beg them to repeat with me: Long live the Republic!] (Anon. 1932: 12). It seems rather implausible that Burgos, who died of heart failure, would have the energy in her last moments to rally her fellow attendees to proclaim loudly their republican fervour (Núñez Rey 2005: 618). The story was nevertheless propagated by the press and helped cement her own myth.

Despite their many differences, several familiar traits bind Burgos to Asensi and Ríos: a liberal legacy courtesy of a father who served as vice-consul for Portugal; the portrayal of counterfeit pedigrees in her fiction; and her role in the shaping of the national mythology.

The breadth of her output leads Burgos to be linked to many genealogies, most prominently feminist ones, but none that explicitly addresses the genealogical imagination in her work and her myth-making role. Few studies address works such as her biographies of Mariano José de Larra and Rafael del Riego, or *Hablando con los descendientes* [Talking with the Descendants] (1929), a compilation of interviews made over the years with descendants of José de Zorrilla, Gustavo Bécquer, Joaquín Costa and Nicolás Salmerón amongst a gallery of prominent writers and politicians who had so decisively influenced the ideological landscape. In the prologue to this work, Burgos presents herself as a curator of past memories and the book an attempt to preserve this legacy: 'Deseaba incluir en mis obras completas este ejemplario de vidas pasadas cuyos últimos vestigios directos he recogido redivivos en las palabras de sus descendientes, o de los que los conocieron, sinceros y amables al mostrarme el relicario íntimo' [I wanted to include in my collected works this exemplar of past lives of which I have collected the last direct vestiges, resurrected in the words of their descendants or those who knew them, all sincere and kind as they showed me their family reliquaries] (1929: 5). Yet she depicts this legacy as paralyzing in *Los huesos del abuelo* [Grandfather's Bones] (1922), in which the descendants of a famous Romantic author live in his shadow, or as an obstacle to national regeneration in *El tío de todos* [Everyone's Uncle] (1925), in which the protagonist is embroiled in a national dispute to prove himself to be the true heir of a mythical missionary. Just as Ríos mocked characters who spun extravagant ancestral plots but furnished Tirso de Molina with a similarly fanciful and doubtful pedigree, Burgos derides the deification of past figures and events whilst contributing to the pantheon herself. It is this tension that I wish to analyze in her output, with an emphasis on how her female protagonists interact with this genealogical imagination and use it to construct their own identities. For this purpose I have selected the novella *La que quiso ser maja* (1924) and the longer *Los anticuarios* (1918), two works that address the interaction with gender more overtly.

They reveal the complex negotiation between several discourses, mainly that of Burgos as subscriber to the status quo — she was after all the daughter of a vice-consul — but also Burgos the tireless advocate of female emancipation. Her literary output is testament to the tensions and struggles of defining the changing identity and role of women during the closing decades of the Restoration (Cibreiro 2005: 56), which another critic summarizes as:

> La modernidad de Carmen de Burgos se ofrece en constante proceso, marcada por los signos de la contradicción y el anhelo, y sin embargo reproduce en muchas ocasiones los lastres ideológicos heredados. Su análisis nos ofrece, en cualquier caso, caminos de gran interés para una comprensión más amplia de este rico y complejo periodo histórico y literario español. (Rodríguez 1998: 397)
>
> [Burgos's modernity is constantly evolving, shaped by contradiction and longing, and yet it still often reveals the ideological burdens she inherited. In any case, its analysis offers us a more comprehensive understanding of this rich and complex historical and literary period in Spain.]

Burgos's *Hablando con los descendientes* (1929) exemplifies this duality that sees her advocating greater female visibility whilst at the same time subscribing to the status quo. On one hand *Hablando con los descendientes* endorses liberal historiography, as when she interviews the son of the famous Carlist leader Ramón Cabrera and is shown a letter by his father in which the famous general acknowledges Alfonso XII as the legitimate monarch, not the pretender Carlos V. At the same time many of these encounters serve to highlight the precarious economic situation of women, often the widows or daughters of these famous men, now forgotten 'por desidia y abandono de los políticos y la sociedad en general' [due to the apathy and neglect of politicians and society in general] (Torres González 2010: 175). Begoña Torres González's analysis is the only full study dedicated to *Hablando con los descendientes*, indicative of the little attention paid to her biographies. Instead Burgos was initially rescued from oblivion thanks to such outwardly feminist works as *La mujer moderna y sus derechos* [On Modern Women and Their Rights] (1927).

This overview of Burgos focuses on three main aspects. The first part provides a brief literary review and explains why Burgos has been so appealing to revisionists, initially at the expense of other aspects of her work that might not prove so overtly feminist. This is followed by a brief biography that foregrounds the liberal inheritance that shaped her historical imagination. The third and last part provides an example of how this is applied — drawing parallels between Burgos and Ríos. Whilst Ríos mainly focused on Tirso de Molina and the Golden Age, the progressive Burgos shifts her attention to the dawn of liberalism and pens biographies of Mariano José de Larra and Rafael del Riego.

Burgos the Feminist Pioneer

Banned by the Francoist regime for her affiliation with the Second Republic, Burgos's writings initially suffered the same fate and her name sank into oblivion. However, in the aftermath of the dictatorship her work became the object of increased scholarly attention, propelled by the pioneering efforts of Elisabeth Starcevic, whose 1976 survey *Carmen de Burgos: defensora de la mujer* [Carmen de Burgos: Champion of Women] paved the way for subsequent studies. Since the 1990s the number of studies has multiplied and so have her biographers, the most recent being Concepción Núñez Rey (2005), whose painstaking research forms the basis of most of my own biographical observations.[1] Such has been the revisionist wave that in a 2010 review of Kirsty Hooper's recovery of the equally forgotten Sofia Casanova, a critic contrasts the obscure status of writers like Casanova — Blanca de los Ríos becomes another illustrative example — to that of 'more mainstream writers such as Emilia Pardo Bazán and Carmen de Burgos' (Romero 2010: 128). Already in an article of 1999, Jennifer J. Wood claims that:

> Recent scholars interested in neglected women writers of the past have worked to restore her reputation and re-establish her importance. Today, Carmen de Burgos ranks with Emilia Pardo Bazán and Concepción Arenal as a pioneer in the defence of women's rights in Spain. (Wood 1999–2000: 373)

While much of her extensive catalogue awaits the republication that would help her achieve public recognition on a par with Pardo Bazán, 'thanks to tireless efforts by scholars from the US and Europe over the past forty years Burgos has become recognized as an important writer and feminist, and is now considered a cornerstone of early twentieth-century Spain' (Louis & Sharp 2017: 5).

For a long time Burgos remained at the margins as, unlike in the case of Pardo Bazán, her work did not follow the trends outlined by literary history. Belonging to a younger generation than Pardo Bazán, her first novel — tellingly-titled *Los inadaptados* [The Misfits] — came out in 1909, long after the heyday of the great novel in the 1880s, when modernist streams had started to make inroads in the literary map. Yet the novel was a genre she held in awe perhaps due to its illustrious pedigree. In a letter to Pérez Galdós, she confesses that 'me voy a atrever a publicar mi primera novela grande (en tamaño). Tengo miedo. La novela es la diosa de la literatura' [I am going to dare to publish my first big novel (in size). I am scared. The novel is the pinnacle of literature] (quoted in Núñez Rey 2005: 218).

Remarks like this demonstrate that Burgos was fully aware of the dynamics of literary criticism, she had after all translated several works by John Ruskin, the leading art critic of the Victorian era.[2] She was similarly well acquainted with the later trends, partly through the writer Ramón Gómez de la Serna, her lover and companion for two decades, and an important figure within the avant-garde movement that replaced the Realist novel as one of the main vehicles for literary legitimacy. Although their styles differed, it did not prevent her from praising the literary innovation of her partner, saying of three of his works in a review that 'en los tres resplandece lo moderno' [modernity shines through in all three] (quoted in Núñez Rey 2005: 441), yet she did not cultivate it herself. Aesthetic experimentation did not sit well with her didactic aims and she preferred instead a more accessible style: 'Escribo para el pueblo más que para los eruditos. Hay que divulgar la verdad en forma sencilla, que pueda llegar a todas las almas' [I write for the people rather than for the learned. The truth has to be spread in the most simple manner so that it reaches everyone] (Burgos 1911a: 12). Because her production did not fit into the parameters of modernity, Burgos was excluded from the canon for a long time. Susan Kirkpatrick, Roberta Johnson and Carmen Arranz are some of the scholars who have in recent years suggested a wider definition of modernity that takes into account the work of women like Burgos. In this way Kirkpatrick urges us to 'reconocer la heterogeneidad de los efectos de la modernidad significa transcender los acercamientos monolíticos y formalistas al [sic] modernismo europeo' [to acknowledge modernity's heterogeneity means transcending the monolithic and formalist approaches of European modernism] (2003:15), echoed by Johnson who observes that 'literary modernism emphasized form and philosophy over social phenomena such as women's shifting roles in the modern world' (2001: 66).

Burgos put her name to a dizzying array of works: novels, novellas, poems, travelogues, reviews, practical manuals, war reports, translations and biographies, as well as countless articles that covered everything from female suffrage to fashion. This eclectic and varied œuvre has spawned a similarly varied bibliographical output.[3] It is easy to see why Burgos would prove so attractive to scholars engaged in recovering the cultural history of women. Her profile as a republican sympathizer and a tireless promoter of progressive policies — she famously campaigned for the right to divorce — makes her more adaptable to modern sensibilities than the conservative Blanca de los Ríos. In the same way that nineteenth-century historians highlighted figures amenable to their conception of nation, it is only understandable that, faced with a vacuum after decades of Francoist repression, feminist scholars would want to fill it with predecessors who helped them legitimize the new democratic project and the participation of women in this transition.

If we were to regard these revisionist efforts as the assembly of a new family tree that accommodates female emancipation, then Burgos occupies a privileged position whilst Blanca de los Ríos and Julia de Asensi continue to perch on more marginal branches. By focusing on how the genealogical imagination informs the work of progressive and conservative writers alike, my aim is to shift the focus away from loaded labels and potential blind alleys. To focus excessively on Burgos as a pioneering feminist can inadvertently lead to new hierarchies wherein Burgos is regarded as more legitimate than the reactionary Ríos. Additionally, not every critic agrees on the scope of Burgos's feminism, which fluctuated and evolved over the course of a long and astoundingly prolific career, with many textual selves borne out of economic or editorial necessity. Again, Rodríguez points out that:

> Hoy nos sorprenden lo que aparentan ser fuertes contradicciones en la ideología de una mujer que tan pronto se declaraba entusiasta republicana y apasionada defensora de los derechos de la mujer como rebatía ardientemente los principios fundamentales de la independencia femenina, recomendando el matrimonio y la maternidad como la fórmula más deseable de desarrollo femenino. (Rodríguez 1998: 382)

> [Nowadays we are surprised by what seem to be strong contradictions in the ideology of a woman who would as easily declare herself an enthusiastic republican and champion of women's rights, as she would passionately refute the basic principles of female independence, suggesting marriage and maternity as the most desirable model for women.]

Burgos was aware of the impact that publishing out of economic necessity had on her literary credentials:

> A mí me ha perjudicado [...] la mayor parte de la labor periodística a que la lucha por la vida me obligó, lo mismo que las obra prácticas para la mujer que he tenido que componer [...]. Cuando algún imbécil pretende hacerme de menos, me llama la ilustre autora de *¿Quiere usted comer bien?* (quoted in Imboden 2001: 17)

> [I have been impaired by much of the journalistic labour to which survival forced me, like the practical manuals for women I have had to compose [...]. When an idiot wants to belittle me, he calls me the illustrious author of *Would You Like to Eat Well?*]

Amy Bell observes how 'Burgos's sometimes tentative, sometimes assertive brand of feminism has raised questions among scholars' (2003: 166). These scholars include Nuñez Rey (2005: 19–20) and Ugarte (1998: 59), who like Rodríguez (1998) mull over the compromises made and the strategies used by Burgos to navigate the social landscape. The ensuing debate, although a necessary one, says more about current conceptions of gender than provides definite answers for any past feminism entertained by Burgos. Such ongoing discussions, whilst expanding and reframing existing critical frameworks, have contributed to make Burgos a central figure in early twentieth-century gender studies. Yet a side effect of this focus has been the occasional neglect of other aspects of her work, facets that link her to women at the other end of the political spectrum like Ríos, as well as wider cultural debates.

Burgos also hailed from a family invested in the new political landscape, a background that perhaps contributes to her own biographical activity centred on men like Larra and Riego, so central to the liberal legacy. However, these are not the male figures with whom she is identified, as for a long time Burgos languished under the 'shadow of the flame' of her companion Gómez de la Serna, as a recent scholar puts it (Mangini 2010: 4). As we will see, Gómez de la Serna's own biography of Burgos romanticized her as a misunderstood loner in a similar fashion to the portraits of past luminaries depicted in *Hablando con los descendientes*. In an effort to break this pattern, later biographers like Núñez Rey outline the familial connections of Burgos in an effort to steer away from romantic readings and better understand her ideological inheritance. This does not imply that either her father's consular career or her father-in-law's political activities determined her own political engagement. But the combination provides a solid foundation upon which to interpret her interest in figures such as Riego or Larra, in the same way that the conservative historicism of her parents might have coloured Ríos's own recreations of the past.

Burgos was born in Almería in 1867, the first child of Don José de Burgos and Doña Nicasia de Seguí. Like Asensi and Ríos, she had access from an early age to the many books collected by her father, who similarly passed on his political leanings to his children. Núñez Rey views his influence as crucial in the early formation of the author's political awareness, above other significant factors such as social class:

> Más transcendencia iba a tener en la formación de la futura escritora Carmen de Burgos la ideología republicana y liberal que le transmitió su padre Don José, unida al gusto por el conocimiento y a la pasión por la lectura, de evidente herencia ilustrada. (Núñez Rey 2005: 29)
>
> [The republican and liberal ideology transmitted by her father Don José would be more important in the education of the future writer Carmen de Burgos, together with a fondness for knowledge and a passion for reading, both clearly legacies of the Enlightenment.]

The family of Burgos, although occasionally liable to financial woes, belonged firmly to the bourgeoisie, particularly her father, attested to by his appointment as vice-consul of Portugal. Burgos would evoke this consular childhood in later years: 'En mi hogar de Almería, que por ser Consulado de Portugal acariciaba con su sombra la bandera blanca y azul' [The shadow of the white and blue flag caressed my home in Almería, being the Consulate of Portugal] (1916: 363). Two years after his appointment, Don José was named Knight of the Order of Christ by the Portuguese authorities, who with this prestigious title acknowledged his consular labour. The early years of Burgos overlap in some respects with those of Asensi, whose father had been the Spanish consul in Tunis. Although their political leanings clearly differ, with Tomás de Asensi being both a centralist and at the centre in Madrid and José de Burgos occupying a more republican fringe at the southern edges of Spain, they both operated within the political cultures of constitutionalism. As for Asensi, the maternal influence on the historical imagination of Burgos remains less tangible, mainly because the activities of women tended to be relegated to the private sphere and were thus less documented than those of men.

Burgos's father-in-law, Don Mariano Robles Álvarez, is another man who played an important role in her formative years. Burgos had married his son Arturo Álvarez Bustos in a union that soon turned sour and would years later form the basis of the novel *La malcasada* [The Unhappily Married Woman] (1923) and other stories with a female protagonist trapped in an unhappy marriage to an abusive husband. Álvarez

Bustos was a journalist like his father but failed to inherit his social conscience or work ethic. Burgos would later describe her husband rather euphemistically as 'esclavo de sus vicios' [slave to his vices] (González Fiol 1922: 20), yet it was the economic penury caused by his dissolute lifestyle that led Burgos to take her first step in the world of journalism. Álvarez Robles headed *Almería Cómica* [Comical Almería], a weekly publication that often became a bi-monthly affair in the hands of its erratic editor. Burgos would take over its running to secure their income:

> En aquel periódico, para ayudar a sostener mi hogar, me vi precisada a trabajar de cajista; y como mi marido, esclavo de sus vicios, no se ocupaba del periódico más que para sacarle provecho, muchas veces, para poder componer original, me valía de la tijera y recortaba de otros periódicos; otras, redactaba yo unas cuartillas, y así fui adquiriendo el entrenamiento periodístico. (Quoted in González Fiol 1922: 20)
>
> [At that newspaper, to support my family, I found myself working as a typesetter; and as my husband, slave to his vices, only took interest in the newspaper for his profit, many times, to publish original content, I made use of scissors and cut from other newspapers; on other occasions I would compose myself some lines, and that is how I acquired journalistic experience.].

Crucially, *Almería Cómica* was published by the printing-house owned by her father-in-law, Don Mariano Álvarez Robles, whom Núñez Rey (2005: 65) describes as 'pionero de la prensa almeriense' [pioneer of the press in Almería]. Don Mariano had started *El Pensil* [The Delightful Garden] in 1845, the first in a string of publications from whose pages he promoted his brand of progressive liberalism, something he would also support as Almería's deputy mayor. His progressive stance culminated in the revolution of 1868, which saw him take an active part in proceedings as a member of the Provisional Revolutionary Junta, later occupying other posts including that of county councillor (Núñez Rey 2005: 68).

Burgos's father-in-law was then, by all accounts, a man actively involved in shaping political discourse, as well as an enthusiastic participant in the city's main literary forums. He might not have collected antiquities like the father of Asensi, but according to a local historian Don Mariano had a few historical artefacts imbued with national significance. Amongst them he claimed to possess a scrap of the banner presented to Almería after its recapture by the Catholic Monarchs, which he kept in a frame, as well as 'un trozo de las cintas del féretro de Prim' [a scrap of the ribbons adorning Prim's coffin] (Santisteban y Delgado 1927: 154). This sacralization of national cohesion embodied by events of symbolic transcendence makes Don Mariano a man of his age. Burgos in turn would later romanticize liberal heroes like Don Mariano, now part of history themselves. Many years later, during a meeting with José da Costa, sentenced for the assassination of the Portuguese would-be-dictator Sidonio Pais, Burgos painted Costa as a liberal martyr:

> Es el tipo de un romántico del siglo XIX. Es uno de aquellos revolucionarios de la época de Fernando VII, uno de los concurrentes a la 'Fontana de Oro'; un enamorado de ideales patrióticos de los tiempos de Olozaga o de Riego; aquellos exaltados que daban la vida por una idea romántica. (Quoted in Núñez Rey 2005: 477)

[He is like a nineteenth-century romantic. One of those revolutionaries from the time of Fernando VII, one of the regulars at the Golden Fountain café; a devotee of the patriotic ideals of Olozaga and Riego; those radicals that gave their lives to a romantic ideal.]

The figure of her father-in-law, who had so energetically taken part in the brief and ill-fated first republic would have influenced her own vision of the past, just as the magazine run by his son gave her a first taste of journalism. Álvarez Bustos was but a pale shadow of his father and Burgos eventually left him after several unhappy years, heading for Madrid with their only daughter. She had obtained a teaching certificate, teaching being one of the few viable options open to women who wished to become economically independent. Ever the consummate storyteller, she amended her own biography and claimed to be ten years younger than she was. Intent on reinventing herself in the capital, the younger age suited better her narrative of a teenage bride trapped in a loveless union in the conservative provinces. Her later companion and writer Ramón Gómez de la Serna highlights this youth in a biographical prologue Burgos asked him to write for her *Confidencias de artistas* [Artists' Confidences] (1917): 'casada a los dieciséis años como suele suceder en Andalucía — su madre se casó a los catorce' [married at sixteen as is often the case in Andalusia — her mother was married at fourteen] (Gómez de la Serna 1917: 14). Such was the success of this reinvention that her date of birth remained uncertain for a long time, only recently confirmed by Núñez Rey (2005: 25–26). In this way, Gómez de la Serna also evokes the humble beginnings of Burgos in the capital and presents us with the picture of a young woman fleeing an abusive marriage with her infant daughter in one hand and a teaching certificate in the other. It is an image that fits with the narrative of Burgos the trail-blazing pioneer which has so enamoured later biographers. A smitten Gómez de la Serna asserts the Spanishness of Burgos comparing her to the female totems of Santa Teresa and Agustina de Aragón in a narration very much mediated by Burgos: '¿Qué quiere usted que yo le pregunte?' [What would you like me to ask you?] (Gómez de la Serna 1917: 20), he asks her at some point. Gómez de la Serna did not know Burgos upon her arrival in Madrid but only hears about her earlier years later as mediated by Burgos herself.

Burgos's account glosses over the figure of her uncle Don Agustín de Burgos y Cañizares, senator and well-known figure in the political world, whose many contacts would have appealed to his niece, who had dedicated to him her first book, a collection of literary essays, hoping for his patronage. However, that Burgos already had contacts within the establishment does not take away from her own achievements; on the contrary, it portrays the author as a woman finely attuned to society and close, like so many other women, to the nexus of power through their fathers, husbands, brothers or uncles. This was certainly a more common figure than that of the maverick ascending through the ranks, a woman ahead of her time, as Burgos is often described. These teleological portrayals connect her with the future, and remove her from her own present and contemporary genealogies, such as the one comprised of Ríos, Asensi and others paving the way for women in literature, or the wider web of men and women forging a shared collective past. Burgos forms part of both of these groups whilst by all accounts being a formidable and enterprising woman. When her uncle allegedly took too many liberties, she left his household but still ordered visiting cards that clearly declared their consanguinity, together with his impressive list of titles (Núñez Rey 2005: 94–95). Like Ríos, who stated her blood relation to her uncle Amador de los Ríos to gain access to archives and libraries, Burgos used her pedigree to open doors at the beginning of her career. Most notably it led to a friendship with Segismundo Moret, also from her native Andalusia, three times prime minister of Spain, as well as occupying other key political roles whenever the Liberal party governed. Contacts like these would shield Burgos from some of the many attacks she had to endure as an outspoken woman in the public eye.

Her rise to prominence came as the first woman to have a column in a national newspaper that she signed 'Colombine', a nom de plume with which she became intrinsically linked in a similarly symbiotic fashion to her admired Larra and his pseudonym 'Fígaro'. The name had been suggested by Augusto Figueroa, the editor of *Diario Universal* [Universal Daily] and did not come from Burgos herself. This first column 'Lecturas para la mujer'[Woman's Review] would later be followed by 'Femeninas' [Women's Section] in *Heraldo de Madrid* [The Madrid Herald] and 'Mundo femenino' [Female World] in the magazine *Nuevo Mundo* [New World], as Burgos carved a space for women defined by her own gender, as indicated by the names of her columns. Her byline appeared in countless other publications, either under her own name, that of Colombine or other pseudonyms including 'Gabriel Luna', 'Perico el de los Palotes', 'Raquel', 'Honorine' or 'Marianela'. In addition to a febrile journalistic activity, Burgos published fiction and, like Ríos, took advantage of a boom enjoyed by the novella, penning close to a hundred.[4] Towards the end of her life, Burgos became part of history herself, portrayed as a progressive pioneer by admirers such as the fellow writer José Montero Alonso. In an interview with Burgos conducted shortly after the establishment of the Second Republic, he describes her home as possessing 'un romántico aire de otro tiempo. Muebles dorados, con terciopelo rojo y azul, con miniaturas en los respaldos' [a romantic air from a bygone age. Golden furniture with red and blue velvet upholstery, with miniatures at the backs] (Montero Alonso 1931: 10). It is reminiscent of the 'terciopelos y moldura dorados' [velvet and gold mouldings] that Fernández Almagro describes upon his visit to the Ríos household (1956: 3).

The main difference between these descriptions of an elderly Burgos and Ríos lie in the decades that separate these two contemporaries. By the 1950s, the long-lived Ríos — almost a centenarian by this point — was seen as a relic of the past and her unwavering monarchism regarded with indulgence as a senile quirk. Burgos, on the other hand, is interviewed as an early proponent of the current political system — 'izquierdista y feminista *de toda la vida*' [a dyed-in-the-wool leftist and feminist] (Montero Alonso 1931: 10).[5] Her sudden death in 1932 spared her from witnessing the end of the republic only a few years later, and above all, the dismantling of the liberal state during the subsequent dictatorship. Burgos's and Ríos's patriotism might take different forms but it nevertheless stems from the same nineteenth-century roots. Both fretted about national decline, both revisited and rewrote the past to accommodate the present and both talked about a need to regenerate the nation with the help of women (Sánchez Dueñas 2013: 239).

Burgos the Biographer

The biographies Burgos penned are thus symptomatic of this shared past that provided historical continuity to the nation and which both Ríos and Burgos invoke in their writings. Whilst Ríos championed Tirso de Molina as a leading exponent of Spanish culture, the progressive Burgos focused her attention on figures more appropriately fitting to her vision, chief amongst them the Romantic writer Mariano José de Larra, whom Burgos similarly helped induct into the hall of fame of national literature. Her biography *Fígaro (revelaciones, 'ella' descubierta, epistolario inédito, numerosos grabados)* [Fígaro (Revelations, 'She' Discovered, Unpublished Epistolary, Numerous Illustrations)] appeared in 1919, a detailed and romanticized vision of a canonical Romantic, in which Burgos reveals the identity of the woman who allegedly was the final trigger for Larra's eventual suicide. As Leonardo Romero Tobar also points out in the only recent study devoted to this work, her identification with Larra also stems from their shared profession. With Larra hailed as the father of modern journalism, it is no wonder that Colombine, the most prominent female byline of the time, would wish to associate herself with him: 'y como periodista, lealmente anclada en la tradición del periodismo hispano, no podía dejar de ser una profunda admiradora de Larra' [as a journalist firmly grounded in the tradition of Spanish journalism, she was bound to be a firm admirer of Larra] (Romero Tobar 2010: 183). The same critic also situates the Larra memoir within the biographical wave of the 1920s, of which Burgos's 1919 offering could be considered a precursor. Yet Burgos's contributions to the field have failed to capture the attention of most critics (Romero Tobar 2010: 187).

Fígaro was well received, as illustrated by the many positive reviews, including that of Pardo Bazán who wrote that 'el libro de la señora de Burgos es un servicio prestado a la historia de las letras y ojalá tuviésemos muchos tan abundantes en noticias sobre los escritores *legítimamente consagrados*' [Mrs de Burgos has done a great service to the history of literature with her book, and if only we had more studies with such abundant information on *legitimately established* writers] (quoted in Núñez Rey 2005: 462, my emphasis).

As in the case of Ríos's archival archaeology in support of Tirso, Burgos also had access to previously unseen documents, now carefully preserved by Larra's descendants well aware of their worth, as remarked by a grandchild: 'nos dejó dos tesoros, su apellido ilustre y... las reliquias' [he left us two treasures, his illustrious surname and... the relics] (Burgos 1919: 9). Faced with the shirt that Larra wore the night he committed suicide, Burgos experiences the same awe her father-in-law must have felt contemplating the preserved ribbon fragment from Prim's coffin (Núñez Rey 2005: 68). Equally, she projects her own political agenda onto Larra as when she muses, 'Tal vez [Larra] entendía la política ideal como la entendía Azorín; en su alma generosa existía tal vez el ensueño de la regeneración de España' [Perhaps [Larra] understood the political ideal as Azorín understood it; perhaps the dream of Spain's regeneration existed in his generous soul] (quoted in Romero Tobar 2010: 188). Like many of the cultivators of this so-called 'nueva biografía' [new biography], Burgos reconstructs her own imaginative version of Larra, sometimes more interested in recalling his spirit than in rigorous documentation. It led Benjamín Jarnés, one of its most prominent practitioners, to summarize this biographical approach as 'tal vez el biógrafo moderno sea peor historiador de una etapa, pero siempre será mejor reconstructor de un individuo' [maybe the modern biographer is the worst historian of a period, but he will always be the best at reimagining a person' (quoted in Romero Tobar 2010: 187).[6]

The same year Burgos published Larra's biography also saw her pen a series of *semblanzas literarias* [literary sketches] on other Romantic writers including Zorrilla, Martínez de la Rosa and Hartzenbusch. Part of the ongoing series *Homenaje a los novelistas españoles del siglo XIX* [Homage to Spanish Novelists of the Nineteenth-Century] published by *La Novela Corta* [The Novella], these brief biographies introduce adaptations of longer novels shortened for the format. Interestingly, all the works Burgos prefaces belong to the genre of the historical novel that Walter Scott had popularized at the beginning of the nineteenth century, and which had significantly helped to mythologize certain historical events. The adapted stories include Martínez de la Rosa's *Doña Isabel de Solís* (1837), Espronceda's *Sancho Saldaña* (1834), Escosura's *El Conde de Candespina* [The Count of Candespina] (1832), as well as later works such as Cánovas's *La campana de Huesca* [The Bell of Huesca] (1851) or Hartzenbusch's *La reina sin nombre* [The Queen Without a Name] (1857).

It is a popular and partisan historiography to which Ríos had contributed only four year earlier with her series *Mujeres en la historia*, published for the popular magazine *Blanco y Negro*. This attempt to reinsert women into the historical landscape by a conservative writer has received as little attention as the progressive Burgos's contributions to the status quo with her biographies of already established men. In other words, the repeated attempts by Ríos to expand national genealogies are sometimes obscured by her otherwise orthodox conservative leanings, whilst Burgos, a progressive self-confessed feminist, advanced mainstream narratives more than studies sometimes give her credit for. As biographer of a string of canonical writers, she testifies once more to a multifaceted and complex engagement with her environment beyond her vindications of the rights of women. It is also worth mentioning that Burgos did dedicate some of her biographical efforts to women, amongst them *La emperatriz Eugenia* [The Empress Eugenia] (1920), published too for *La Novela Corta*, together with *Vida amorosa de Jorge Sand* [The Love Life of George Sand], *María de Zayas (estudio)* [María de Zayas (Study)], *Doña Gertrudis Gómez de Avellaneda (estudio)* [Doña Gertrudis Gómez de Avellaneda (Study)], three works that Núñez Rey (2005: 638) has not been able to localize. However, unlike Ríos, Burgos's commitment to wider female representation has rarely been questioned.

Similarly, her little studied biography *Gloriosa vida y desdichada muerte de Don*

Rafael del Riego [The Glorious Life and Unfortunate Death of Don Rafael del Riego] reveals a Burgos, keen to find earlier sympathizers of the republican state model. It is no coincidence that the biography coincided with the proclamation of the Second Republic. With this work, Burgos claimed to have recovered the memory of Riego as a man who had been so prominently hailed as a freedom martyr by progressives in the nineteenth century, executed for his attempt to restore the 1812 constitution and dismantle the absolutist monarchy of Fernando VII. The publication of Riego's biography, concomitant with a new republic and two years before the centenary of his execution, shows Burgos exalting those figures who fit her vision of the past. In fact, *Gloriosa vida y desdichada muerte de Don Rafael del Riego* was followed by the subheading '*(Un crimen de los Borbones)*' [A Crime by the Bourbons] and could be seen as part of a republican wave that contains such works as the *Himno y marcha fúnebre de Riego* [Riego's Hymn and Funeral March] (1930). Or the similarly subtly-titled *El demonio intenta asesinar a Pi y Margall* [The Devil Tries to Assassinate Pi y Margall] (1930), that centres on one of the presidents of the first republic.[7] As Manuel Moreno Alonso points out in the only re-edition of Burgos's political hagiography:

> El libro de Colombine, publicado apresuradamente a comienzos de la Segunda República, se inscribe dentro de una coyuntura política en la que se trató de fabricar una 'memoria inicial republicana' de la sociedad que celebraba el fin de la monarquía mezclando el Himno de Riego con vivas a Nicolás Salmerón. (Burgos 2013: 118)

> [Colombine's book, released in a rush at the beginning of the Second Republic, is part of a political period that tried to create a 'republican origin myth' for a society that was celebrating the end of the monarchy mixing Riego's Hymn with cheering Nicolás Salmerón.]

In her portrayal of Riego, Burgos paints him as a cultured man of the world with only Spain's best interests at heart. Even his alleged humble pedigree is rectified, a restoration reminiscent of the one implemented by Ríos with Tirso de Molina. Quoting Francisco Pi i Margall, Burgos repeats claims that Riego 'nació de familia noble, su padre era administrador de Correos de Oviedo y en su Universidad cursó don Rafael algunos años, *hasta acabar su carrera literaria*' [born to a noble family, his father was the postmaster of Oviedo and Don Rafael studied in its university for some years *until he finished his literary degree*] (Burgos 2013: 164, my emphasis). Whether Riego descends from a noble family as Pi i Margall alleges, she is more interested in emphasizing his impeccable liberal pedigree — a civil servant father with a university degree and a literary vocation. It echoes Julia de Asensi's father earlier on when he claims that a literary education was the greatest legacy his father left him ('el mejor patrimonio que podía legarle era una educación literaria' [the best legacy that he could leave him was a polished literary education)] (quoted in Díez Ménguez 2006: 21). That Pi i Margall emphasizes in turn the alleged literary legacy passed on to Riego by his father follows the same tradition, a coincidence far from accidental. After all, Pi i Margall was the inaugural president of Spain's first attempt at republicanism and would have been eager to establish new genealogies of power wherein nobility was conferred by a liberal education rather than blood ties. Burgos herself expands on this genealogy when she claims that 'yo puedo añadir a estos datos el que la familia de Riego se distinguía por su cultura; su padre era poeta y sus tíos y sus hermanos escritores' [and I can add to this information that Riego's family distinguished themselves by their culture; his father was a poet and his uncles and brothers were writers] (2013: 164). As Moreno Alonso points out, Burgos provides no proof for this new proposed family tree. There are other examples. Two years before the proclamation of the Second Republic, Burgos had interviewed the sons of Nicolás Salmerón for the *Heraldo de Madrid* — later included in *Hablando con los descendientes* (1929). In her exchange with the eldest son, Burgos describes him as someone who had inherited his father's intellect: 'hijo heredero de su nombre y de su claro talento' [heir to his name and to his bright talent] (1929: 151), recipient then of an impeccable republican pedigree. The erudition and altruistic patriotism of Salmerón father are foregrounded in the son, as if these qualities were transferable and legitimized his interventions: 'es la suya figura de un hombre de estudio, un filósofo y patriota, que dedicó su existencia a trabajar por el bien de la humanidad' [his profile is that of a learned man, a philosopher and a patriot, who dedicated his life for the good of humanity] (1929: 151).

Nowadays neglected, Burgos's biographical labour did not go unnoticed by contemporary critics. In fact, it contributed to her own cultural legitimacy. In a 1931 *ABC* article arguing for the admission of women to the Real Academia, Cristóbal de Castro picks out Burgos amongst those overdue the honour in a passage often cited by her biographers: 'Entre las escritoras de hoy destacan en labor academicista, de erudición, de investigación, de aportación crítica y documental, de eficacia para las letras puras, Blanca de los Ríos, Concha de Espina y Carmen de Burgos' [Blanca de los Ríos, Concha de Espina and Carmen de Burgos are among the women writers of today who stand out for their academic labour, for their erudition, for their research, for their criticism and documentation, and for their contribution to the literary field] (1931: 11).

To justify his choice, Castro singles out the Larra biography penned by Burgos, and compares her to the heroines of the War of Independence, Agustina de Aragón and the Countess of Bureta. In other words, Castro praises her role in the cultural canonization of Larra and legitimizes her efforts by anointing her defender of the patria. In the same vein, Ríos is praised for her work on Tirso de Molina: 'ella ilumina los orígenes de Tirso con descubrimientos sensacionales de bastardía' [she casts light on the origins of Tirso with her sensational discovery of illegitimacy] (Castro 1931: 11). Even Concha Espina, the third woman Castro shortlists for the honour, is lauded for her contribution to the genealogical imagination. Thus, Castro highlights Espina's *Mujeres del Quijote* [Women in The Quixote] (1916), a title reminiscent of Ríos's *Las mujeres de Tirso* (1910), both of which can be classified as belonging to a gynocentric literary history cultivated by the likes of all three authors: Espina, Ríos and Burgos. None of them would be elected members of the Royal Academy despite the enthusiastic backing of people like Cristóbal de Castro, who concludes his passionate plea by appealing to the female deity who according to classical mythology presides over the arts: 'A los académicos de la Española, que no están presididos por Apolo, sino por Minerva; este alegato en pro de las escritoras españolas' [to the academicians of the Royal Academy, which is not presided over by Apollo, but by Minerva; this is a plea in favour of Spanish women writers] (1931: 11). Despite this rhetorical strategy, favoured particularly by Ríos, with its invocation of a female genesis, the Royal Academy would not admit a woman to its ranks until 1977.[8]

Whilst this introduction has partly focused on her work as a biographer, the following two chapters are both informed by her labour as an art critic, another facet of her life similarly neglected. Here I wish to examine in more detail how Burgos dealt with this exclusion of women from key centres of legitimacy, with particular reference to her works *La que quiso ser maja* (1924) and *Los anticuarios* (1918). The progressive politics of Burgos are evident in her output, yet the characters in her fictions are encumbered with a historical imagination that does not always reflect this. So far, the works discussed have been arranged in chronological order. The next chapter, however, begins with *La que quiso ser maja* (1924), whose exploration of the Goyaesque *maja* by the republican Burgos seems a suitable follow-on by way of contrast with *Madrid goyesco* by the conservative Ríos.

Notes to Chapter 7

1. A line-up of biographers that includes Castañeda Ceballos (1994), Establier Pérez (2000) and Bravo Cela (2003), amongst others.
2. See Núñez Rey for a complete list of her Ruskin translations (2005: 638–41).
3. Louis (2005) has focused on Burgos's ongoing efforts for legal equality between the sexes, as well as analyzing her contribution to popular fiction and the boom of the novella, as have Martínez Garrido (1999), Rodríguez (1998) and Imboden (2001), among others. Imboden (2001), Zubiaurre-Wagner (2003) and Núñez Rey (2005) are among those who highlight the theme of travel as flight from convention and the search for a female self as central in the literary and journalistic production of Carmen de Burgos. Her stint as a war correspondent in the Second Moroccan War (1920–26) forms the basis for studies that analyze colonial discourse in her work, including Wood (1999–2000), Pozzi (2000), Zaplana (2005) and Zapata-Calle (2011). Even her hitherto little-studied cookery manuals have been recently analysed by Ingram (2009), who sees them as a product of modernization.
4. Núñez Rey lists them all (2005: 627–33). This figure does not include the ten novels she also authored between 1909 and 1931.
5. Although always progressive, Burgos did not always define herself as a feminist. It is hard to ascertain whether this was self-censorship or because she did not identify with the label earlier in her career. Thus, in a 1911 speech she claims that 'No he logrado fijar aún la verdadera acepción de la palabra feminismo. [...] Así que en realidad yo no sé si soy feminista' [I have yet to fix the true definition of feminism. [...] So actually I do not know if I am a feminist] ([1911b]: 7).
6. For a more historical context for the so-called 'new biography', see Pulido Mendoza (2009), Serrano Asenjo (2002) and Soguero García (2000).
7. Both of these are titles from the *Novela Política* [The Political Novel], a cheap collection that dramatized past clashes between progressive and monarchist with clear republican sympathies. It is but one example of the many books, pamphlets and other publications that proliferated in the years running up to the Second Republic and that reflected a wider political mobilization and the emergence of mass politics (Villares & Moreno Luzón 2009: 548).
8. Carmen Conde (1907–96) would be the first woman to occupy a seat in the Royal Academy.

CHAPTER 8

❖

La que quiso ser maja: Creating a Female Legacy

Nearly two decades after Ríos penned *Madrid goyesco*, her contemporary Burgos published in 1924 *La que quiso ser maja* [The Woman Who Wanted to be a *Maja*]. We meet Carola, a young woman who comes to live with her aunt in Madrid after her parents pass away. It is the same familial arrangement encountered in *Madrid goyesco* but with a crucial difference, in that here both niece and aunt have a steady income in the form of an inheritance and pension. Like Aurora in *Madrid goyesco*, Carola has a mercenary view of marriage common in a society where it was still the only path to financial stability for many women: 'El matrimonio se le aparecía sólo como una necesidad económica' [she regarded marriage only as an economic necessity] (Burgos 2000: 10). Yet unlike Ríos's protagonist, Carola does not need to consider marriage for her survival. Instead the drama in this story stems from Carola's failed attempts to create a legacy within the narrow confines of her gender, where she is still hampered by the passive roles allocated to women. *La que quiso ser maja* figures amongst the last group of novellas Burgos wrote, out of over eighty in total. It is also one of her many works awaiting a more thorough critical analysis, although it has received a certain amount of interest in recent years due to its publication as part of *La Novela Pasional* [The Passion Novel], and as part of a renewed interest in Spanish erotic production, illustrated by its inclusion in Zubiaurre-Wagner's *Cultures of the Erotic in Spain: 1898–1939*.[1]

Her surname symbolically absent, Carola lacks a pedigree with which to prop herself up, and she does not attempt to graft herself onto more august family trees as Aurora Reinaldos did. Carola pursues a more modern way to inscribe herself in the public imagination, at first attempting to run an asylum for under-privileged boys, together with another single woman. The initiative is met with hostility and suspicion so Carola defaults to the traditional route of marriage and children. Her inability to conceive leads her to seek yet another way of leaving an imprint — she starts to frequent the Prado Museum where she goes regularly to admire the paintings of the old masters, and concocts here the idea of being depicted as a *maja* alongside the canonized Goya as another way to impress herself on history: 'Las únicas mujeres que quedaban eran aquellas perpetuadas allí por el genio de un gran pintor' [the only women that remain are those immortalized there by the genius of a great painter] (Burgos 2000: 37). As Carola cannot biologically perpetuate herself, she decides to preserve herself in the form of a painting reminiscent of Goya and in this way become part of a much larger family tree — the artistic patrimony labelled Spanish and housed in El Prado. This stab at immortality forms the basis of this chapter. Carola's plan to be immortalized in paint establishes an interesting dialogue with the artistic legacy of Goya and the place of women in the national art canon.

Just as literature became nationalized during the second part of the nineteenth century, mapped out in genealogical terms with Cervantes as one of the founding fathers, so did art, with Goya and other painters occupying similarly patriarchal roles. The cataloguing of literature and the curation of art stem from the same impulse for nationalization. Writing on the parallels between literary canons and the pictorial ones assembled by museums, Stuart Davies observes how 'the story of great authors and their works is a narrative that echoes the wider history of the nation: the canon is both a memorialization of the cultural past and also a representation of it for new generations' (2012: 6). *La que quiso ser maja* reflects the role played by museums, in particular the Prado, in the canonization of art. It is a world Burgos knew well in her extensive work as an art critic, an activity that has attracted very little scholarly attention, save a few notable examples such as Kirkpatrick (2003) and Cabanillas Casafranca (2005–06), particularly when compared to the attention received by her more overtly feminist output. However, as Cabanillas Casafranca observes, the role of women as creators and muses, in particular, seems to occupy a central theme in female art criticism during this period (2005–06: 386).

Cabanillas Casafranca highlights *La maja desnuda*, with its infamous muse, amongst the paintings that Burgos revisited both in her fiction and in her journalism, although fails to mention explicitly *La que quiso ser maja*. In an article titled 'La vuelta a Goya' [The Return to Goya], Burgos claims that 'es extraordinario, para el que analiza la psicología en las bellas artes, el hallazgo que hizo Goya de la mujer en toda su gracia española y castiza' [for those who analyze the psychology in the fine arts, it is extraordinary how Goya managed to capture women in all of their pure Spanish glory] (1910a: 22). Such declarations remind us of the similar praise Ríos had lavished upon both Goya and above all Tirso for their abilities to capture the essence of Spanish women. Goya also features among Burgos's favoured painters together with Velázquez and El Greco, all of whom she often praises in her writing and all three comfortably entrenched in the Spanish canon in part due to this steady stream of recognition from herself and others. Like her little-studied output as a biographer, her labour as curator of art reveals a Burgos actively contributing to the nationalization of the past and of cultural production.[2] Yet *La que quiso ser maja* also reveals the struggle of women to inscribe themselves within this patrimony. Carola fails in her quest to become a *maja*, a figure that by the 1920s had become almost a caricature 'on the verge of losing their allegorical aura and their prestige as patriotic landmarks' (Zubiaurre-Wagner 2012: 279). Carola also fails to be preserved in El Prado. Her portrait, painted by an up-and-coming artist, proves too avant-garde for official taste and instead ends up displayed in the secluded privacy of the living room, much to her chagrin. Carola fails to transcend the domestic space of home and occupy the very public one of El Prado.

Museums in Nation Building

The pivotal role played by museums like El Prado in nation formation demands further clarification in order to better contextualize the strategy pursued by Carola. This is because a familiarity with such mechanics of legitimacy clearly informs *La que quiso ser maja* — not content with her transformation into a *maja*, Carola's ultimate goal is to be exhibited in the Prado Museum in a strategy of double legitimacy. Without the blessing of this institution, Carola cannot achieve the sort of artistic pedigree she craves. The cultural clout exercised by the Prado reflects its key function in nationalizing artistic production. Moved by a similar impulse to that which led literary historians like Amador de los Ríos to identify native genres, José de Madrazo, one of the first directors of the museum, would invest similar energy in isolating a Spanish School of painting. In her study 'Painted in Spanish: The Prado Museum and the Naturalization of the Spanish School in the Nineteenth Century', Eugenia Afinoguénova examines precisely this strategy and remind us how 'museums are now viewed as foundations which exemplified the rupture in transnational circuits of elite cultures by developing national canons and furnishing the image-repertoires of nations' (2009: 320).

The creation of a Spanish School was in itself a bit of a family affair, championed by the previously mentioned José de Madrazo and later by his eldest child Federico Madrazo, also a director, together with Carlos de Madrazo, another member of the clan who had helped disseminate this nationalistic nomenclature to a wider public through the several museum catalogues he put together. In the assembly of a unified pictorial tradition that erases previous regional differences or influences, Federico de Madrazo resorted to a genealogical analogy, imagining it as a family tree retroactively rooted in a set of national motifs or preoccupations. Once again, the family comparison appears, which Afinoguénova also identifies as one of the most evocative cognitive metaphors used to bind the 'imagined communities' of modern nationalism. As she remarks: 'Federico de Madrazo's genealogy of the "Spanish School" was complemented by another naturalizing metaphor: that of an "artistic family", which set the foundation of an ancestry national in scale and political by nature' (2009: 328). Burgo herself contributed to this process of canonization with her public lectures on art in prestigious venues such as the Louvre, where she in 1922 read 'Pintores españoles' [Spanish Painters] (Cabanillas Casafranca 2005–06: 398; Núñez Rey 2005: 636).

Afinoguénova charts this trajectory of the Prado from private royal collection to privileged public site for the enunciation of national symbolism, and shows how art in a museum setting fulfils a different function to that privately displayed in aristocratic *Wunderkammers*. As Andrew McClellan observes in his book *Inventing the Louvre*:

> The purpose or 'mission' of the museum was, as it still is, to educate and conserve. Therein lies the 'modernity' of the museums [...], and it is that which distinguishes them from other prominent art collections in Europe. All royal and princely collections in the eighteenth century manifested the wealth and taste of their owners. (McClellan 1994: 2)

This view of the Louvre also applies to its Spanish counterpart the Prado, which had opened its doors to the public in 1819 as Museo Real or Museo Fernandino [Royal Museum or Fernandine Museum], and derived the main bulk of its collection from the symbolically fraught Hapsburgs and Bourbons.[3] The nationalization project had been initiated by King Amadeo I, who in 1872 declared it the property of the nation, an act completed by the government of the First Republic that followed his abdication under a 1873 legal initiative, and which formally entrusted the management of the collection to the state. To signal its new status, the institution was rechristened as the Museo Nacional de Pintura y Escultura [National Museum of Painting and Sculpture] but would be retained in the popular imagination as the Museo del Prado.

The increasing cultural clout enjoyed by the museum can be seen in the literature of the time, stories which in turn helped cement El Prado's status as home of the national artistic patrimony. Amongst other examples, El Prado makes an appearance in Pérez Galdós's *La desheredada* (1881) wherein the protagonist Isidora Rufete claims that the affinity she feels contemplating these paintings is indicative of an artistic sensibility only somebody of noble ancestry can possess. Inspired by the canvases she encounters, Isidora easily pictures herself as a Roman patrician or a Venetian noble (Pérez Galdós 2000: 420), images that echo Carola conceiving herself as a *maja* in the style of Goya. Yet a key characteristic distinguishes Isidora from Carola: in *La desheredada*, Pérez Galdós mocks the storyline of the foundling with noble roots that proliferated in serialized novels, and of which *Oliver Twist* is the canonical example. As we have seen, it was a popular motif that legitimated a more abstract take on 'noble', such as moral integrity or an appreciation of culture that the new ruling classes could claim in the absence of an aristocratic pedigree. Isidora has consumed too many of these stories that lead her to believe that she too is of noble ascendancy in a quest for distinction, with tragic consequences. Carola, on the other hand, does not cling to a noble pedigree (or aspirations to one), the only female character studied who does not invoke the authority of ancestry to justify her actions or inject credibility into their arguments. Inés had defended El Encubierto by partly alluding to his consanguinity with the Catholic Monarchs, Melita Palma posed as the noble Clara de Alvarado to gain approval from her prospective mother-in-law, Doña Aurora dreams up a whole family tree to destigmatize her occupation as a pawnbroker, as well as to secure an advantageous marriage for her niece. As we will see, even the protagonist of *Los anticuarios*, although not keen herself, humours the noble aspirations of her husband who shares with Doña Aurora a penchant for ostentatious surnames and dubious family trees.

Carola does not pursue this path, although it becomes increasingly clear that the portrait for which she now longs will occupy the same space as the coat of arms Doña Aurora so proudly displayed. In the absence of descendants, the painting functions as both her progeny, 'aquel retrato que representaba su sobreviviente; un hijo que encarnaba ella misma' [that portrait which represented her offspring; a child that she herself embodied] (Burgos 2000: 64), and a precious heirloom that she will donate to the Prado, so she too can join the ranks of her chosen artistic family.

To be inducted into the Prado, Carola is aware she must fulfil certain criteria: 'Un retrato de fotografía, o un vulgar retrato al óleo, no resuelven nada. Cuando no se tiene familia que los conserve, van a parar al Rastro' [a photographical portrait, or a mere oil painting did not solve anything. When one has no family to keep them, they end up in the Rastro] (36).

Carola fears that after her passing, her portrait might end up as a cheap antique sold at the flea market in the Rastro park, joining other orphaned and discarded objects.[4] It brings us back to the noble aspirations of Isidora in *La desheredada* and her conception of art. As Luis Fernández Cifuentes remarks in a recent essay on the role of art museums in the construction of class, entitled 'Isidora in the Museum', it is suggestive that the aspiring aristocrat should start her survey of Madrid by first visiting the Prado (Fernández Cifuentes 2005: 82). Not only instrumental in shaping a shared national culture, the art museum also mirrors and supports a social hierarchy that benefits those on the upper echelons. Not everyone was equal within its walls. Only the privileged classes were allowed to display their works of art, propped up by their historical credentials. The lower classes, on the other hand, were expected to admire them, regarded as models to emulate, in a well-rehearsed civics exercise in which everyone was told their place (Fernández Cifuentes 2005: 87). The museum scene at the beginning of *La desheredada* reminds the reader of the position occupied by Isidora, condemned to be the admirer rather than the emulator. A similar destiny awaits the protagonist of *La que quiso ser maja*, whose social class will equally prevent her from hanging on the walls of the Prado.

Becoming a *Maja*

Unfazed or wilfully ignorant of the social obstacles she faces, Carola convinces her husband to support her dream of being depicted as a *maja* and gets his consent to use his inheritance towards funding her latest bid for immortality. Don Salvador had originally suggested 'Franzen' as a candidate, an allusion to August R. Franzén (1863–1938), who had become an established portraitist at the turn of the century. Carola rejects this idea, finding him too common, as she pores over the different painters she finds in the Prado to find someone — in her words — versed in the art of depicting women (words that echo those of Burgos in her article 'La vuelta a Goya' that praises his portrait skills). Although reliant on the sketching skills of a man, Carola still wishes to find a visual language that reflects her inner concept of herself, settling finally for Goya's *La maja desnuda* [The Naked *Maja*]. The allure exerted by the *maja* as a key signifier of Spanish identity is clearly a strong factor in her attraction to Goya's painting, but so is her state of undress. Carola opts for *La maja desnuda* rather than her more demure counterpart *La maja vestida*, to the slight alarm of her husband who feels uncomfortable with this level of exposure. Carola does not emulate this pose or even the state of undress, but tries instead to recreate the effect with an eclectic assemblage of symbols she has harvested from different traditions, perhaps in an attempt to reclaim artistic discourse away from male monopoly.

That Carola picks *La maja desnuda*, despite not wishing to disrobe, is a suggestive choice laden with symbolism that feeds into several threads and reveals Burgos as a playful surveyor of the cultural map she outlines. As a privileged benchmark for all things Spanish, Goya was a contested figure, meaning different things to different parties. His work has been the subject of numerous interpretations, a veritable cornucopia that leads Nigel Glendinning to remark in *Goya and his Critics* that 'often the viewpoint has been more obvious than the view, and criticism has revealed more about the critics than about Goya' (1977: 198). Glendinning analyses the major patterns in Goya criticism, revealing particularly febrile activity during the decades preceding *La que quiso ser maja*, ranging from psychological and pathological interpretations to racial and political ones. In this way, Burgos's contribution could be seen as yet one more piece in the colourful mosaic of criticism.

Yet it also hints at more personal connections, as both her long-term friend and mentor Vicente Blasco Ibáñez and her partner Ramón Gómez de la Serna had authored stories called 'La maja desnuda'. While Blasco Ibáñez had produced a longer novel, the version by Gómez de la Serna is a brief vignette placed at the centre-fold of the erotic magazine *Flirt*. It narrates the breaking in of an artist into the Prado Museum to admire the *maja desnuda*. Besotted, he allegedly molests the painted *maja* in a surreal turn of events. In Blasco Ibáñez's version, the protagonist, a celebrated painter, convinces his reluctant wife to pose as the *maja desnuda*, only for her to later regret her decision and destroy the image. Against the traditional theory of jealousy, Katharine Murphy reads this act as 'a response to the violation of her freedom and selfhood within the canvas, and to the artist's drive for possession' (2010: 950). That the protagonist in Burgos's story refuses flat-out from the beginning to disrobe raises an interesting intertextual dialogue with Blasco Ibáñez's version, as does the fact that it appeared in an erotic publication as did Gómez de la Serna's significantly cruder take.

Carola's refusal to pose as a naked *maja* could also be read as a reaction against the profusion of images depicting women in the nude, bar a strategically placed mantilla, that flourished in the first decades of the twentieth century — as observed by Zubiaurre-Wagner (2012: 260–61, 264–72) and discussed earlier in *Madrid goyesco*. Illustrative examples in high art include Ignacio de Zuloaga's *Desnudo de la mantilla y el clavel* [Nude with a Mantilla and a Carnation] (1915), Federico Beltrán Masses's *La maja maldita* [The Cursed *Maja*] (1918), a portrait of the legendary dancer Carmen Tórtola Valencia or Julio Romero de Torres's *La Venus de la poesía* [The Venus of Poetry] (1913) that features the cuplé singer Raquel Meller dressed in only a diaphanous veil, sitting next to her fully-clothed husband Enrique Gómez Carillo, a well-known writer. Romero Torres would later depict Carmen de Burgos in the same fashion as Gómez Carillo, soberly dressed and with a book in her hand denoting her profession as a writer. The portrait would become a status symbol, mentioned in interviews as a prestige prop ('cuando fui a inteviuvarla, la encontré trabajando en su salón romántico, en donde lucía su esplendidez dos lienzos maravillosos de Romero Torres' [when I went to interview her, I found her working in her romantic salon, where two wonderful paintings by Romero Torres stood out in their splendour], Aragonés 1933: 5).

Carola decides to pose not merely covered, but standing up, which can be read both as a defiant gesture against the traditional practice of reclining, but also as a playful jab at the ultimately pedestrian dimension of *La maja de pie* [The Standing *Maja*] , as Carola already christens this future work. At the same time, her wish to be depicted standing up can also be read as an attempt to emulate the pose adopted by the Duchess of Alba, also dressed as a *maja* in a 1797 Goya portrait. The duchess occupies a privileged space in the historical imagination. Part of the fascination with *la maja desnuda* stems from the popular legend that has the Duchess of Alba as the model. Even the republican Burgos observes in an article how:

> La leyenda repite sin recatarse mucho que uno de sus modelos fue la duquesa de Alba, la aristócrata de más genuina cepa española, la mujer que conservaba, por esa condición que tienen los títulos conseguidos en los tiempos heroicos, todo el troquel antiguo, tradicional y fortísimo de la raza. (Burgos 1910a: 24)

> [The legend maintains without hesitation that one of his models was the Duchess of Alba, the aristocrat of purest Spanish stock, the woman who retained the age-old blueprint of the race, powerful and traditional, as a result of having acquired her titles of nobility during heroic times.]

It should come as no surprise that Carola should wish to emulate such a totem of the Spanish race, hoping that some of her aura might rub off on her.

However, the aesthetic of the work, iconography and delusions of grandeur sit incongruously with a middle-class woman of the 1920s, a decade associated with streamlined art deco and abstract avant-garde. Carola looks for inspiration in Renaissance painters such as Titian, whom she admires for his allegorical *mise en scène*, taking it upon herself to improve on Goya, perceived as too austere, with the incorporation of a peacock into her own portrait. The choice of a bird associated with royalty in many cultures, and specifically with immortality in Christianity (its flesh was once believed not to decay), is not accidental, and reveals the scope of her ambitions.[5] Finding such a bird in Madrid proves impossible, and Carola has to content herself with a ragged stuffed one that has seen better days, incidentally found in the Rastro market, foreshadowing the ironic fatalism suffered by the ill-fated portrait. The latter is conceived in the following terms:

> Quedó convenido que el retrato sería vestida de negro, con peina de teja y mantilla española. Había que exagerar un poco el descote para lucir el collar con la gran cruz de oro sobre el seno. Llevaría aretes largos, un grueso alfiler de brillantes en la mantilla y pulseras. El pavo real debía estar a su lado, sobre la alfombra. (Burgos 2000: 46)

> [It was decided that she would be dressed in black for the portrait, with the traditional Spanish comb and mantilla. The cleavage had to be exaggerated a little to showcase the necklace with the large golden cross. She was to wear drop earrings, a thick diamond pin in the mantilla and bracelets. The peacock should be by her side, on the carpet.]

So before finding a painter, she has already assembled all the iconography with which she wishes to be depicted, creating a visual language that owes much to Renaissance paintings, with their rich allegorical tradition, as well as more recent symbolism denoting pedigree. Carola delves into the popular imagination and plunders it for any element that evokes pedigree, be it the patrician peacock, or a black mantilla as donned by the Duchess of Alba, concocting a semiotic supernova similar to the one forged by Doña Aurora with her litany of patriotic patronymics. The result is equally overwhelming, bordering on pastiche, and in the case of Carola gets lost in translation after the painter fails to recreate this inner vision. Overwrought or not, Carola is trying to piece together an alternative to both *The Naked Maja* and *The Dressed Maja* with her *The Standing Maja*.

Having now a more accurate visual representation of how she wishes to be memorialized, she contacts the famous portraitist Marcelo. But Marcelo only sees Carola as another amorous conquest, not considering her on a par with the aristocracy and luminaries who constitute the bulk of his subjects. Besides, Marcelo claims to like his models naked, 'a mí me gusta pintar mujeres frescas..., pero sin ropa' [I like to paint loose women..., but without clothes] (Burgos 2000: 49), which conflicts with the requirements of Carola.

Burgos relates how Marcelo had infamously painted a fictional English aristocrat as a naked Venus, an example briefly worth exploring as it echoes a cause célèbre that would have been known to readers, as well as providing an interesting parallel to the resulting painting that Carola eventually manages to commission. Some readers might have thought of an equally rebellious Spanish noble, María de Gloria de Collado y de Alcázar, who descended from one of the country's most noble families and had posed for Federico Beltrán Masses with only a mantilla on her head in *La maja marquesa* [The Marchioness *Maja*] (1915). Its execution coincides with that of Zuloaga's painting mentioned above, *Desnudo de la mantilla y el clavel,* painted a couple of years after Torres's *La Venus de la poesía*. However, such representation found no favour with the more conservative members of the judging panel, and the picture was rejected for the annual Exposición Nacional de Bellas Artes [National Exhibition of Fine Arts], a veto that raised its profile and piqued public interest.

The image was widely disseminated by many newspapers that reproduced the infamous painting, and was also printed on thousands of postcards. Its risqué cachet was further highlighted by such captions as '"La maja marquesa", cuadro de Federico Beltrán que fue rechazado por el Jurado de la Exposición de Bellas Artes' [The Marchioness *Maja*, painting by Federico Beltrán, which was rejected by the Jury of the Fine Arts Exhibition] (Mori 1915: 1), the phrasing chosen by *El País*, which featured it prominently on its cover. In the same vein, *El Heraldo de Madrid* provided detailed instructions to its readers on where to find the infamous painting that 'como es sabido por haberlo publicado la prensa, lo rechazó el Comité de la Exposición Nacional de Bellas Artes por considerarlo inmoral' [as everyone knows, was rejected by the committee of the National Exhibition of Fine Arts after having been published by the press] (Anon. 1915: 2). Prominent artists such as Ignacio Zuloaga and Julio Romero de Torres rallied in its favour, and *La maja marquesa* was instead exhibited at the Sala de Arte Moderno [Modern Art Salon] in Madrid to queues around the block of people eager to catch a glimpse of the controversial picture. Despite its initial rejection by the judging panel of the National Exhibition, the picture received the ultimate seal of approval after another exhibition by Beltrán was attended the following year by none other than King Alfonso XIII and the queen mother. It is precisely this kind of recognition Carola craves but fails to garner.

After having been turned down by Marcelo, Carola manages to convince the up-and-coming artist Jacinto Pimentel to paint her portrait as his entry for that year's National Exhibition. She now sees her induction into the Prado assured and revels in imagining her future legacy on its walls, historicizing her portrait as it becomes national patrimony: 'Tendría lugar cuando pasara sobre su retrato el tiempo que había pasado sobre los de Velázquez, por ejemplo. Entonces era fácil que se discutiera si la *Maja de pie* era más linda que la *Maja desnuda*' [it would happen with her portrait when enough time had passed as it was the case with Velázquez for example. Then it would be easy to debate whether *The Standing Maja* was lovelier than *The Naked Maja*] (Burgos 2000: 61–62). However, the avant-garde Jacinto Pimentel espouses a very different artistic agenda and paints Carola in a distorted Expressionist style, to the disappointment of both Carola and her husband who would have preferred a more realist aesthetic.[6] Resigned, she consoles herself by hoping it might still win first prize and join the Prado, despite its departure from her own vision. But the picture proves too experimental for the judging panel, dashing any remaining hopes of entering the Prado and being consecrated as national patrimony. Hoping to replicate the media coverage given to other rejected works — *La maja marquesa* being the canonical example — an affronted Jacinto Pimentel resorts to the press to vent his indignation:

> Quiso recurrir a los periódicos, dar escándalo, que se le hiciera justicia; pero en vista de que no conseguía nada, y de que en Madrid no existía, como en Francia, un *Salón de Rechazados*, para que el público pudiera convencerse de la mala fe del Jurado de la Exposición, pensó en colgar su cuadro de un árbol del Retiro. (Burgos 2000: 67)
>
> [He wanted to go to the newspapers, stir up a scandal, to have justice done; but given that he was not getting anywhere, and that unlike in France, there was no *Salon des Refusés* in Madrid so that the public could see the Exhibition Jury's erroneous ways, he thought of nailing his painting to a tree in the Retiro park.]

The recipe that had proven so successful for *La maja marquesa* fails in the case of *La maja de pie*, which struggles even to find an alternative display space. Jacinto blames it on the lack of a Salón de los Rechazados, a reference to the Parisian Salon des Refusés that had been established in 1863 by Napoleon to house the increasing number of works that did not meet the requirements of the Salon. As many critics have observed, its creation ultimately contributed to the legitimation of avant-garde streams to the point that, as Robert Jensen remarks in *Marketing Modernism in Fin-de-siècle Europe*, 'all later "avant-gardes" required the label of "refusés" whether they earned it or not' (1994: 36). It is this label to which Jacinto appeals but without the desired effect. Madrid might not have had an actual Salón de los Rechazados but it contained other spaces that fulfilled a similar role, as demonstrated by the successful display of *La maja marquesa* at the Sala de Arte Moderno. Failing that, Jacinto decides to hang it from a tree in the Retiro, thus stripping the painting of any claims it might have had to enter the sacred space of the Prado. It is rescued by Don Salvador to spare his wife from the prying eyes of onlookers in a public space not explicitly demarcated for the aesthetic contemplation of art. Carola must content herself with exhibiting it in her own private living room: 'Así rescatado el gran cuadro, fue a ocupar el testero principal del salón; pero tristemente, sin la gloria a que estaba destinado' [After its rescue, the large painting ended up occupying a place of honour in the sitting room, but without the glory for which it was destined] (Burgos 2000: 69).

Through her portrait, Carola had tried to transcend this domestic sphere and insert herself into national consciousness by deliberately fashioning herself as a Spanish totem. Yet she lacks some crucial ingredients. Most importantly, she lacks the august pedigree of someone like María de Gloria de Collado y de Alcázar when she decided to pose for the infamous *La maja marquesa*. It echoes the frisson that surrounds the *Maja desnuda* in part due to the rumours that the Duchess of Alba was its subject. But Carola lacks this pedigree, and there remains the fact that she does not model naked. Carola is no Duchess of Alba despite attempts to emulate her in portrait form. It leaves her reliant on the unpredictable course of history that might lead to a posthumous recognition and so finally vindicate her claims: '¡Quién sabe! Al Greco tardaron siglos en hacerle justicia' [Who knows! It took centuries before they did El Greco justice] (Burgos 2000: 69). Despite a finely tuned historical awareness, Carola loses control of her narrative and is proved unable to manufacture the legacy for which she longs. The resulting painting with its eclectic symbolism — part traditional allegory, part modern nationalism filtered through an avant-garde aesthetic — does not easily fit into any category. Its style proves too experimental for the establishment who rejects it, yet neither is it scandalous enough to properly *épater la bourgeoisie* and be labelled a *refusé*, so ends up back in the domestic sphere where it was painted. It shows how even in the roaring 20s women are still saddled with a legacy that restricts their roles within the national imagination. Part of the problem resides in Carola's insistence on being fashioned as a *maja*, resorting to an iconography that by the 1920s is suffering from exhaustion through sheer overuse, verging on parody. Symbolic saturation threatens the project of Carola, who fails to realize that the *maja* figure no longer occupies such a privileged position in the visual language of modernity, which favours instead a more abstract and internationalist take on art (Zubiaurre-Wagner 2012: 309). Yet Carola also fails in her project to become a fully-fledged New Woman, as her initial fruitless attempt to create the asylum shows. It leaves her in limbo since 'she does not fit into the old cast of the patriotic *maja* (and no doubt looked ridiculous in that extemporaneous portrait built around peinetas, mantillas, and fans), but she is equally unable to become a modern woman' (Zubiaurre-Wagner 2012: 309).

It is this limbo that Burgos often explored in her narrative and in which she must occasionally have felt herself, as she describes, '¿Tendencias? Yo soy *naturalista romántica*, variable como mis *yoes*' [Trends? I am a *romantic naturalist*, as varied as my different selves] (1910b: xii). As we know, this difficulty in cataloguing her output resulted later in neglect as Burgos fell between the cracks of nomenclature or, as Kirkpatrick remarks, 'hasta hace poco Burgos ha sido invisible dentro de la historia literaria española porque su escritura y su identidad autorial no encajaban adecuadamente en ninguna de sus categorías principales' [until recently Burgos was invisible in Spanish literary history because her writing and identity as an author did not fit neatly into any of the main categories] (2003: 21). Burgos was aware that as a creative woman she occupied a precarious and indeterminate position in a space dominated by men, a concern that often surfaces in her narrative. Short stories and novellas such as 'El último deseo' [The Last Desire] (1908), 'La incomprensible' [The Misunderstood Woman] (1908) and 'El perseguidor' [The Persecutor] (1917) explore the ideological baggage with which her protagonists are saddled throughout their journeys to Classical Italy, Romantic Germany and the Modernist metropolises of London and Paris in search of a space and literary language that reflects their identity as women and artists in a cartography — both discursive and geographical — drawn by men. This constant limbo is summarized at the end of 'La incomprensible' when the protagonist Isabel rejects the advances of a renowned painter, which leads him to exclaim: '¡Cristiana! ¡Burguesa! [...] No serás jamás artista ni conocerás la felicidad' [Christian! Bourgeois! You will never be an artist or know happiness] (Burgos 1908: 96.) It is an accusation illustrative of the limbo in which Burgos's heroines often find themselves (the protagonist of *La que quiso ser maja* being no exception) and shows that women are not only excluded from conservative creeds but also from liberal tenets that are tailored to fit male needs and interests. Trapped in a discursive field that condemns them as either too transgressive or too boringly bourgeois, women like Isabel or Carola end up marooned in a no-man's land — or perhaps 'all-woman's land', since we find so many of them there. The rejected painter carries on to the infamous Fornos Café, an artist's haven and therefore a safe discursive space, whilst we see Isabel vanish into her doorway, her future uncertain.

Although written with much humour and satire, *La que quiso ser maja* shows the limbo many women faced in their attempt to create a legacy, stranded between nineteenth century narratives that seemed increasingly out-dated and exhausted, and an incipient modernity that was not sufficiently developed to support new female models or reflect their experiences. Carola's oscillation between old customs and newer ones such as postponing marriage until her thirties shows the complex landscape women like Carola had to negotiate, reinforcing the status quo and undermining it, rejecting the idea of marriage but pursuing maternity, fashioning themselves as objects of desire but wanting to be fully in charge of their objectification. The way in which Carola articulates her desire for immortality owes much to the genealogical imagination and the new mechanisms of legitimacy that underpinned the liberal state: she refers to her prospective portrait as a child and dreams of joining the Spanish artistic family of the Prado. Yet her modus operandi reveals her to be an independent, assertive woman, economically independent, who faced with a catalogue too restrictive to leave her imprint tries expanding her options to reflect this new-found agency but without much success. Having failed as a philanthropist, and then as a mother, Carola decides that being a muse will guarantee her a place in history. This conscious appropriation of the muse role appears in both *Melita Palma* and *Madrid goyesco*, which also shows the potential dangers of 'using the tools of the master'. It backfires in *Madrid goyesco* when the internal narrative logic of the trope Doña Aurora had invoked ultimately overrides the alternative ending she had devised. Carola takes a more proactive approach, eagerly seeking out artists who will draw inspiration from an image she has fashioned, rather than having to mould herself to a pre-existing projection, as was the case for Melita Palma. Yet regardless of the degree of agency exercised by the woman, a muse still remains a passive party. Ultimately Carola loses control of her artistic vision when the painter's depiction diverges from her inner projection.

Notes to Chapter 8

1. Published between 1924 and 1928, *La Novela Pasional* includes 186 titles, and is one of the approximately 250 known collections that appeared during this period according to Guereña (2000: 199); see also Guereña (2001). Despite its appearance in such collections, *La que quiso ser maja* contains few if any sexual references, an exiguity of the explicit only amplified by the borderline pornographic passages of other titles. Instead, any erotic cues are provided by some of the gratuitous illustrations that accompany the text, featuring women in various stage of undress, and often completely disassociated from the action narrated (Pujante 2014: 205)
2. Together with Velázquez and Goya, El Greco (1541–1614) features amongst those painters rediscovered in the nineteenth century as visual distillers of the Spanish spirit. Originally from Greece, but relocated to Toledo, El Greco was hailed by the intellectuals associated with the Generation of '98. In his work they seem to gauge the mysticism and decadence that permeated the Spanish spirit. Burgos subscribed to this vision, as illustrated in the article 'Las mujeres del Greco' [The Women of El Greco], in which she describes the women as 'esencialmente místicas e idealistas' [essentially mystic and idealistic] (1914: 2). For the reception of El Greco in the nineteenth century, see Álvarez Lopera (1987) and Boone (2007).
3. Although faithful to its civic function, the idea of displaying national treasures had first been raised by Joseph Bonaparte during his brief stint on the Spanish throne (1808–14). In this way the inception of the Prado is tied to the Louvre in more ways than both belonging to the zeitgeist. It was however King Ferdinand VIII that brought the idea to fruition (Afinoguénova 2010: 210).
4. This is the outcome in Ramon de Mesonero Romanos's short story 'El retrato' [The Portrait] (1832), in which the narrator finds the portrait of a deceased friend languishing in a pawn shop years after his death.
5. In her analysis of *Venus with an Organist and Cupid* (c. 1555), the Titian picture that probably inspires Carola to include a peacock in her own portrait, Simona Cohen reads the presence of the bird as a symbol of deceptive vanity, in a perhaps deliberate move to undermine its association with immortality (2008: 149).
6. In a recent study Thomas R. Franz reads this distorted version of Carola as a snub by Jacinto Pimentel after Carola declines to have an affair with him, satirizing her vain bid for immortality (2017: 84). However, I disagree: Pimentel's male pride might have taken a knock but he seems genuinely upset that the establishment refuses to recognize his avant-garde vision of art.

CHAPTER 9

Counterfeit Genealogies and Forged Patrimony in *Los anticuarios*

Published in 1918, Burgos's fourth novel *Los anticuarios* [The Antiques Dealers] centres on the picaresque exploits of the two eponymous antiques dealers. Based in Paris, the former civil servant Fabián de las Navas y Marchamalo and his enterprising wife Adelina run a shop that specializes in Spanish antiques. Burgos showcases once more her knowledge of art, displaying a detailed grasp of the merchandise peddled by the couple, from chinoiserie to paintings and brocade. Whilst in *La que quiso ser maja*, the author had explored the role of museums in legitimizing national narratives and consecrating certain art as native, in *Los anticuarios* Burgos satirizes the growing interest in antiques that can be seen as another manifestation of this interest in a shared past. A longstanding interest in the national patrimony meant that this was not the first time antiques had appeared in Burgos's narrative, nor would it be the last. Núñez Rey points out how 'la preocupación de la autora por el patrimonio artístico español era muy antigua' [the author's concern for Spain's artistic patrimony was well established] (2005: 465) and mentions the investigation by Burgos into the disappearance of some El Greco paintings from a church. If these works of art are metonyms for the country, logic dictates that their exit from the country would dilute the national spirit. Burgos thus remarks in *Los anticuarios* that 'todas las naciones se preocupaban cada vez más de evitar que las obras de arte fueran llevadas al extranjero' [all nations were increasingly taking steps to avoid artworks being taken abroad] (1989: 139). Like Goya's paintings, antiques transcend their physical presence to stand for more abstract qualities associated with nationalism and cultural cohesion. In *Los anticuarios*, this national patrimony becomes a platform upon which to discuss the contribution of women to its arsenal. Once again, the novel reveals the entanglement of women in several often contradictory discourses. The enterprising protagonist Adelina strives for economic independence for herself and her daughters, and often espouses views very different from those of her husband. On the other hand, Adelina never neglects her domestic duties and through her later role as an antiques dealer, she becomes a purveyor of furniture, embroidery, vases and other objects of interior decoration. In other words, she monetizes a domesticity she is simultaneously undermining with her emancipatory efforts.

Los anticuarios is the main text analyzed in this chapter, although it should be noted that in the hands of Burgos antiques are malleable and recurring metaphors, used to frame different debates. Thus, in the later *El tío de todos* [Everyone's Uncle] (1925), Burgos portrays antiques dealers in a rather unflattering light, with only their own economic interests at heart. In *El tío de todos*, two women belonging to the profession convince an elderly pair of sisters to dispose of their family heirloom, a so-called 'mantón de Manila' [Manila shawl], to raise funds to pursue a fraudulent inheritance claim against the fabled uncle of the title. However, as the title equally reveals, they are not the only ones who believe themselves to be the rightful heirs. The mythical relative bears the common surname of Garcilaso, which leads to the creation of an industry centred round identifying the true family branch, as genealogists and opportunistic antiques dealers monetize these aspirations. The conflation of the genealogist and the antiques dealer reveals how both ultimately promise pedigree, whether that of a family tree or a physical object imbued with its own valuable history. Burgos satirizes a Spain that is victim of its own historical imagination, fixated on finding a single origin story, giving up traditional Spanish shawls and other emblematic tokens of Spanish culture for something less tangible.[1] It rests upon the naive assumption that if only the gold of Garcilaso — clearly a placeholder for the country's imperial past — could be tracked down, then all current problems would disappear. Yet this search in the past to solve the present proves fruitless. It leads an exasperated character to conclude: 'Pero si ahora parece que somos Garcilaso media España. ¿Cómo vamos a ser parientes todos?' [But now it seems like half of Spain is a Garcilaso. Are we really all related?] (Burgos 1925: 73). As it turns out, the main obstacle to locating this chimeric Garcilaso is the absence of his second surname, the maternal one, which remains unknown. With this observation, Burgos seems to warn against attempts to reconstruct family trees if these trees exclude women. Or as another character puts it, the ancestral chart will remain incomplete in its current state, 'porque también hay que contar *con la madre*' [because one also has to include *the mother*] (74, my emphasis).

Such instances show how Burgos conceptualizes the marginalization of women in national narratives in genealogical terms, yet it is the earlier *Los anticuarios* that foregrounds this gendered exclusion. This is partly because Burgos suggest ways to overcome it in the figure of Adelina, who has an approach to the genealogical imagination very different from that of her husband. Predictably, Fabián has a habit of foregoing the second surname in his reconstructions, illustrated by the separate matrilineal line for women he likes to recite:

> Y aprovechaba [...] para repetir una vez más el árbol genealógico de las mujeres, que él había compuesto.
> — Son hijas de mujer, nietas de mujer, biznietas de mujer, madres de mujer, y siempre mujeres. (Burgos 1989: 219)
>
> [And he took the opportunity [...] to recite once more the genealogical tree of women he had composed.
> — They are daughters of women, granddaughters of women, great-granddaughters of women, mothers of women, and always women.]

To which Adelina retorts: 'Lo mismo podríamos decir de vosotros [...] Hijos de mujer, nietos de mujer, biznietos de mujer, padres de mujer... con la agravante de que sois también *los maridos de las mujeres*' [The same could be said of you men [...] Sons of women, grandsons of women, great-grandsons of women, fathers of women... and to make things worse you are also *husbands of women*] (219). With this comeback, Adelina not only reclaims the female presence, but engulfs her husband in the separate lineage he had drawn, one of the many instances throughout the story that sees her trying to tweak the terms of discourse. *Los anticuarios* also introduces the element of economic necessity into any attempts at self-fashioning, a concern that had preoccupied Ríos's female protagonists as well. Like them, Adelina also follows the route of marriage but pressed by the demands of a growing brood does not content herself with the increasingly stretched salary of her husband, seeking instead her own income. As we will see, it is at her initiative that the couple enter the world of antiques, and she retains a key role in the family business: 'Todo el complicado mecanismo de su oficio pesaba sobre Adelina' [the whole complicated mechanism of their work rested on Adelina's shoulders] (92). If the household is seen as a microcosm of the nation, then in Burgos's vision, women occupy an important position in this *patria chica*. *Los anticuarios* reminds us that matrimony still constitutes the safest guarantor of economic stability for women. In the work of Burgos, it becomes a popular platform for discussion of the place of women, as observed by Johnson in a suggestive but tantalizingly brief essay titled 'Carmen de Burgos: Marriage and Nationalism', which features *Los anticuarios* amongst those novels that 'intertwined nationalism and domesticity' (2000: 142). Johnson highlights the figure of the enterprising Adelina, whom she too sees as Burgos's attempt to create a female model with greater impact than those traditionally on offer. Yet the lucrative business of forging antiques in which Adelina takes part is interpreted as a critique of the fetishized 'national essence' pursued by some as the holy grail of authenticity. 'Spain's historical heritage,' Johnson writes, 'so avidly sought by the male members of the Generation of '98' — is as slippery as defining gender roles within marriage or in society at large' (2000: 145). In this aspect, my reading diverges from that of Johnson, because while Burgos questions the overwhelmingly male bent of national patrimony, she does not dismiss the idea of a national essence. In fact, women like Burgos took a keen interest in shaping this patrimony despite its androcentric bent. She derived considerable discursive authority this way, yet she was also interested in expanding this patrimony to make it more inclusive.

How Adelina succeeds in establishing such a niche for herself constitutes the axis of this chapter, approached once more through the prism of genealogy. As in *La que quiso ser maja*, Burgos uses different spaces to illustrate the different paths to legitimacy, from the private domestic sphere to the public arena of the museum. Not all spaces are open to women, and we may recall that Carola has to content herself with displaying her portrait at home. In *Los anticuarios*, Burgos attempts to weave a new future with the threads of previous discourses, from the concept of a fixed national culture to the sacralization of certain historical episodes or objects as proofs of this national cohesion.

To gain this agency, Adelina becomes an *anticuaria*, that is a female antiques dealer, and repackages the past to carve herself a niche in the present. From a strictly lexical point of view, this is a rather innovative move. Whereas the Real Academia Española had accepted, in its *Diccionario de la lengua castellana* of 1803, the female modifier of 'historian', *anticuario* remained in the masculine form into the beginning of the twenty-first century, and it had yet to acknowledge the female presence in the profession despite women like Adelina.[2] Her transition from ambulant seller to fully-fledged antiques dealer sees her safely circulating in the private sphere, albeit those of other women, until eventually entering the public arena with a shop that on the inside still resembles a domestic interior, with its old furnishings and countless knick-knacks. Such hybridity blurs the boundaries between the public male and private female realm that underpinned the cult of domestic ideology.[3] The practice of pitching merchandise within the safe confines of the home, free from the disapproving public gaze, was already a common activity for women in Spain at the time. Doña Aurora had to a certain extent followed this model, allocating part of her house to the pawnbroking business, although ensuring it remained separated from her private life so as not to be tainted by its crass commercialism.

Initially Fabián entertains misgivings about his wife's trading ambitions, fearing that it might tarnish their reputation. He compares Adelina to those:

> Vendedoras de ropas usadas que van por los escenarios y por las casas de las burguesas, que desean figurar con poco dinero y compran los trajes de deshecho de las elegantes, *esos vestidos que siempre tienen historia* y son de la esposa del Banquero que ha caído de luto; de la Marquesa o de la Duquesa, que no se los ha puesto; y hasta proceden del Palacio. (Burgos 1989: 34, my emphasis)

> [Female sellers of second-hand clothing who frequent theatre backstages and the homes of middle-class women who wish to keep up appearances with little money, and who buy the cast-offs of fashionable ladies, *those dresses that always have a history*, and that belonged to the Banker's wife who had to go into mourning; or to the Marchioness or Duchess, who have not worn them; some even coming from the Palace.]

Lacking a pedigree themselves, Fabián mocks those who buy these 'dresses with a history' in the hope that some of the legitimacy may rub off. This is a more democratic, and thus less exclusive, way of acquiring legitimacy and augmenting their social capital. As the liberal project expanded the meaning of family ties to more abstract bonds that encompassed the citizens of a nation, so the concept of family heirlooms expanded to include antiques, which could be regarded as *national* heirlooms. To possess a painting belonging to the Spanish School, or a piece of furniture with its own pedigree was in a way to belong to the national family. In his disquisitions on power dynamics the sociologist Pierre Bourdieu includes antiques as an important status signifier in a passage that is worth quoting at length:

> To possess things from the past, i.e. accumulated, crystallized history, aristocratic names and titles, châteaux or 'stately homes', paintings and, collections, vintage wines and antique furniture, is to master time, through all those things whose common feature is that they can only be acquired in the course of time, by means of time, against time, that is, by inheritance or through dispositions

which, like the taste for old things, are likewise only acquired with time and
applied by those who can take their time. (Bourdieu 1984: 63–64)

The purchase of antiques can be seen as a shortcut to accessing these coveted
deposits of time, hence predictably the best clients are nouveau riche who 'pagaban
espléndidamente los retratos de prelados, de hidalgos o de nobles damas con el
pañolito de encaje en la mano' [paid handsomely for the portraits of prelates, and
of noblemen and women holding a lace handkerchief] (Burgos 1989: 188). In his
conception of antiques, Jerome de Groot observes how:

> Antiques demonstrate a complex commodification of the past — the fetishisation
> of the object due in the main to its age and historical context as well as any
> innate value of craftsmanship [...]. They are measures of cultural capital, objects
> which enhance the owners' sense of worth and allow them entry to particular
> discourses on taste. (Groot 2009: 67)

Rather than creating history, as Carola had attempted with her portrait in *La que
quiso ser maja*, one can acquire portraits with a pre-packed pedigree, as in the case
of antiques. They do not need to be displayed in the Prado first to attain their
status, they already carry the aura of antiquity and can thus safely adorn the homes
of their owners, an outcome Carola had regarded as a failure. This focus on the
domestic space and interior decoration to signal status partly explains the attraction
of the antiques trade to Adelina, seen from this perspective as a less transgressive
occupation than other professions completely removed from domesticity. Such
gendered connotations are described by Barrett Kalter in his *Modern Antiques*, in
which he analyzes the rise of mass consumption of the past: 'while medals and
carved gems were locked up in the secluded *masculine* space of the cabinet, newly
purchased antique furniture and decorative ornaments spread the past throughout
domestic interiors, in some cases to create the illusion of inherited wealth' (2012:
19, my emphasis).

Taking advantage of these mechanisms of legitimacy, intimately associated with
the increased purchasing power of the bourgeoisie and their demands for accompanying paraphernalia, Adelina decides to become an *anticuaria*.[4] *Los anticuarios*
reflects a heightened historical consciousness that had created a favourable climate for
antiques to prosper. The Industrial Revolution had shifted a part of the population
to urban centres where new arrivals had to share space with strangers. Antiques
became repositories of this shared past that characterizes nationalist narratives.
Antiques were also *physical* manifestations of these abstract bloodlines. If individuals
were no longer bonded by actual bloodlines or belonged to the same village, at
least they could be linked by objects that represented a common heritage, even an
imagined one. An antique could be defined as an artisanal creation, 'something that
has endured over time: it carries some of the past into our present and has a story to
tell. In fact, an antique has many stories to tell' (Rosenstein 2009: 1). These are the
stories that both Fabián de las Navas y Marchamalo and his wife Adelina recount to
potential buyers — an antique has to have a past and possess historical pedigree as
part of its ontological allure. However, Fabián, a born raconteur, not merely content
to convince a buyer that a shred of stained lace belonged to the ill-fated Marie

Antoinette or an old rusty sword to El Cid himself, also weaves his own fabled ancestry. He fashions himself as a unique object that cannot easily be replicated. Fabián claims aristocratic blood, which makes him an antique too, before the rise of less exclusive national lineages.

Such a strategy brings to mind Doña Aurora and her penchant for constructing dubious family trees with branches in all the major aristocratic families. With this repositioning, Ríos's character had attempted to elevate herself from her lowly status as a pawnbroker and remove the sordid implication of any mercantile profit from the equation. Fabián relies on even more inflated claims: upon introducing himself as a duke, a potential seller confesses, 'Es para mí un goce que esas alhajas vayan a parar a un noble como el señor Duque, en lugar de ir a manos de un anticuario inmundo' [it is my pleasure that these treasures end up with a nobleman like the Duke, instead of in the hands of a foul antiques dealer] (Burgos 1989: 71).

Nobility belongs in popular imagination to a pre-capitalist era and is therefore not tainted by the commercial ambition associated with the bourgeoisie. This exchange reveals much about the dynamics of social prestige, the rise of the middle classes and how the past should be approached, that is, 'how a society consumes its history is crucial to the understanding of contemporary popular culture, the issues at stake in representation itself, and the various means of self- or social construction available' (Groot 2009: 2). Fabián, a former civil servant — a representative of the new nation-state — is aware of the appeal exerted by the aristocracy, by the human embodiment of an antique.

While an initially sceptic Fabián frets over his wife's commercial ventures, concerned about the impact they may have on his social aspirations, and moreover his family name, Adelina is not only not afraid to seek new openings available to women, but also seems less concerned with family trees than her husband, partly due to her own lowly origins. This prevents her from being anchored in the past and frees her to pursue a future not dictated by ancestral expectations. Fabián by contrast shows great pride in his family links, specifically to an uncle, a senator in Madrid and his initial benefactor, to the point that Fabián occasionally compresses this link by introducing himself as the son rather than the nephew of Senator Don Andrés Marchamalo de las Navas (Burgos 1989: 40). To strengthen the pedigree of his nephew, his uncle had initially arranged a marriage with 'la segundona de una familia linajuda a la cual se unió Fabián sin conocerla apenas' [the youngest daughter of a noble family whom he wed barely knowing her] (32). This first marriage proves to be an unhappy one, with a distant wife, pious to the point of caricature, who dies within a year of their union from a 'indigestión de santidad' [self-righteous indigestion] according to Fabián, or from his mortifying lack of patrician parentage according to her disapproving family (32). Although of impeccable pedigree, Clarita Zaragüeta embodies an outmoded type of woman with no stake in the future of the nation, not only failing to contribute to the conversation with her silent passive demeanour but also turning out to be predictably infertile. Burgos literally removes Clarita from the gene pool, having her succumb to a vague consumption and fulfil her narrative destiny as befits a character with saintly aspirations.

The widowed Fabián falls for Adelina, the daughter of a Civil Guard captain, who in the absence of a noble lineage has inherited an 'arrogancia marcial y una decisión masculina' [martial arrogance and a masculine decisiveness] (33) from her military father. Adelina is a child of the liberal establishment eager to leave her mark, represented partly by her relentless initiative and partly by a prodigious fecundity. One could interpret the remark 'la verdad era que dar a luz no le costaba gran trabajo' [the truth is that giving birth was no great effort] (33) in both a biological sense and a figurative sense. Adelina will both renew the race and shape the future of the nation.

In this way, the plebeian and proudly Spanish Adelina is cut from the same cloth as Ríos's heroines: Melita and the ill-fated Maravillas. It shows that both Burgos and Ríos embraced the idea of the *pueblo*, or the people, as a repository of the national spirit, reformulated during this period by Unamuno and other intellectuals associated with the Generation of 98 through the concept of *intrahistoria* [intrahistory].[5] It denoted the idea that the 'real Spain' was to be found in the daily goings-on of the *pueblo*, away from the battles and kings of traditional history books. Coined by Unamuno, the term *intrahistoria* is reminiscent of the *Kulturgeschichte* championed by German intellectuals, or what the French called 'history of civilization' (Boyd 1997: 130). The difference is that Ríos and Burgos, each with their own ideological standpoint, were keen to carve out a more significant role for the female representatives of this national essence. Adelina thus promptly produces a male heir for Fabián but all their subsequent offspring turn out to be girls, and are taught the ropes of the profession. In fact, Adelina explicitly trains her many daughters so that they do not have to rely on matrimony as their only source of economic stability, an inequality between genders that does not bypass her: '¡Qué contenta estaría si todas hubieran sido hombres! Esos van siempre bien por todas partes' [How happy would she be had they all been men! Men fare well wherever they go] (137).

Adelina occupies a strategic interstice that enables her to pursue a more egalitarian agenda whilst complying with certain expectations, such as producing the requisite scion, but having met that requirement, she bears only girls. Similarly, the resolution to supplement their income from the sale of antiques might come from Adelina, but she must obtain the backing of her husband to open a shop. In other words, she still needs to be chaperoned to enter the public arena fully. Burgos praises the organizational talent of a woman who does not neglect her domestic duties, but rather performs them so well that it leaves her with spare time to throw herself into the sale of antiques with gusto. Her modus operandi might thus not be such a radical departure from traditional gender roles, she still marries, still organizes the household, still dutifully produces descendants. And yet she also relentlessly probes frontiers whenever the opportunity arises. She manages to convince her husband to formalize the business by opening an establishment in Madrid, achieving this by exploiting his genealogical pretensions to her advantage, so that an antique shop ceases to be a blemish on the pedigree and becomes rather a source of income to guarantee the family's social standing. Fabián constantly invokes his ancestry: 'él hablaba siempre de sus ilustres antepasados, de sus nobles amigos, de los honores de su familia. Su tío, el senador, su antiguo protector, era un Dios en su recuerdo' [he was always talking about his illustrious ancestors, of his noble friends, of the honour of his family. His uncle, the senator, past protector, was a god in his memory] (39–40). Adelina delves into this past to convince her husband gradually of a strategy for financial security that would not reduce them to 'traperos distinguidos' [glorified hawkers] (39), as Fabián sometimes fears. Instead she appeals to this allegedly distinguished family history to justify any attempts to restore their previous standing or even legitimize social mobility. In this respect she is no better than her husband, resorting to the same ploys as him to improve her own standing in society. It is another example of the complexity of women's bid for emancipation.

This appropriation of her husband's genealogical fixation serves to expand Adelina's own field of operation, whose circumference expands from the domestic circle to include the public circle of the Madrid shop window. Not yet satisfied, Adelina sets her eyes on Paris, a city she begins to frequent in her hunt for valuable antiques, despite not speaking the language. Her initial inability to speak French does not deter her: she claims that 'las mujeres lo aprendemos todo en seguida' [we women pick up everything quickly] (38). To navigate this new environment, she relies on intuition, a trait that had been identified by Darwin as particularly female, so too imitation (1981: 326–27).

The motif of the business woman who is instinctive has a long tradition in literature. An example worth highlighting is that of Isabel Arnáiz, from the ensemble cast featured in Pérez Galdós's *Fortunata y Jacinta*. Isabel is also prodigiously fecund, described as a 'ama de gobierno' [head of the government] , an image that firmly places the matriarch of the Arnáiz household within the allegorical tradition of the mother country: 'Aquella gran mujer, Isabel Cordero de Arnáiz, dotada de todas las agudezas del traficante y de todas las triquiñuelas económicas del ama de gobierno, fue agraciada además por el Cielo con una fecundidad prodigiosa' [that great woman, Isabel Cordero of Arnáiz, gifted with all the cunning of a trader and all the budgetary tricks of the head of government, was also blessed with a prodigious fecundity] (Pérez Galdós 2011: 256–57). Married into a bourgeois dynasty of textile merchants, she successfully updates her husband's business model thanks to her intuition and half-digested facts gathered here and there, as opposed to an informed business acumen. She *senses* that the colonial trade centre is shifting to Singapore with the rise of the British Empire, but does not know the exact location of the English colony (Pérez Galdós 2011: 252–53). Similarly, Adelina soon establishes important contacts in the French capital despite very little previous knowledge of the culture or language. Like the consecration of maternity, the identification of intuition as a female trait forms part of a gendered essentialist conception of women that Burgos shared with many of her contemporaries which should not undermine the validity of her emancipatory pursuits.

The Paris envisioned by Burgos becomes a space where Adelina sees the opportunity to reinvent herself. Because she specializes in Spanish antiques, the move could be seen as a transplant of the nation on a micro-scale, carrying a chunk of its history embodied by these objects across the border. Here Adelina could in turn expand the discursive borders of the new national outpost to include more female participation. In some ways this is a revolutionary path. Her decision to relocate and to train her numerous daughters to follow in her professional footsteps differentiates her from earlier literary counterparts such as Isabel Arnáiz. Challenged with a similar number of daughters, Galdós's character frets about their future, one that can only be secured with an advantageous match, or any match. Although both Isabel and Adelina are modelled on the trope of the national matriarch, the three-decade gap that separates the two novels empowers Burgos to propose a more active role for the daughters of the nation. It is also worth noting that although published in the last years of the 1880s, Galdós's family saga takes place even earlier, between 1869 and 1874, the so-called revolutionary six-year-period before the rehabilitation of the Bourbons. By 1918, Burgos, a republican sympathizer like Galdós, takes up the baton and foregrounds the marginal role still occupied by women in the liberal nation-state. The similarities between Adelina and Isabel Arnáiz, whether intentional or not, show Burgos engaging in a trans-textual dialogue with her own literary legacy. Brought up on the great family sagas of Realism, Burgos recognizes the textual framework that has different generations tailgating the national narrative, so that personal and civic history conflate and the family becomes simultaneously a private and a public space where the author can explore both individual and collective identities. It is within this tradition that one should read Adelina as the matriarch who does not merely repackage and commodify history, but also passes this skill onto her daughters. *Los anticuarios* does not merely revolve around how the Marchamalos manipulate the past to ensure their future, but how Spain should approach its historical legacy.

Of all Burgos's female creations, Adelina seems to embody many of the qualities promoted by her to guarantee the renewal and prosperity of Spain. Adelina and her creator certainly share an aesthetic affinity. Gómez de la Serna has left us with a description of Burgos's study that resembles an antique shop such as the one run by Adelina, a 'gran salón cubierto de tapices *gobelinos*' [a great salon covered with Gobelin tapestries] filled with casts of famous statues by the likes of Rodin or Donatello and presided over by a massive antique table with spiral legs (1998: 362). Like her creator Burgos, Adelina treasures the past but never loses sight of the future and is, in the words of Imboden, 'capaz de conciliar las mejores cualidades de la española arraigada con los valores modernos de la sociedad parisina, en la que se integra sin problemas con su familia' [able to combine the best qualities of an entrenched Spanish identity with the modern values of Parisian society, in which she seamlessly settles with her family] (2001: 33).

Adelina thrives in Paris, imagined as a blank canvas on which to redraw Spanish identity away from representations that Burgos regards as fossilized and exclusionary. This portrayal of Paris as a more progressive place is acknowledged by Johnson (2000: 144), who reads the decision to remain in France as the only way to guarantee the 'new marital gender balance they have achieved'. A return to Spain would entail a significant loss of Adelina's hard-won independence. This is seen in Burgos's unforgiving representation of Toledo, depicted in *Los anticuarios* as the antithesis of the modernity and openness of Paris. In this respect Adelina differs from her husband, with Fabián enamoured with the historical pedigree of Toledo as he revels in its past and Adelina far less captivated by what she sees as a stagnating city slumbering in its past imperial glories. During one of their visits there Fabián exclaims: 'Cuando me canse del negocio [...] compraré una de estas casas y la arreglaré al estilo de los reyes godos [...] y me vendré a acabar mis días tranquilo con mi mujercita' [When I tire of the business [...] I will buy one of these houses and refurbish it in the style of the Goth kings [...] and I will come here to spend the remainder of my days with my sweet little wife] (Burgos 1989: 53).

Adelina is less enthusiastic about recreating this medieval past:

> Adelina sonreía ¡qué terrible vivir allí! Con el contraste acudía más atractivo a su evocación el recuerdo de París, la ciudad amplia, donde parecía correr alegremente el viento de la libertad, tan distinto de este viento encañonado de los callejones. (Burgos 1989: 53)
>
> [Adelina smiled, how awful would it be to live there! The contrast made Paris seem even more attractive in her memories, the vast city in which the wind freely roamed, so different to the wind scrambling through these narrow streets.]

Toledo with its narrow streets and hostile male clergy leaves little room for Adelina to manoeuvre, either spatially or discursively. It is therefore no surprise that she seems less taken by its heritage than her husband, given its predominantly male characterization. Fabián, on the other hand, attempts to graft himself to this privileged branch of the national tree in a similarly distorted fashion to that of Doña Aurora (who had distilled this longing for legitimacy in the surname Afanes de Toledo). Not content with the title of duke, Fabián also bestows upon himself the title of count and baron to form an aristocratic triptych, and reveals to his Toledo host that 'descendemos de doña Urraca y del Cid, por línea recta de Wamba y Godofredo el Velloso y más posteriormente del Duque de las Victorias' [we descend from Doña Urraca and El Cid, direct descendants of Wamba and Godfrey the Hairy One, and later of the Duke of las Victorias] (69). Like Doña Aurora, this ancestry heaves with symbolism to the point that it resembles an abridged version of Modesto Lafuente's history of Spain rather than a mere enumeration of forefathers. Fabián, a former civil servant with a law degree, is well acquainted with liberal mythology, a knowledge he clearly uses to his advantage. '¡De algo ha de servir saber de historia!' [Knowing history has its uses!] (99) he later confesses, after conniving with the genealogical fantasies of a buyer with yet another tale generously filled with national mythology.

All Fabián's merchandise boasts elaborate origin stories that make them an indispensable part of history whilst he punctuates his own ancestry with liberal landmarks such as the aforementioned title of Duque de las Victorias, literally 'Duke of the Victories'. As many readers would have humorously remarked, this was a title Isabel II had bestowed upon General Baldomero Espartero (1793–1879) for defending the vulnerable new constitutional monarchy against the Carlist uprising.

The strategy pursued by Fabián highlights in all its hyperbolic glory the essentially narrative nature of the nation — Homi K. Bhabha's adage that nation is narration (1990). None of the objects he sells is worth anything without the accompanying tale, a point literally illustrated by a buyer's insistence that Fabián write down the story just related and attach it to the purchased antiquity. His wife Adelina, however, does not share his passion for this counterfeit genealogy and shows more interest in the possibilities a modern metropolis like Paris offers to build more inclusive lineages, ones that acknowledges the female presence.

Weaving a New Future

As we have seen, the path to this more inclusive place is not always straight and sees Adelina relying on many of the strategies employed by Fabián. She cannot make a clean break with the past in part because to create a new future, she needs to commodify the past in the antiques she sells. A similarly complex relationship emerges in Adelina's interest in old lace and embroidery, antiques that she pursues as obsessively as her husband collects statues. With this appreciation for needlework, a traditionally female pursuit, Burgos suggests it should receive a parity of esteem in the cultural patrimony that defines a country. Such a standpoint is once again empowering, claiming cultural clout for women whilst not veering significantly from the status quo. After all, sewing constitutes one of the founding stones of domesticity; women writers often invoke sewing metaphors to appease any suspicions that their literary pursuits might prove disruptive, despite distractions. 'Yo hilvano mis artículos y las prendas de vestir de mi familia' [I baste my articles and the clothes for my family] writes Pilar Contreras tellingly in *Mis distracciones* (1910), and continues:

> Tanto es así, que muchas veces dejé el hilo de zurcir, para coger el hilo de una idea y en bastante ocasiones, mientras he devanado una madeja para hacer un ovillo, me he devanado los sesos toda deshilvanada y desmadejada con la busca y captura de una consonante — por ejemplo — para empalmarla a una poesía resultando yo hecha el 'ovillo' si no he dado con él. (Quoted in Ramírez Almazán 2009: 177)

> [To such an extent, that many times I dropped the thread of mending to pick up the thread of an idea, and on several occasions, whilst I have wound a skein for a ball of yarn, I have wound up myself, lost the thread, incoherent, in the search and capture of a consonant — for example — to add the finishing stitches to a poem, getting all tangled up if I fail to find it.]

The city of Toledo, a proxy for Spain as a whole as well as housing a substantial part of the national patrimony, becomes the setting for Burgos's ode to embroidery. The many pages dedicated to the art of the needle, described in loving detail, attest to the author's genuine admiration for this activity. Thus, during one of their visits to Toledo, Adelina leaves Fabián behind recounting his genealogical reveries, building castles in the air in the absence of real ones. Her destination is a convent she visits in the hope that the impoverished nuns might be willing to part with some relic.

This constitutes Chapter V, tellingly titled 'En el convento' [In the Convent], in which Adelina has the opportunity to delight in some dazzling examples of needlework. That the place should be inhabited mostly by women who address each other as 'sister' regardless of an absence of blood bonds is quite suggestive within the discourse of nationalism. Here we have an almost exclusively female-populated space where a group of women arranged within a social hierarchy employ kinship terms such as 'sister' or 'mother superior' to reflect the power dynamic. It is this female congregation who look after a priceless collection of richly embroidered altar tunics, mantels, cloths and other examples of female craftsmanship. More concretely, they are all jealously guarded by the so-called *sacristana*, the church officer in charge of the sacred vessels and objects. Again, one is tempted to draw parallels between the sacred items under her purview and the sacralization of objects within nationalism. The reverence displayed by Burgos towards the bloodied shirt of Larra springs to mind. So too does the memorial ribbon from the coffin of General Prim that her father-in law Don Mariano Bustos Álvarez treasured as a relic. The difference lies in that the articles Adelina admires are preserved by women.[6]

On learning of the presence of another expert, the *sacristana* cannot help but display her collection with the pride of a connoisseur in a moving passage in which she shows Adelina the full extent of the vast collection: 'Abrió cajones de ropa blanca, albas, toallas, paños de altar, con magníficos encajes antiguos. Ya de aquello entendía ella tanto como la anticuaria, y le gustaba ver que los admiraba una inteligente' [She opened drawers full of white clothing, albs, towels, altar cloths with magnificent old embroidery. She knew as much about these as the antiques seller, and enjoyed seeing them be appreciated by an expert.] (Burgos 1989: 60).

In this passage, Burgos resorts to the same register used in the many articles dedicated to loftier artistic disciplines. Taking as a vantage-point embroidery already imbued with a sacred dimension, she was perhaps trying to spread this solemnity to all embroidery. This was not her first attempt to elevate embroidery to an art form nor was she the first to do so. It echoes, amongst others, the words of Ernest Lefébure, lace manufacturer and administrator of the Musée des Arts Décoratifs in Paris, who in 1887 had authored a popular volume on the subject devised in part to highlight the role played by women in the production of art, an aim explicitly stated in the preface. Translated into Spanish the same year, Lefébure finishes his introduction hoping 'to instigate in many directions a progress of knowledge and opinion through which it may be recognized that the production of embroidery and lace-making are worthy of standing upon the same level with those of painting, engraving and sculpture, and of being represented in our public museums' (1888: vii–viii). His claim that 'lace is the most poetic of all textile issues' (1888: vi) is echoed by Pardo Bazán who praises elaborate needlework by comparing it to a poem in her short story 'Casi artista' [Almost an Artist] (1897) (1964: 1692). The title encapsulates the frustration felt by many women, a baton that would be picked up by the following generation of writers. Thus, Kirkpatrick remarks how both Rosa Chacel and Carmen Baroja celebrate sewing in their work as an outlet for female creativity on a par with other artistic endeavours (2003: 81–82). Carmen Baroja, in particular, championed it in her *El encaje en España* [Lace in Spain], released in 1933 during the Second Republic, perhaps as a reminder of the contribution of women at a time when the political landscape was being significantly reshaped.

A relationship between women, texts and textiles can be traced back to classical antiquity. The most salient examples within this tradition are Helen of Troy and, above all, Penelope, both of whom occupy a space between complying with patriarchy and questioning their allocated roles in their weaving/unweaving of complex tapestries. Both of these mythical figures, particularly Penelope, have spawned their own revisionist tradition. They are what early feminist critics Sandra M. Gilbert and Susan Gubar call 'needlers', that is, 'querulous about their derivative status but adamant about asserting their influence in even most inauspicious situations' (Gilbert & Gubar 1979: 521). Nearly four decades later, Paula A. de la Cruz-Fernández picks up this thread in an article on the role of sewing in the separation of the sexes entitled 'Embroidering the Nation: The Culture of Sewing and Spanish Ideologies of Domesticity'. Herein she proposes that 'sewing needs to be examined as a powerful equalizing activity as it homogenized women's participation in the nation-building project without necessarily divorcing the image of women from the domestic sphere' (2014: 250). As an example, Cruz-Fernández mentions the freedom martyr Mariana Pineda, one of the few women featured in the secular hagiographies, as someone who embodies this position. Executed for embroidering 'Equality, Freedom and Law' on a banner that would later become the symbol of republicanism, she was mythologized in Federico García Lorca's play *Mariana Pineda* (1923–25). Lorca narrates how Mariana, busy stitching the flag, is berated for transgressing the domestic realm and using her sewing for political purposes:

> ¿Qué le importan las cosas de la calle?
> Y si borda, que borde unos vestidos
> para su niña, cuando sea grande.
> Que si el Rey no es buen Rey, que no lo sea;
> las mujeres no deben preocuparse. (García Lorca 1991: 142)

> [Why does she care about the word on the street?
> If she does embroidery, she should be embroidering dresses
> for her daughter for when she grows up.
> If the King is not a good King, so be it;
> women should not worry.]

Yet despite this conception of sewing in *Mariana Pineda* as an act of subversion to compensate for political powerlessness, its promotion could equally be understood within a more conventional framework. In other words, the case of Mariana shows the role of women in producing such potent symbols of nationhood as a flag, but only via the domestic pursuit of sewing.

Embroidery becomes a way for women to participate in nation-building, but only from the safe confines of domesticity. In this way the 1857 Moyano Bill that made the education of girls compulsory stipulated needlework as a core subject. Later, women writers and journalists like Burgos would help consecrate home economics as a science aimed exclusively at the female gender (Cruz-Fernández 2014: 264).

In her book, *La mujer en el hogar* [The Woman at Home] (1909), republished a year before *Los anticuarios*, Burgos contributes to the notion that the running of the home fell to women. Yet far from relegating women to second place, Burgos praises this role, which she sees as essential for the well-being of society (Burgos 1909: 20–21). Thus, despite being an indefatigable campaigner for women's rights, Burgos also subscribed to domestic ideologies that offered a way for women to participate in nation-building, albeit one that seems rather essentialist to modern eyes.

The centrality of embroidery can thus be interpreted both as a continuation of women's domesticity and as a wish to expand their role. *Los anticuarios* undoubtedly wishes to claim a stake for women, carved out symbolically in the heart of Toledo. The centrality of the convent episode to the narrative arc can be gleaned from the decision to preserve it in the later adaptation to a novella, when a rather rushed and compressed version was released in 1921 as part of the novella collection *Los contemporáneos* [The Contemporaries], with its original twenty-three chapters reduced to thirteen sections, of which a mangled version of Chapter V forms one. In spite of this hurried pruning, no doubt driven by economic necessity, the admiration for the art of sewing remains, now promoted to a position nearer the beginning of the story.

A Modern Novel

This overlooked novel thus constitutes an illuminating example of how Burgos scouts for new spaces within monolithically male family trees. Her partner Gómez de la Serna declared it one of her best works, 'esos *Anticuarios*, en que se concreta una novela de espléndida picardía' [those *Antiques Dealers* that make such a splendid picaresque novel] (quoted in Núñez Rey 2005: 533–34), and helped it be published by the Biblioteca Nueva, of which he was director. Yet its conservative format explains in part the later neglect by critical models oriented towards aesthetic innovation that fail to consider *Los anticuarios* as representative of its age. With its third-person omniscient narrator and extensive descriptive passages that minutely record the daily life of the antiques dealers, the novel brings to mind the literary macrocosmos of Galdós. It is therefore not regarded as a particularly radical departure from nineteenth-century narrative. Such readings enshrine innovative content at the expense of its conventional packaging, as is often the case with Burgos. As observed by Rita Felski in her *Beyond Feminist Aesthetics*:

> The assumption that the political value of a text can be read off from its aesthetic value as defined by modernist paradigm, and that a text which employs experimental techniques is therefore more radical in its effects than one which relies on established structures and conventional language is too simple. (Felski 1989: 161)

While *Los anticuarios* relies on traditional story-telling, its subjects, the trafficking of national patrimony and preoccupation with authenticity are all by-products of a heightened historical conscience and a concern with origins that underpin modern nationalism. In other words, whilst its format might not follow the precepts of modernism, its topic is certainly modern and reflects the zeitgeist. Despite initial dissimilarities, it would have sat well with the remaining offerings of Biblioteca Nueva, one of the many publishing houses set up at the turn of the century to disseminate the latest continental tendencies (Simón Palmer 2010: 165). Its back catalogue contains translations of works by Guillaume Apollinaire, Gabriele D'Anunzio and other writers who cultivated an array of avant-garde aesthetics familiar to Burgos but not present in her own work. The eclectic inventory of Biblioteca Nueva suggests a more inclusive definition of 'new' or 'modern' than the one drafted by later literary historians, in the same way that Biblioteca Mignon harboured both the melodrama of *Melita Palma* and the aesthetically disparate *Jardín umbrío*. Once more, reconstructing the context of the original publication of these works provides a more nuanced understanding of the discursive mechanisms of the time, stripped away later and sacrificed to satisfyingly simple common denominators. In the case of Ríos, her domestic melodramas do not fit the Realist mould whereas *Los anticuarios* could be described as *Realismo rezagado* [late Realism] in a literary panorama that now valued avant-garde experimentation as a more legitimate vehicle. Even critics like José María Marco, responsible for the first new edition of *Los anticuarios*, gets hampered by conventional literary classification, leading him to overlook occasionally some of her complexity at the expense of compressing her into the rigid constraints laid out by dominant narratives. Thus Marco (1989: 24) labels the work 'naturalismo feliz' [happy naturalism] due to its attention to minutiae but upbeat outcome. This narrow nomenclature does not do *Los anticuarios* justice. It is thanks to the ongoing efforts of researchers since that Burgos's work can be read within wider parameters. Thus, nearly thirty years after Marco's edition, *Los anticuarios* was published once more, its editor Teresa Muñoz Pinillos now highlighting it as valuable example of feminist art criticism (2018).

Burgos's book is thus a valuable thread in reconstructing a more nuanced vision of the past — it maps out the complex topography Burgos had to negotiate. She promotes embroidery as a way of providing women with a more substantial role in the curation of the national patrimony, whilst subscribing to domestic ideologies, even further coding it as an exclusively female pursuit in her role as a home economics teacher, and thus contributing to a separation of spheres. Equally she denounces an ancestral fever and fixation with a shared historical imagination reduced to trite tropes such as El Cid or Don Pelayo, and from which the antiques dealers draw their profit. Yet Burgos herself contributed to the popularization of the past and of seminal nation-building episodes with her romanticized reconstructions of Riego and Larra, or the pocket-sized editions of historical romance novels that she prefaced, now reduced to an accessible thirty-two pages. The three hundred plus pages of *Los anticuarios*, on the other hand, meander through a complex landscape that at times endorses domesticity and at other times undermines it, that mocks banal historicism but through satire acknowledges its ubiquity. The digressive, detailed prose of *Los anticuarios* might seem out-dated, but many of its issues still remain unresolved today. It is fitting that *Los anticuarios* never properly concludes: it simply stops and one must imagine Adelina and her descendants still in an ongoing battle to carve out a female space in the national patrimony.

Notes to Chapter 9

1. The shawl or *mantón* acquires significant symbolism during the latter half of the nineteenth century and beginning of the twentieth. In the first decades of the 1900s the media published a profusion of images showing the *mantón de Manila* wrapped around women as a patriotic prop. As the name reveals, the textile originally came from the Philippines, part of the Spanish empire until 1898. Its fetishization can thus be read as a reluctance to let go of the imperial past, as suggested by Zubiaurre-Wagner (2012: 272). In *Fortunata y Jacinta*, Galdós makes it a metaphor for creeping Europeanization of customs and a diminishing international projection of the country. No longer favoured by the upper-classes and the bourgeoisie, it remains a bastion of the popular classes who 'defendía la prenda española como defendió el parque de Monteleón y los reductos de Zaragoza' [who defended this Spanish item of clothing like they had defended the park of Monteleón or the strongholds of Zaragoza] (Pérez Galdós 2011: 250–51).
2. The female variant of 'historian', *historiadora*, appears in 1803 as a variant in the fourth edition of the *Diccionario de la Real Academia Española* [Dictionary of the Spanish Royal Academy] (*DRAE*). *Anticuaria* would have to wait until 2002, in the twenty-second edition of *DRAE*, although it should be noted that it appears as an acceptable variant in *Diccionario de la lengua española* [Dictionary of the Spanish Language] (1917) edited by José Alemany y Bolufer, who was also a member of the Real Academia Española. Interestingly, despite a long history of antique trading, *DRAE* listed *anticuario* only as somebody with a purely academic interest in the past, closely related to a historian. The 1925 edition would provide a second definition of *anticuario* as somebody who collects or trade with antiques, thus reflecting its mercantile aspect. I owe this observation to Dra Mercedes Bengoechea, who, after the presentation of my paper at the Women in Spanish and Portuguese Studies annual conference, noted the late incorporation of *anticuaria* into *DRAE*.
3. With such feminine connotations, the figure of the antiques dealer can itself be seen as transgressive, blurring the gender binary. It is no coincidence that Burgos portrays many of the Parisian dealers as effeminate, as if an affinity for domestic interiors had diluted their masculinity, a gendering also noted by Johnson (2000: 144–45).
4. On the link between capitalism and commodification of the past, Kalter observes once more how 'the first usage of "antique" to mean an odd, valuable furnishing dates to 1771 — less than a decade after the appearance of the neologism "shopping"' (2012: 19).
5. Miguel de Unamuno and Ángel Ganivet develop the concept of *intrahistoria* in 'El porvenir de España (1898–1912)' [The Future of Spain (1898–1912)] (Unamuno 1968: 662).
6. Ironically, they might not have been manufactured by women. Cruz-Fernández (2014: 255) points out how, despite the glorification of sewing as a female talent, it was often a domestic pursuit. Women were not allowed into guilds until a Royal Decree of 1799, and even then they were relegated to more 'womanly' activities such as decorative embroidery and sewing.

EPILOGUE

A Bone of Contention

In December 1922, the ever-prolific Burgos published yet another novella. Released in the same collection for which she had adapted *Los anticuarios* the year before, *Los huesos del abuelo* [Grandfather's Bones] parodies a similar fetishizing of past artefacts. Yet instead of a Ming vase or Flemish embroidery, the object of veneration is a dead Romantic poet, his posthumous fame carefully cultivated by his descendants for maximum social recognition. With no fortune, the family relies on this fame, particularly the women, dependent on the illustrious surname Campo Grande in the absence of other opportunities. As if the poet's heritage is not guarantee enough, the granddaughter Concha shows a similar interest to Doña Aurora in expanding the family tree to bolster her status, with similarly hyperbolic claims. Concha commissions a genealogist to produce an ancestral chart; he, for a handsome sum, concludes that 'Campo Grande resultaba, por línea materna, descendiente directo de Guzmán el Bueno, y por la paterna, de Santo Domingo de Guzmán' [Campo Grande was, on the mother's side, a direct descendant of Guzmán the Good, and on the father's side, descended from Saint Domingo of Guzmán] (Burgos 1922: 7). Always eager to firm up their pedigree, subject to the whims of collective memory, she campaigns to have her predecessor interred in the Panteón de Hombres Ilustres [Pantheon of Illustrious Men]: 'Representaba para ella algo como un seguro de muerte de que el muerto seguiría siendo gran muerto por eternidad. Estar en el Panteón era dar carácter oficial a una gloria, que no le negaban, pero que tampoco reconocían ampliamente' [To her this was akin to death insurance, a guarantee that the dead would remain great in death for eternity. To be in the Pantheon was to give an official stamp to a greatness that was not denied but neither was it sufficiently acknowledged] (10).

Her ambitions are thwarted when a collapse of the tombs accidentally mixes the bones of her grandfather with less revered remains. A desperate Concha claims to have identified the skeleton of the poet based on his clothing and dispatches a box of bones to its new burial place. But the authenticity of the reconstruction is questioned by a journalist, who upon closer inspection drily remarks that 'el señor de Campo Grande tiene tres fémures y dos esternones' [Campo Grande has three thighbones and two breastbones] (25). With more pity than sarcasm, the narrator concludes that 'para aquellas desgraciadas acababa toda su influencia y toda su importancia al desaparecer el prestigio de los huesos del abuelo' [those unfortunate women had all their influence and importance taken when the prestige of grandfather's bones vanished] (25). Concha and her daughter might have been the driving force of a cult of personality that would have left them forever in the shadow of their great predecessor but that also would have provided them with social clout and represented a source of income. It highlights the precarious situation in which many female descendants found themselves, as Burgos would later expose in *Hablando con los descendientes* (1929), in which she interviews the widow of José Zorrilla and other women related to Romantic icons. At the same time, Burgos herself cannot resist contributing to this aura 'con ese respecto que profeso a las mujeres-reliquias, monumentos vivos de un pasado glorioso' [with that respect that I profess to relic-women, living monuments to a glorious past] (quoted in Núñez Rey 2005: 456). As we have seen, her critique of a paralyzing compulsion to look back, turning people into pillars of salt when they should be fixing their gaze on the future, coexists with her own fascination with this past and her own contributions to the historical imagination.

Published in December, *Los huesos del abuelo* may have been influenced partly by the exhumation of the poet and statesman Manuel José Quintana (1772–1857), and the transfer of his remains to the Almudena Cemetery earlier in the year. (It is worth noting that Quintana enjoyed a more canonical status at the beginning of the twentieth century than he does nowadays, on a par with Cervantes or Lope de Vega as illustrated by Rubén Darío's preface to his influential *Prosas profanas y otros poemas* [Profane Prose and Other Poems] (1896). Taking stock of his literary influences, imagined once more as a family tree, the Nicaraguan-born Darío describes the Spanish branch as 'El abuelo español de barba blanca me señala una serie de retratos ilustres: "Este, me dice, es el gran don Miguel de Cervantes Saavedra, genio y manco; este es Lope de Vega, este Garcilaso, este Quintana"' [The Spanish grandfather with the white beard points towards a series of illustrious portraits: 'This one, he says, is the great don Miguel de Cervantes Saavedra, genius and one-armed; this is Lope de Vega, this is Garcilaso, this is Quintana'] (1917: 10).) As in *Los huesos del abuelo*, Quintana had been buried in a now-decaying graveyard, which made his move urgent. But unlike his fictional counterpart, the body of Quintana had been embalmed and was thus not in danger of being diluted by less revered remains. On 11 March, marked by an official ceremony, Quintana was moved to his new mausoleum in the Madrid Almudena Cemetery. Not everyone agreed with such an initiative; Manuel Azaña, who would later become first President of the Second Republic, joined the critics, maintaining that exhuming the dead was a trait peculiar to Spain: 'No hay duda, desenterrar a los muertos es pasión nacional' [There is no doubt, exhuming the dead is a national passion], he concludes in that navel-gazing lament characteristic of reformers, in which Spain trails behind other countries but is also *sui generis* in its failure (1922: 168). Myopic assessments such as these, described by Nuñez Seixas (1997: 489) as the '"ensimismamiento" de la historiografía insular con su(s) propio(s) nacionalismo(s)' ['self-absorption' of an insular historiography with its/their own nationalism(s)], overlook the fact that the exhumation of secular relics is a symptom of nationalism, and therefore not particular to the country alone. If Quintana had been reburied with such pomp and circumstance, Azaña imagines the commotion the discovery of Cervantes could cause: '¡Ah, si el esqueleto del Manco apareciese! [...] cómo nos revolcaríamos en la fosa abierta, poseídos de furia patriótica sepulcral!' [Oh, if the skeleton of the One-Armed Man appeared! [...] how we would roll around in the open grave possessed by a sepulchral patriotic fever!] (1922: 168).

In 2015, nearly a century later, and also in the month of March, the media reported that the author of *Don Quixote* had been found. Azaña's forgotten article was enthusiastically exhumed by a new generation of dissenting journalists who highlighted his prophetic voice and echoed the old adage that Spain is indeed different (Pousa 2015). Similarly, the *New Yorker* commented that 'disinterring famous people has become a kind of sport in the Hispanic world', in remarks that conjure up the well-trodden image of a macabre Catholic sensibility (Stavans 2015). Yet such a conclusion is undermined by the elaborate re-interment of Richard III a week later in England, five hundred years after his death. Faced with such an elaborate burial, a columnist bemoaned that 'royalty forever drags us back to a feudal state of mind from which we have never quite escaped', a phrase that could equally have been uttered by a despondent nineteenth-century reformist, wondering why 'this fantasy of anointed genes persists' (Toynbee 2015).

As we have seen, part of the answer lies in the fact that the replacement of the feudal order with the liberal state did not eliminate blood ancestries. On the contrary, it expanded them to include painters, politicians, war heroes, writers and other representatives of these new values, creating in a way a cultural aristocracy. It is this ancestral logic that drives journalists to contact the descendants of Cervantes upon the discovery of their forefather, the same impulse that had driven Burgos to contact relatives of the Romantics a century earlier. Thus almost four hundred years after the death of his distant relative, *El Mundo* interviewed Manuel de Parada de Luca Tena under the sensationalistic headline of 'Habla el último descendiente de Cervantes' [The Last Descendant of Cervantes Speaks], a claim not strictly true upon further reading but which lends the family narrative a more dramatic air (Sala & Salas 2015). A specialist in genealogy and heraldry, Parada produced a detailed chart to demonstrate his kinship to the Spanish icon. Not content with one illustrious ancestor, Parada bolstered his national pedigree by claiming a blood affiliation to Hernán Cortés, in a bid for double legitimacy reminiscent of the fictional Concha Campo Grande in *Los huesos del abuelo* and her descent from Guzmán el Bueno, although Parada appears positively restrained when compared to Fabián de Marichalar in *Los anticuarios* or Aurora Reinaldos in *Madrid goyesco* and their overblown, concocted coats of arms.

In any case Parada is not a direct descendant of Cervantes. That line allegedly died out with the early passing of the granddaughter of the writer, losing not only the celebrated surname, but also a direct ancestral line to Cervantes. Hence the detailed family tree shown to journalists that traces the connection in the absence of a DNA match that would materially confirm it — the gene in 'genealogy' now the main source of legitimacy. With the rise of genetics in the last decades, 'the gene itself has become, at once, a dominant cultural referent for processes of social and biological reproduction and a key cultural metaphor for the rearticulation of "race", nation and otherwise imagined bodies and communities' (Steinberg 2000: 137). Not descended from the direct line, Parada is unable biologically to prove his parentage and, more crucially, neither can the remains of Cervantes be properly identified without the support of matching DNA. As articles repeatedly explain to readers, in order to identify Cervantes the forensic archaeologists need to isolate mitochondrial DNA, a strand passed from mother to offspring without recombination, and which had been lost with the death of the granddaughter.

The urgency to determine the exact remains of Cervantes is because the writer was buried in a common grave with fifteen other people in a situation reminiscent of *Los huesos del abuelo*. Had Burgos's story taken place a few decades later, a genetic profiling of the granddaughter Concha would had identified the real Campo Grande. As it stands, the bones of Cervantes exude enough allure that a common grave cannot completely obscure them. Not able to isolate his bones, the archaeologists have assembled a so-called 'reduction of his bones', a stock that aims to preserve his essence. Yet doubt remains whether any of the remains belong to the writer of *Don Quixote*, an uncertainty a DNA profiling could have cleared up. In this way genetics is used to ascertain the existence of a metaphysical concept. A forensic puzzle on paper, presented as a scientific exercise, the whole enterprise has been driven by the quasi-mystical qualities attributed to his remains, with a particular interest in localizing the hand that authored *Don Quixote*. It leads the historian Moreno Luzón to remark that 'en la segunda década del siglo XXI, y con las novedades técnicas pertinentes, se reproducen comportamientos propios del XIX, cuando los despojos de glorias y héroes nacionales sufrían continuos trasiegos' [in the second decade of the twenty-first century, and with the relevant technical advances, we see a return to behaviours more characteristic of the nineteenth century, when the remains of past glories and national heroes were constantly relocated] (2015). After much debate and failed attempts to assert his identity, Cervantes, or part of him, was given a ceremonial send-off presided over by the outgoing mayor of Madrid, Ana Botella. Many objected to this commemoration that the Cervantista Francisco Rico acerbically described as 'en la tradición más castizamente patriótica' [in the purest Spanish tradition] (2015). The ceremony was overseen by the Conservative Ana Botella who generously peppered her eulogy with patriotic incantations — 'por España y siempre por España, como el propio Cervantes' [for Spain now and always, like Cervantes himself] (quoted in Anon. 2015).

Botella's oratory could have come from Blanca de los Ríos herself. After all, both are women of a conservative persuasion invoking nationalist imagery to assert their authority. As we know, Ríos's efforts paid off in her time. She is the only woman yet to be interred in the Parthenon of Illustrious Writers and Artists, yet her orthodox leanings and tacit support of the Francoist regime would conspire to obscure her legacy. More popular is the tomb of the Republican Carmen de Burgos, in the Civil Cemetery of Madrid. Burgos represents a strand of liberalism more amenable to modern sensibilities, even though she also enthusiastically contributed to a national mythos. But as many scholars now point out, before the irruption of the Spanish Civil War, nationalism was the property of both the right and the left (Núñez Seixas 1997: 490; Dougherty 2004: 67).

Meanwhile the more forgotten Asensi has an equally neglected tomb in the now decaying cemetery of San Lorenzo in Madrid. One doubts that should the grave collapse, and the bones be mixed with those of others, a team of forensic archaeologists would be dispatched to isolate them from less sacred ones. The exhumation of secular relics remains an important strategy to justify the existence of a national genealogies but is only reserved for those bones considered canonical, as is patent in the remains of Cervantes becoming such a bone of contention in the second decade of the twenty-first century. However, this study has not sought to sacralize the remains of Asensi, Ríos or Burgos, but rather to make visible the genealogical imagination that continues to underpin national constructs even today. It has highlighted the gendered logic that turns women into the mother country, metonyms for the nation, whereas men become founding fathers. The logic lends women some legitimizing authority but confines it to their biology. The pattern repeats itself. As the media keeps reminding us, Cervantes, hailed as father of the modern novel, needs the actual bodily remains of his female relatives to confirm his identity in the ultimate modern legitimizing ceremony: a DNA profiling.

Despite these passive portrayals, women participated actively in the construction of the modern state through all the mediums available to them. They exploited the pedagogical powers bestowed upon them by cultivating children's literature, as did Julia de Asensi. Exposed to the same historical imagination as their male counterparts, they offered their own reconstructions of the past to include more women, a strategy actively pursued by Ríos, who retroactively inserts women in all foundational episodes, from medieval Spain to the War of Independence. Others such as Asensi lamented women's lack of agency in her historical legends, even questioning the epistemological certainty of historiography in *El encubierto*. Burgos and Ríos feature amongst those who knowingly parodied ancestral fever in the figure of Fabián de Marichalar or Doña Aurora, perhaps in an effort to establish their intellectual credentials against a backdrop that disenfranchised women. Burgos attempted to lay new foundations for future generations of women to thrive outside the domestic confines, whilst at the same time hailing domestic skills such as sewing as core pieces in the assembly of these new genealogies. Both Burgos and Ríos advocated for more female visibility whilst replicating old patterns and firmly supporting the maternal trope. Yet their very public presence created a new precedent and encouraged other women to step into the public arena. Not that they figured as lone figures in the cultural landscape, in fact, they formed part of a growing number of women whose contributions have often been overlooked by traditional and revisionist models that took the division between politics and the domestic space at face value. Yet instead of a rigidly enforced binary between public and private, we find that the private was often considered public property.

Family imagery pervades everything, from immediate blood relations to the more figurative but no less emotive bonds that tied citizens to the mother country.

It informs literary canons with patriarchs such as Cervantes and Tirso, and the Spanish School as identified by Madrazo with patriarchs such as Velázquez and Goya. It imbues foundational episodes with a quasi-mystical aura and turns any person or object involved in these historical events into secular saints and relics. It is hard to escape an epistemological filter with such a long-established pedigree and with such a ubiquitous presence. The immediacy and malleability of the family metaphor explains its perennial popularity but should not blind us to the gendered foundations upon which it was established and to a certain extent continues to operate. If we cannot entirely escape the narratological appeal of family sagas, perhaps we should exhume more texts of past women, rather than bodies, to prove the cultural legitimacy of men. Doing so will at least make any resulting family tree more inclusive and representative.

BIBLIOGRAPHY

AFINOGUÉNOVA, EUGENIA. 2009. 'Painted in Spanish: The Prado Museum and the Naturalization of the Spanish School in the Nineteenth Century', *Journal of Spanish Cultural Studies*, 10.3 (September): 319–40

——2010. 'The Nation Disrobed: Nudity, Leisure and Class at the Prado', in *National Museums: New Studies from Around the World*, ed. by Simon J. Knell and others (London: Routledge), pp. 207–24

ALAS, LEOPOLDO, 'Clarín'. 1885. *Sermón perdido: crítica y sátira* (Madrid: Fernando Fé)

——2002 [1896]. 'El rana', in *Obras completas*, ed. by Carolyn Richmond, vol. 3 (Oviedo: Nobel), pp. 938–43

ALEMANY Y BOLUFER, JOSÉ (ed.). 1917. *Diccionario de la lengua española* (Barcelona: Ramón Sopena)

ALONSO, CECILIO. 2010. *Hacia una literatura nacional 1800–1900*, in *Historia de la literatura española*, ed. by José-Carlos Mainer and Gonzalo Pontón, vol. 5 (Barcelona: Crítica)

ALTER, STEPHEN G. 1999. *Darwinism and the Linguistic Image: Language, Race, and Natural Theology in the Nineteenth Century* (Baltimore, MD, & London: Johns Hopkins University Press)

ÁLVAREZ JUNCO, JOSÉ. 2001. *Mater Dolorosa: la idea de España en el siglo XIX* (Madrid: Taurus)

ÁLVAREZ LOPERA, JOSÉ. 1987. *De Ceán a Cossío: la fortuna crítica del Greco en el siglo XIX* (Madrid: Fundación Universitaria Española)

ALZOLA, PABLO DE. 1898. 'El problema cubano', *Revista Contemporánea*, 111 (July): 561–87

ANDERSON, BENEDICT. 1983. *Imagined Communities: Reflections on the Origin and Spread of Nationalism* (London & New York: Verso)

ANDREU MIRALLES, XAVIER. 2009. 'Retrats de família (nacional): discursos de gènere i de nació en les cultures liberals espanyoles de la primera meitat del segle XIX (1808–1850)', *Recerques: història, economia i cultura*, 58–59: 5–30

——2010. 'Figuras modernas del deseo: las majas de Ramón de la Cruz', in *Género y modernidad en España: de la Ilustración al liberalismo*, ed. by Mónica Bolufer and Mónica Burguera (Madrid: Marcial Pons, Ediciones de Historia), pp. 25–46

——2011. 'Retratos de familia (nacional): discursos de género y de nación en las culturas liberales españolas de la primera mitad del siglo XIX', in *Estudios sobre nacionalismo y nación en la España contemporánea*, ed. by Ismael Saz Campos and Ferran Archilés i Cardona (Saragossa: Prensas Universitarias de Zaragoza), pp. 79–111

ANON. 1822. 'Biografía: Doña María de Molina, reyna y regente de Castilla', *Periódico de las Damas*, 15.4: 10–26

ANON. 1880. 'Revista bibliográfica', *El Globo*, 25 August, p. 3

ANON. 1883. 'Libros nuevos: Leyendas y tradiciones en prosa y verso por Julia de Asensi', *La Época*, 7 May, p. 4

ANON. 1912. 'Intelectualitats femenines espanyoles', *Feminal, Ilustratió Catalana*, 25 February, p. 7

ANON. 1915. 'Arte y artistas: La maja marquesa', *El Heraldo de Madrid*, 9 May, p. 2

ANON. 1932. 'Muerte de una escritora ilustre', *El Sol*, 9 September, p. 12

Anon. 1956a. 'Anoche falleció en Madrid Doña Blanca de los Ríos', *ABC*, 14 April, p. 31
Anon. 1956b. 'Honras fúnebres: ha fallecido la escritora española Blanca de los Ríos', *Noticiarios y Documentales*, 23 April
Anon. 2015. 'Los restos de Cervantes descansan desde hoy en la iglesia de San Ildefonso', *Europa Press*, 11 June, <http://www.europapress.es/madrid/noticia-restos-cervantes-descansan-hoy-iglesia-san-ildefonso-20150611113013.html> [accessed 27 July 2015]
Aragonés, Galiana. 1933. 'En el aniversario de su muerte: lo que me contó la gran escritora Carmen de Burgos (Colombine)', *El Heraldo de Madrid*, 7 October
Archilés i Cardona, Ferrán. 2008. 'Vivir la comunidad marginada: nacionalismo español e identidades en la España de la Restauración', *Historia de la educación: Revista interuniversitaria*, 27: 57–85
Aresti, Nerea. 2007. 'Shaping the Spanish Modern Man: The Conflict of Masculine Ideals through a Court Case in the 1920s', *Feminist Studies*, 33.3 (Fall): 606–31
Arranz, Carmen. 2010. 'Boundaries of Modernity: Spanish Women Writers at the Turn of the Twentieth Century', University of Kentucky Doctoral Dissertations, paper 28, <https://uknowledge.uky.edu/gradschool_dis/28> [accessed 3 December 2018]
Arteaga Soler, María Jesús. 2006. '¡Tal vez cuando era cuerpo los astros me envidiaban! Discurso y representación femenina en la poesía de Blanca de los Ríos', in *Sin carne: representaciones y simulacros del cuerpo femenino: tecnología, comunicación y poder*, ed. by Mercedes Arriaga Flórez (Seville: Arcibel), pp. 434–46
Asensi, Julia de. 1876. 'A.S.M. el Rey D. Alfonso XII', in *Albúm poético dedicado a S.M. el Rey D. Alfonso XII y al Ejército con motivo de su entrada en la capital de la Monarquía* (Madrid: Imprenta Oficial)
—— 1880. *Tres amigas* (Madrid: Biblioteca Universal)
—— 1883. *Leyendas y tradiciones en prosa y verso* (Madrid: Biblioteca Universal)
—— 1890. 'Tus cantares', *El Album Iberoamericano*, 14 December
—— 1897. *Brisas de primavera: cuentos para niños y niñas* (Barcelona: Antonio J. Bastinos)
—— 1901. *La hija de Villoria* (Barcelona: Antonio J. Bastinos)
—— 1905. *Victoria y otros cuentos, por Julia de Asensi*, ed. by Edgar S. Ingraham (Boston: D. C. Heath)
Azaña, Manuel. 1922. 'Quintana, en la infausta remoción de sus huesos', *La Pluma*, 22 (March): 168–69
Bacon, Kathy. 2007. *Negotiating Sainthood: Distinction, Cursilería and Saintliness in Spanish Novels* (Oxford: Legenda)
Baker, Edward. 2000. 'Fin de Siècle Culture', in *Spanish History Since 1808*, ed. by José Álvarez Junco and Adrian Shubert (London: Arnold; New York: Oxford University Press), pp. 155–77
Ballarín Domingo, Pílar. 1989. 'La educación de la mujer española en el siglo XIX: historia de la educación', *Revista interuniversitaria*, 8: 245–60
Bastinos, Antonio J. (ed.). 1903. *Parnaso Español* (Barcelona: Julián Bastinos)
Bécquer, Gustavo Adolfo. 1986. *Leyendas*, ed. by Pascual Izquierdo (Madrid: Catédra)
Belda, Joaquín. 1922. *La piara* (Madrid: Librería Renacimiento)
Bell, Amy. 2003. 'Razing Their Voices: Carmen de Burgos's Subtextual Revisions of the Works of José Zorrilla and Gustavo Adolfo Bécquer in "El veneno del arte"', *Letras Femeninas*, 29.2 (Winter): 166–81
Berkin, Carole. 2006. *Revolutionary Mothers*, 2nd edn (New York: Vintage)
Bernstein, Richard B. 2009. *The Founding Fathers Reconsidered* (New York & Oxford: Oxford University Press)
Berzal de la Rosa, Enrique. 2008. *Los comuneros: de la realidad al mito* (Madrid: Silex Ediciones)
Bhabha, Homi K. (ed.). 1990. *Nation and Narration* (London & New York: Routledge)

BIEDER, MARYELLEN. 1992. 'Woman and the Twentieth-Century Spanish Literary Canon: The Lady Vanishes', *Anales de la literatura española contemporánea*, 17: 301–24

BIGGANE, JULIA. 2000. *In a Liminal Space: The Novellas of Emilia Pardo Bazán* (Durham: University of Durham)

BLANCO, ALDA. 1995. 'Gender and National Identity: The Novel in Nineteenth-Century Spanish Literary History', in *Culture and Gender in Nineteenth-Century Spain*, ed. by Lou Charnon-Deutsch and Jo Labanyi (Oxford: Clarendon Press), pp. 120–37

BLANCO GARCÍA, FRANCISCO. 1899. *La literatura española en el siglo XIX*, 2nd edn, vol. 2 (Madrid: Saénz de Jubera)

BLASCO HERRANZ, INMACULADA. 2013. 'Mujeres y nación: ser españolas en el siglo XX', in *Ser españoles: imaginarios nacionalistas en el siglo XX*, ed. by Javier Moreno Luzón and Xosé M. Núñez Seixas (Barcelona: RBA), pp. 168–206

BLASCO IBAÑEZ, VICENTE. 1998 [1906]. *La maja desnuda*, ed. by Facundo Tomás (Madrid: Cátedra)

BLASCO PASCUAL, J. 1993. 'De "oráculos" y de "cenicientas": la crítica ante el fin de siglo español', in *¿Qué es el modernismo? Nueva encuesta, nuevas lecturas*, ed. by Richard A. Cardwell and Bernard McGuirk (Boulder, CO: Society of Spanish and Spanish-American Studies), pp. 59–86

BLOM, IDA, KAREN HAGEMANN and CATHERINE HALL (eds). 2000. *Gendered Nations: Nationalisms and Gender Order in the Long Nineteenth Century* (Oxford & New York: Berg)

BOIX, VICENTE. 1921 [1852–59]. *El encubierto de Valencia: leyenda histórica del siglo XVI* (Valencia: El Mercantil Valencia)

BOLUFER, MÓNICA, and MÓNICA BURGUERA (eds). 2010. *Género y modernidad en España: de la ilustración al liberalismo* (Madrid: Marcial Pons Ediciones de Historia: Asociación de Historia Contemporánea)

BOONE, ELIZABETH M. 2007. *Vistas de España: American Views of Art and Life in Spain, 1860–1914* (New Haven, CT, & London: Yale University Press)

BORDONADA, ANGELA ENA (ed.). 1990. *Novelas breves de escritoras españolas, 1900–1936* (Madrid: Castalia)

——2006 [1908]. 'Introducción', in Vicente Ángeles, *Los buitres* (Murcia: Editora Regional de Murcia), pp. 7–37

BOSS, CAROLINA DEL. 1878. *Margarita* (Seville: Gironés y Orduña)

BOURDIEU, PIERRE. 1984. *A Social Critique of the Judgement of Taste*, trans. by Richard Nice (Cambridge, MA: Harvard University Press)

BOYD, CAROLYN P. 1997. *Historia patria: Politics, History, and National Identity in Spain, 1875–1975* (Princeton, NJ: Princeton University Press)

BRAVO CELA, BLANCA. 2003. *Carmen de Burgos (Colombine): contra el silencio* (Madrid: Espasa Calpe)

BROWN, JOAN L., and CRISTA JOHNSON. 1998. 'Required Reading: The Canon in Spanish and Spanish American Literature'. *Hispania*, 81.1 (March): 1–19

BURDIEL, ISABEL (ed.). 1998. 'Isabel II: un perfil inacabado', *La política en el reinado de Isabel II*, special issue of *Ayer*, 29: 187–216

——1998. 'Myths of Failure, Myths of Success: New Perspectives on Nineteenth-Century Liberalism', *Journal of Modern History*, 70 (December): 892–912

——2000. 'The Liberal Revolution, 1808–1843', in *Spanish History since 1808*, ed. by José Álvarez Junco and Adrian Shubert (London: Arnold; New York: Oxford University Press), pp. 17–32

——2004A. *Isabel II: no se puede reinar inocentemente* (Madrid: Espasa-Calpe)

——2004B. 'The Queen, The Woman and The Middle Class: The Symbolic Failure of Isabel', in *Spain*, ed. by Mónica Burguera and Christopher Schmidt-Nowara, special issue of *Social History*, 3.29 (Autumn): 301–19

——2018. 'La revolución del pudor: escándalos, género y política en la crisis de la monarquía liberal en España', *Historia y Política*, 39: 23–51
BURGOS, CARMEN DE. 1908. *Cuentos de Colombine: (novelas cortas)* (Valencia: Sempere)
——1909. *La mujer en el hogar* (Valencia: Sempere)
——1910A. 'La vuelta a Goya', in *Al balcón* (Valencia: Sempere), pp. 22–24
——1910B. 'Autobiografía', in *Al balcón* (Valencia: Sempere), pp. vii–xiv
——1911A. *La voz de los muertos* (Valencia: Sampere)
——[1911B]. *Misión social de la mujer: conferencia pronunciada por D ͣ Carmen de Burgos Seguí el día 18 de febrero de 1911* (Bilbao: Sociedad El Sitio)
——1914. 'Las mujeres del Greco', *Heraldo de Madrid*, 6 April, p. 2
——1916. *Peregrinaciones* (Madrid: Alrededor del Mundo)
——1919. *Fígaro: (revelaciones, 'ella' descubierta, epistolario inédito)* (Madrid: Alrededor del Mundo)
——1922. *Los huesos del abuelo*, *Los Contemporáneos*, 224
——1925. *El tío de todos* (Barcelona: Ribas y Ferrer)
——1929. *Hablando con los descendientes* (Madrid: Renacimiento)
——2000 [1924]. *La que quiso ser maja* (Seville: Renacimiento)
——2013 [1931]. *Gloriosa vida y desdichada muerte de Don Rafael del Riego: (un crimen de los Borbones)* (Seville: Centro de Estudios Andaluces; Valencina de la Concepción: Renacimiento)
——1989 [1918]. *Los anticuarios*, ed. by José María Marco (Madrid: Biblioteca Nueva)
BURGUERA, MONICA. 2006. 'Mujeres y soberanía: María Cristina e Isabel II', in *Historia de las mujeres en España y América Latina: del siglo XIX a los umbrales del XX*, ed. by Isabel Morant, vol. 3 (Madrid: Cátedra), pp. 85–116
——2012. *Las damas del liberalismo respetable: los imaginarios sociales del feminismo liberal en España, 1834–1850* (Madrid: Cátedra)
BUTT, JOHN. 1980. 'The "Generation of 1898": A Critical Fallacy?', *Forum for Modern Language Studies*, 16: 136–53
CABANILLAS CASAFRANCA, ÁFRICA. 2005–06. 'Carmen de Burgos "Colombine", crítica feminista de arte', *Espacio, Tiempo y Forma*, series 7, Historia del Arte, 18–19: 385–406
CANAL, JORDI. 2000. *El carlismo: dos siglos de contrarrevolución en España* (Madrid: Alianza Editorial)
CARNERO, GUILLERMO. 1998. 'Introducción', in *Historia de la literatura española*, ed. by Víctor G. de la Concha, vol. 7 (Madrid: Espasa Calpe)
CASANOVA, SOFÍA. 1910. *La mujer española en el extranjero: conferencia dada en el Ateneo de Madrid el 9 de abril de 1910* (Madrid: Regino Velasco)
CASTAÑEDA CEBALLOS, PALOMA. 1994. *Carmen de Burgos 'Colombine'* (Madrid: Horas y Horas)
CASTRO, CRISTÓBAL DE. 1931. 'El sexo y la academia', *ABC*, 22 February, p. 11
CASTRO, FERNANDO DE. 1869. *Discurso inaugural leído por Don Fernando de Castro, rector y catedrático de la Universidad, 21 de Febrero de 1869*, 2nd edn (Madrid: Rivadeneyra)
CASTRO ANTONIO, ANA. 2010. *Julia de Asensi: el camarada* (Vigo: Trymar)
CEJADOR Y FRAUCA, JULIO. 1915. *Historia de la lengua y literatura castellana*, vol. 3 (Madrid: Tip. de la 'Rev. de arch., bibl., y museos')
CÉPEDA GÓMEZ, JOSÉ, and ANTONIO CALVO MATURANA (eds). 2012. *La nación antes del nacionalismo en la monarquía hispánica (1777–1824)* (Madrid: Publicaciones Universidad Complutense de Madrid)
CHARNON-DEUTSCH, LOU. 1996. 'Pornography and the Bécquer Brothers' Bourbons in the Raw', in *Bodies and Biases: The Representation of Sexualities in Hispanic Cultures and Literatures*, ed. by Roberto Reis and David William Foster (Minneapolis: University of Minnesota Press), pp. 274–93

——2000. *Fictions of the Feminine in the Nineteenth-Century Spanish Press* (University Park: Pennsylvania State University Press)
——2004. 'Nineteenth-Century Women Writers', in *The Cambridge History of Spanish Literature*, ed. by David T. Gies (Cambridge: Cambridge University Press), pp. 461–69
CIBREIRO, ESTRELLA. 2005. 'De "ángel del hogar" a "mujer moderna": las tensiones filosóficas y textuales en el sujeto femenino de Carmen de Burgos', *Letras Femeninas*, 31.2 (Winter): 49–74
CLOSE, ANTHONY. 1978. *The Romantic Approach to 'Don Quixote': A Critical History of the Romantic Tradition in 'Quixote' Criticism* (Cambridge: Cambridge University Press)
COHEN, SIMONA. 2008. *Animals as Disguised Symbols in Renaissance Art* (Leiden & Boston, MA: Brill)
CORONADO, CAROLINA. 1991. *Poesías*, ed. by Noël Valis (Madrid: Castalia, Instituto de la Mujer)
COSSÍO, JOSÉ MARÍA DE. 1960. *Cincuenta años de poesía española: 1850–1900* (Madrid: España-Calpe)
COUGH, FRANCIS. 2007. 'El arte y la literatura al servicio de la humanidad', in *El malestar juvenil: raíces, contextos y experiencias*, ed. by Carlos Mingote Adán and Miguel Requena (Madrid: Díaz de Santos) pp. 461–91
CRUZ, JESÚS. 1996. *Gentlemen, Bourgeois, and Revolutionaries: Political Change and Cultural Persistence among the Spanish Dominant Groups, 1750–1850* (Cambridge & New York: Cambridge University Press)
CRUZ-FERNÁNDEZ, PAULA A. DE LA. 2014. 'Embroidering the Nation: The Culture of Sewing and Spanish Ideology of Domesticity', in *Memory and Cultural History of the Spanish Civil War: Realms of Oblivion*, ed. by Aurora G. Morcillo (Leiden & Boston, MA: Brill), pp. 249–84
CRUZ ROMEO, MARÍA. 2014. 'Domesticidad y política: las relaciones de género en la sociedad posrevolucionaria', in *La España liberal, 1833–1874*, ed. by María Cruz Romeo and María Sierra (Madrid: Marcial Pons Historia; Saragossa: Prensas de la Universidad de Zaragoza), pp. 89–130
CUESTA FERNÁNDEZ, RAIMUNDO. 1998. *Clío en las aulas: la enseñanza de la historia en España entre reformas, ilusiones y rutinas* (Madrid: Akal)
DANVILA Y COLLADO, MANUEL. 1884. *La Germanía de Valencia: discursos leídos ante la Real Academia de la Historia en la recepción pública del Excmo. Señor Don Mauel Danvila y Collado el día 9 de noviembre de 1881* (Madrid: Manual Gines Hernández)
DARÍO, RUBÉN. 1917. *Prosas profanas y otros poemas* (Madrid: Mundo Latino)
DARWIN, CHARLES. 1981 [1871]. *The Descent of Man* (Princeton, NJ: Princeton University Press)
DAVIES, CATHERINE. 2006. *South American Independence: Gender, Politics, Text* (Liverpool: Liverpool University Press)
DAVIES, CATHERINE, CLAIRE BREWSTER and HILARY OWEN. 1998. *Spanish Women's Writing 1849–1996* (London: Athlone Press)
DAVIS, RYAN A. 2012. 'Suggestive Characters: Hypnotism and Subjectivity in Blanca de los Ríos's *Las hijas de Don Juan* (1907)', *Decimonónica*, 9.1: 1–16
DAVIS, STUART. 2012. *Writing and Heritage in Contemporary Spain: The Imaginary Museum of Literature* (Woodbridge & Rochester, NY: Tamesis)
DES JARDINS, JULIE. 2003. *Women and the Historical Enterprise in America: Gender, Race, and the Politics of Memory, 1880–1945* (Chapel Hill: University of North Carolina Press)
DÍEZ MÉNGUEZ, ISABEL. 1999. 'Leyendas y tradiciones de Julia de Asensi y Laiglesia: una manifestación más del Romanticismo rezagado', *Anales de literatura hispanoamericana*, 28: 1353–85

———2006. *Julia de Asensi (1849–1921)* (Madrid: Orto)
DOUGHERTY, DRU. 2004. 'Deconstructing the Patriarch: Eduardo Marquina's "Las hijas del Cid" (1908)', *España contemporánea: revista de literatura y cultura*, 17.1: 67–80
———2001. 22ND EDN (Madrid: Espasa Calpe)
DUPONT, DENISE. 2010A. 'Introducción', *Siglo diecinueve: literatura hispánica*, 16: 7–11
———2010B. 'Blanca de los Ríos, Emilia Pardo Bazán, Francisa Larrea y Cecilia Böhl de Faber: hijas, madres, y la creación de un modelo de mujer estudiosa, o "ángel del archivo"', *Siglo diecinueve: literatura hispánica*, 16: 219–40
———2012. *Writing Teresa: The Saint from Ávila at the Fin-de-siglo* (Lewisburg, PA: Bucknell University Press; Lanham, MD: Rowman & Littlefield)
DURAN I SANPERE, AGUSTÍ. 1952. *Centenario de la Librería de Bastinos* (Barcelona: José Bosch)
ESCOSURA, PATRICIO DE LA. 1835. *Ni rey ni roque: episodio histórico del reinado de Felipe II, año de 1595* (Madrid: Repullés)
ESPADAS BURGOS, MANUEL. 2000. 'Los orígenes de la Restauración', in Ramón Menéndez Pidal, *Historia de España. Tomo XXXVI. La época de la Restauración*, ed. by Manuel Espadas Burgos, vol. 2 (Madrid: Espasa Calpe)
ESPIGADO TOCINO, GLORIA. 2010. 'El discurso republicano sobre la mujer en el Sexenio Democrático, 1868–1874: los límites de la modernidad', in *Género y modernidad en España: de la ilustración al liberalism*, ed. by Mónica Bolufer and Mónica Burguera (Madrid: Marcial Pons), pp. 143–68
ESPINA, CONCHA. 1916. *Al amor de las estrellas: (mujeres del Quijote)* (Renacimiento)
ESTABLIER PÉREZ, HELENA. 2000. *Mujer y feminismo en la narrativa de Carmen de Burgos 'Colombine'* (Almería: Instituto de Estudios Almerienses)
EZAMA GIL, MARÍA DE LOS ÁNGELES. 1993. 'Algunos datos para la historia del término "novela corta" en la literatura española de fin de siglo', *Revista de literatura*, 55.109: 141–48
———2001. 'Blanca de los Ríos, escritora de cuentos', *El cuento español en el siglo XIX. Autores raros y olvidados*, special issue of *Scriptura*, 16: 171–87
———2008. 'El concepto de literatura nacional en la prosa de don Juan Valera', in *Literatura y nación: la emergencia de las literaturas nacionales*, ed. by Leonardo Romero Tobar (Saragossa: Prensas Universitarias de Zaragoza), pp. 351–72
FELSKI, RITA. 1989. *Beyond Feminist Aesthetics: Feminist Literature and Social Change* (Cambridge, MA: Harvard University Press)
FERNÁNDEZ BREMÓN, JOSÉ. 1889. 'Crónica', *La Ilustración Española y Americana*, 15 April, p. 218
FERNÁNDEZ ALMAGRO, MELCHOR. 1956. 'Doña Blanca', *ABC*, 19 April, p. 3
FERNÁNDEZ CIFUENTES, LUIS. 2005. 'Isidora in the Museum', in *Visualizing Spanish Modernity*, ed. by Susan Larson and Eva Woods (Oxford & New York: Berg), pp. 81–93
FERNÁNDEZ HERREROS, MANUEL. 1870. *Historia de las germanías de Valencia: breve reseña del levantamiento republicano de 1869* (Madrid: la Viuda e Hijos de M. Álvarez)
FERNÁNDEZ Y GONZÁLEZ, MANUEL. 1974 [1862]. *El cocinero de su Majestad* (Madrid: Círculo de Amigos de la Historia)
FINCH, JAMES AUSTIN. 1886. 'Cesare Cantù', *The Catholic World*, 43.256: 525–34
FINN, MARGOT, MICHAEL LOBBAN and JENNY BOURNE TAYLOR. 2010. 'Introduction: Spurious Issues', in *Legitimacy and Illegitimacy in Nineteenth-Century Law, Literature and History*, ed. by Margot Finn, Michael Lobban and Jenny Bourne Taylor (Basingstoke: Palgrave Macmillan), pp. 67–92
FITZMAURICE-KELLY, JAIME. 1901. *Historia de la literatura española traducida del inglés y anotada por A. Bonilla y San Martín, con un estudio preliminar por M. Menéndez y Pelayo* (Madrid: La España Moderna)
FONTANA, JOSEP. 1982. *Historia: análisis del pasado y proyecto* (Barcelona: Crítica)

——2007. *La época del liberalismo*, in *Historia de España*, ed. by Josep Fontana and Ramón Villares, vol. 6 (Barcelona: Crítica; Madrid: Marcial Pons)

FONTANA, JOSEP, and RAMÓN VILLARES. 2007. 'Introducción General', in *Historia de España*, ed. by Josep Fontana and Ramón Villares, vol. 1 (Barcelona: Crítica; Madrid: Marcial Pons), pp. vii–xiii

FORCADELL ÁLVAREZ, CARLOS, and MARÍA CRUZ ROMEO (eds). 2006. *Provincia y nación: los territorios del liberalismo* (Saragossa: Institución Fernando el Católico)

FOX, INMAN. 1997. *La invención de España: nacionalismo liberal e identidad nacional* (Madrid: Cátedra)

FRANZ, THOMAS R. 2017. 'Carmen de Burgos and Her Virtual Dialogues with Pío Baroja and Miguel de Unamuno', in *Multiple Modernities: Carmen de Burgos, Author and Activist*, ed. by Anja Louis and Michelle M. Sharp (London: Routledge), pp. 77–92

FREIRE LÓPEZ, ANA MARÍA. 1999. *La Revista de Galicia de Emilia Pardo Bazán (1880)* (La Coruña: Fundación Barrié de la Maza)

FUSI AIZPURÚA, JUAN PABLO. 2000. *España: la evolución de la identidad*. Madrid: Temas de Hoy

GALAÍN, ROBERTO DE. 1912. 'Una escritora ilustre: Blanca de los Ríos', *Mundo Gráfico*, 15 May, p. 7

GARCÍA CÁRCEL, RICARDO. 1981. *Las germanías de Valencia* (Barcelona: Península)

GARCÍA CARRAFFA, ALBERTO. 1922. *Diccionario heráldico y genealógico de apellidos españoles y americanos*, vol. 7 (Madrid: Antonio Marzo)

GARCÍA DELGADO, JOSÉ LUIS, JUAN PABLO FUSI AIZPURÚA and JOSÉ MANUEL SÁNCHEZ RON. 2008. *España y Europa*, in *Historia de España*, ed. by Josep Fontana and Ramón Villares, vol. 11 (Barcelona: Crítica; Madrid: Marcial Pons)

GARCÍA GUTIERREZ, ANTONIO. 1840. *El encubierto de Valencia, drama en cinco actos y en verso* (Madrid: Yenes)

GARCÍA LORCA, FEDERICO. 1991 [1923–25]. *Mariana Pineda*, ed. by Luis Martínez Cuitiño (Madrid: Cátedra)

GIES, DAVID THATCHER. 1994. *The Theatre in Nineteenth-Century Spain* (Cambridge & New York: Cambridge University Press)

GILBERT, SANDRA M., and SUSAN GUBAR. 1979. *The Madwoman in the Attic* (New Haven, CT: Yale University Press)

GILMARTIN, SOPHIE. 1998. *Ancestry and Narrative in Nineteenth-Century British Literature: Blood Relations from Edgeworth to Hardy* (Cambridge: Cambridge University Press)

GIMENO DE FLAQUER, CONCEPCIÓN. 1900. *Evangelios de la mujer* (Madrid: Fernando Fé)

GINGER, ANDREW. 2007A. *Painting and the Turn to Cultural Modernity in Spain: The Time of Eugenio Lucas Velázquez (1850–1870)* (Selinsgrove, PA: Susquehanna University Press)

——2007B. 'Spanish Modernity Revisited: Revisions of the Nineteenth Century', *Journal of Iberian and Latin American Studies*, 13.2–3: 121–32

GLANTZ, MARGO. 1998. *Las genealogías* (Mexico: Alfaguara)

GLENDINNING, NIGEL. 1977. *Goya and his Critics* (New Haven, CT: Yale University Press)

GLENN, KATHLEEN M. 1999. 'Demythification and Denunciation in Blanca de los Ríos' "Las hijas de Don Juan"', in *Nuevas perspectivas sobre el 98*, ed. by John P. Gabriele (Frankfurt am Main: Vervuert; Madrid: Iberoamericana), pp. 223–30

GÓMEZ, MATILDE. 1886. 'Biografía de Julia de Asensi', in *Las mujeres españolas, americanas y lusitanas pintadas por sí mismas*, ed. by Faustina Sáez de Melgar (Barcelona: Juan Pons), pp. 639–40

GÓMEZ DE AVELLANEDA, GERTRUDIS. 2001 [1841]. *Sab*, ed. by Catherine Davies (Manchester & New York: Manchester University Press)

GÓMEZ DE BAQUERO, EDUARDO. 1912. 'Revista literaria', *Los Lunes de El Imparcial*, 28 October, p. 4

GÓMEZ DE LA SERNA, RAMÓN. 1917. 'Prólogo', in Carmen de Burgos y Seguí, *Confidencias de artistas* (Madrid: Sociedad Española de Librería), pp. 7–23

—— 1922. 'La maja desnuda', *Flirt*, 9 (centrefold)
—— 1998. 'Colombine', in *Obras completas*, vol. 1 (Barcelona: Círculo de Lectores), pp. 360–62
GÓMEZ-FERRER MORANT, GUADALUPE (ed.). 2005–. *Del siglo XIX a los umbrales del XX*, in *Historia de las mujeres en España y América Latina*, ed. by Isabel Morant, vol. 3 (Madrid: Cátedra)
—— 2011. *Historia de las mujeres en España: siglos XIX y XX* (Madrid: Arco/Libros)
GONZÁLEZ FIOL, F. 1922. 'Domadores del éxito', *La Esfera*, 422.24 (June): 19–20
GONZÁLEZ LÓPEZ, MARÍA ANTONIETA. 2001. *Aproximación a la obra literaria y periodística de Blanca de los Ríos* (Madrid: Fundación Universitaria Española)
GROOT, JEROME DE. 2009. *Consuming History: Historians and Heritage in Contemporary Popular Culture* (London: Routledge)
GUEREÑA, JEAN-LOUIS. 2000. 'La producción erótica española en los siglos XIX y XX', in *Actas del XIII Congreso de la Asociación Internacional de Hispanistas, Madrid 6–11 de julio de 1998*, ed. by Florencio Sevilla Arroyo and Carlos Alvar Ezquerra, vol. 2 (Madrid: Castalia), pp. 195–202
—— 2001. 'Literatura y prostitución en la España del siglo XIX: de la novela folletinesca a la literatura clandestina', in *Historia social y literatura: familia y clases populares en España (siglos XVIII–XIX): Primer Coloquio Internacional Acción Integrada Francoespañola, Université Jean Monnet, Saint-Etienne, septiembre de 2000*, ed. by Jacques Soubeyroux and Roberto Fernández (Lleida: Milenio), pp. 157–76
GUERRERO CABRERA, MANUEL, and JOSÉ ANTONIO VILLALBA MUÑOZ. 2007. 'La historia en la poesía de Blanca de los Ríos', in *Escritoras y pensadoras europeas*, ed. by Mercedes Arriaga Flórez (Seville: Arcibel), pp. 349–56
GULLÓN, RICARDO. 1969. *La invención del 98 y otros ensayos* (Madrid: Gredos)
HAIDT, REBECCA. 2011. *Women, Work and Clothing in Eighteenth-century Spain* (Oxford: Voltaire Foundation)
HOBSBAWM, ERIC, and TERENCE RANGER. 1983. *The Invention of Tradition* (Cambridge & New York: Cambridge University Press)
HOOPER, KIRSTY. 2007. 'Death and the Maiden: Gender, Nation and the Imperial Compromise in Blanca de los Rios's "Sangre española" (1899)', *Revista Hispánica Moderna*, 60.2: 171–85
—— 2008. *A Stranger in My Own Land: Sofía Casanova, a Spanish Writer in the European Fin de Siècle* (Nashville, TN: Vanderbilt University Press)
—— *The Atlantis Project: Women and Words in Spain, 1890–1936*, <https://web.archive.org/web/20130516094807/http://atlantis.kirstyhooper.net/> [accessed 11 January 2019]
HURTADO, ÁMPARO. 1998. 'Biografía de una generación: las escritoras del noventa y ocho', in *Breve historia feminista de la literatura española (en lengua castellana) Vol. 5. La literatura escrita por mujer (del. s.XIX a la actualidad)* (Barcelona: Anthropos), pp. 139–54
HURTADO, JUAN, and ANGEL GONZÁLEZ PALENCIA. 1921. *Historia de la literatura española* (Madrid: Tip. de la "Revista de Arch., bibl. y museos")
HUYSSEN, ANDREAS. 1986. *After the Great Divide: Modernism, Mass Culture, Postmodernism* (Bloomington: Indiana University Press)
IAROCCI, MICHAEL P. 2006. *Properties of Modernity: Romantic Spain, Modern Europe, and the Legacies of Empire* (Nashville, TN: Vanderbilt University Press)
ICHIJO, ATSUKO, and GORDANA UZELAC (eds). 2005. *When is the Nation? Towards an Understanding of Theories of Nationalism* (London: Routledge)
IMBODEN, RITA CATRINA. 2001. *Carmen de Burgos 'Colombine' y la novela corta* (Bern: Peter Lang)
INFANTES DE MIGUEL, VICTOR, MIGUEL FRANÇOIS LOPEZ and JEAN-FRANÇOIS BOTREL (eds). 2003. *Historia de la edición y de la lectura en España: 1472–1914* (Madrid: Fundación Germán Sánchez Ruipérez)

INGRAM, REBECCA ELIZABETH. 2009. 'Spain on the Table: Cookbooks, Women, and Modernization, 1905–1933' (doctoral dissertation, Duke University)
JAGOE, CATHERINE. 1993. 'Disinheriting the Feminine: Galdós and the Rise of the Realist Novel in Spain', *Revista de Estudios Hispánicos*, 27.2: 225–48
JENSEN, ROBERT. 1994. *Marketing Modernism in Fin-de-Siècle Europe* (Princeton, NJ, & Chichester: Princeton University Press)
JOHNSON, ROBERTA. 1998. 'The Domestication of Don Juan in Women Novelists of Modernist Spain', in *Intertextual Pursuits: Literary Mediations in Modern Spanish Narrative*, ed. by Jeanne P. Brownlow & John W. Kronik (Lewisburg, PA: Bucknell University Press; London: Associated University Presses), pp. 222–38
—— 1999. 'The Domestic Agenda of the Generation of '98', in *Nuevas perspectivas sobre el 98*, ed. by John P. Gabriele (Frankfurt am Main: Anthropos)
—— 2000. 'Carmen de Burgos: Marriage and Nationalism', in *La Generación del 98 frente al nuevo fin de siglo*, ed. by Jesús Torrecilla (Amsterdam & Atlanta, GA: Rodopi), pp. 140–51
—— 2001. 'Carmen de Burgos and Spanish Modernism', *South Central Review*, 18.1–2 (Spring-Summer): 66–77
—— 2003. *Gender and Nation in the Spanish Modernist Novel* (Nashville, TN: Vanderbilt University Press)
JOVER, JOSÉ MARÍA. 1984. 'Carácteres del nacionalismo español, 1854–1874', *Zona Abierta*, 31 (April-June): 1–22
JUSDASNIS, GREGORY. 1991. *Belated Modernity and Aesthetic Culture: Inventing National Literature* (Minneapolis: University of Minnesota Press)
KALTER, BARRETT. 2012. *Modern Antiques: The Material Past in England, 1660–1780* (Lewisburg, PA: Bucknell University Press; Lanham, MD: Rowman & Littlefield)
KEEFE UGALDE, SHARON. 1997. 'Reconfigurations of the Female Lyric Subject in "Canto de Ofelia" de Blanca de los Ríos', *Monographic Review/Revista Monográfica*, 13: 182–89
KERBER, LINDA K. 1980. *Women of the Republic: Intellect and Ideology in Revolutionary America* (Chapel Hill: North Carolina University Press)
KIRKPATRICK, SUSAN. 1989. *Las románticas: Women Writers and Subjectivity in Spain, 1835–1850* (Berkeley: University of California Press)
—— 2003. *Mujer, modernismo y vanguardia en España: 1898–1931*, trans. by Jacqueline Cruz (Madrid: Cátedra)
LABANYI, JO. 2005. 'Horror, Spectacle and Nation-Formation: Historical Painting in Late-Nineteenth-Century Spain', in *Visualizing Spanish Modernity*, ed. by Susan Larson and Eva Woods (Oxford & New York: Berg), pp. 64–80
LAFUENTE, MODESTO. 1850. *Historia general de España, desde los tiempos más remotos hasta nuestros días*, vol. 1 (Madrid: Mellado)
—— 1852. *Historia general de España, desde los tiempos más remotos hasta nuestros días*, vol. 9 (Madrid: Mellado)
LANDES, JOAN B. 2001. *Visualizing the Nation: Gender, Representation, and Revolution in Eighteenth-Century France* (Ithaca, NY: Cornell University Press)
LATORRE, MARIANO DE LA. 1901. 'Libros nuevos', *El Álbum Ibero-Americano*, 22 February, pp. 82–83
LÁZARO, REYES. 2000. 'El "Don Juan" de Blanca de los Ríos y el nacional-romanticismo español de principios de siglo', *Letras Peninsulares*, 13: 467–83
LEFÉBURE, ERNEST. 1888. *Embroidery and Lace: Their Manufacture and History from the Remotest Antiquity to the Present Day*, trans. by Alan S. Cole (London: H. Grevel)
LEGGOT, SARAH. 2008. *The Workings of Memory: Life-Writing by Women in Early Twentieth-Century Spain* (Lewisburg, PA: Buckell University Press)
LÓPEZ-VELAZ, ROBERTO. 2004. 'De Numancia a Zaragoza: la construcción del pasado

nacional en las historias de España del ochocientos', in *La construcción de las historias de España*, ed. by Ricardo García Cárcel (Madrid: Marcial Pons), pp. 195–298

LOUIS, ANJA. 2005. *Women and the Law: Carmen de Burgos, An Early Feminist*. Woodbridge: Tamesis

LOUIS, ANJA, and MICHELLE M. SHARP. 2017. 'Introduction: Multiple Modernities: Carmen de Burgos, Author and Activist', in *Multiple Modernities: Carmen de Burgos, Author and Activist*, ed. by Anja Louis and Michelle M. Sharp (London: Routledge), pp. 1–14

LUXENBERG, ALISA. 1999. 'Regenerating Velázquez in Spain and France in the 1890s', *Boletín del Museo del Prado*, 17.35: 125–50

MAINER, JOSÉ-CARLOS. 1994. 'La invención de la literatura española', in *Literaturas regionales en España: historia y crítica*, ed. by José María Enguita and José-Carlos Mainer (Saragossa: Institución Fernando el Católico), pp. 23–45

MALIN, MARK R. 2003. 'Of Beginnings and Endings, Prólogos y Despedidas: Julia de Asensi's *Tres amigas*', *Confluencia*, 19.1: 103–11

MANGINI, SHIRLEY. 2010. *Maruja Mallo and the Spanish Avant-Garde* (Farnham: Ashgate)

MARAVALL, JOSÉ ANTONIO. 1977. 'El mito de la "tradición" en el constitucionalismo español', *Cuadernos hispanoamericanos*, 329–30: 547–67

MARCILHACY, DAVID. 2010. *Raza hispana: hispanoamericanismo e imaginario nacional en la España de la Restauración* (Madrid: Centro de Estudios Políticos y Constitucionales)

MARCO, JOSÉ MARÍA. 1989. 'Prólogo', in *Los anticuarios* (Madrid: Biblioteca Nueva), pp. 9–24

MARTÍNEZ GARRIDO, ELISA. 1999. 'Amor y feminidad en las escritoras de principios de siglo', in *Carmen De Burgos: aproximación a la obra de una escritora comprometida*, ed. by Miguel de Naveros and Ramón Navarrete-Galiano (Almería: Publicaciones del Centro de Estudios Almerienses), pp. 8–56

MARTÍNEZ MARINA, FRANCISCO. 1813. *Teoría de las Cortes ó grandes Juntas nacionales de los Reinos de Leon y Castilla [...]: con algunas observaciones sobre la lei fundamental de la Monarquía Española [...] promulgada en Cádiz á 19 de Marzo de 1812* (Madrid: Collado)

MARTÍNEZ SIERRA, GREGORIO. 1916. *Cartas a las mujeres de España* (Madrid: Renacimiento)

MASIELLO, FRANCINE. 1992. *Between Civilization and Barbarism: Women, Nation and Literary Culture in Modern Argentina* (London & Lincoln: University of Nebraska Press)

MCCLELLAN, ANDREW. 1994. *Inventing the Louvre: Art, Politics, and the Origins of the Modern Museum in Eighteenth-century Paris* (Cambridge & New York: Cambridge University Press)

MCCLINTOCK, ANNE. 1993. 'Family Feuds: Gender, Nationalism and the Family', *Feminist Review*, 44 (Summer): 61–80

MCWILLIAM, ROHAN. 2010. 'Unauthorised Identities: The Impostor, the Fake and the Secret History in Nineteenth-Century Britain', in *Legitimacy and Illegitimacy in Nineteenth-Century Law, Literature and History*, ed. by Margot Finn, Michael Lobban & Jenny Bourne Taylor (Basingstoke: Palgrave Macmillan), pp. 67–92

MELLOR, ANNE K. 2000. *Mother of the Nation: Women's Political Writings in England 1780–1830* (Bloomington &: Indiana University Press)

MENÉNDEZ Y PELAYO, MARCELINO. 1890. *Historia de las ideas estéticas en España*, 2nd edn, vol. I (Madrid: A. Pérez Dubrull)

MOI, TORIL. 1999. *What Is a Woman?: And Other Essays* (Oxford: Oxford University Press)

MONTERO ALONSO, JOSÉ. 1931. 'Carmen de Burgos ("Colombine") fue la autora de la primera encuesta periodística en torno al divorcio', *Nuevo Mundo*, 24 October, p. 10

MONTOTO Y RAUTENSTRAUCH, LUIS. 1929. *'En aquel tiempo...': vida y milagros del magnífico caballero Don Nadie* (Madrid: Renacimiento)

MORALES MOYA, ANTONIO. 2013. 'La nación católica de Menéndez Pelayo', in *Historia de la nación y del nacionalismo español*, ed. by Antonio Morales Moya, Juan Pablo Fusi Aizpurúa and Andrés de Blas Guerrero (Barcelona: Galaxia Gutenberg, Círculo de Lectores), pp. 502–24

MORENO LUZÓN, JAVIER (ed.). 2007. *Construir España: nacionalismo español y procesos de nacionalización* (Madrid: Centro de Estudios Políticos y Constitucionales)

—— 2015. 'Los huesos de Cervantes', *El País*, 13 April, <http://elpais.com/elpais/2015/03/30/opinion/1427723899_463059.html> [accessed 27 July 2015]

—— 2018. 'The Restoration 1874–1914', in *The History of Modern Spain: Chronologies, Themes, Individuals*, ed. by Adrian Shubert and José Álvarez Junco (London: Bloomsbury Academic), pp. 46–63

MORETO, AGUSTÍN. 1999 [1654]. *El desdén, con el desdén*, ed. by John E. Varey (Barcelona: Crítica)

MORI, ARTURO. 1915. 'Exposición de Bellas Artes de 1915', *El País*, 9 May, p. 1

MORO ABADÍA, OSCAR. 2006. *La perspectiva genealógica de la historia* (Santander: Ediciones de la Universidad de Cantabria)

MÜLLER-WILLE, STAFFAN, and HANS-JÖRG RHEINBERGER. 2012. *A Cultural History of Heredity* (Chicago: University of Chicago Press)

MUÑOZ PINILLOS, TERESA. 'Carmen de Burgos y "Los anticuarios" regresan a Toledo', *ABC Toledo*, 16 May, <https://www.abc.es/espana/castilla-la-mancha/toledo/abci-carmen-burgos-y-anticuarios-regresan-toledo-201805141420_noticia.html> [accessed 28 August 2018]

MUÑOZ SEMPERE, DANIEL. 2011. 'Historia como novela y novela como historia en *Ni rey ni Roque* (1835) de Patricio de la Escosura', *Bulletin of Spanish Studies*, 88.7–8: 57–71

MURPHY, KATHARINE. 2010. 'Images of Pleasure: Goya, Ekphrasis and the Female Nude in Blasco Ibáñez's *La maja desnuda*', *Bulletin of Spanish Studies*, 87.7: 939–57

NASH, MARY. 1994. 'Experiencia y aprendizaje: la formación histórica de los feminismos en España', *Historia Social*, 20: 151–72

NOYES, DOROTHY. 1998. 'La Maja Vestida: Dress as Resistance to Enlightenment in Late 18th-Century Madrid', *Journal of American Folklore*, 111.440: 197–218

NÚÑEZ REY, CONCEPCIÓN. 2005. *Carmen de Burgos, 'Colombine' en la Edad de Plata de la literatura española* (Seville: Fundación José Manuel Lara)

NÚÑEZ SEIXAS, XOSÉ MANOEL. 1997. 'Los oasis en el desierto: perspectivas historiográficas sobre el nacionalismo español', *Bulletin d'histoire contemporaine de l'Espagne*, 26: 483–533

—— 1999. *Los nacionalismos en la España contemporánea (siglos XIX y XX)* (Barcelona: Hipòtesi)

OUTRAM, DORINDA. 2013. *The Enlightenment* (Cambridge & New York: Cambridge University Press)

O'TOOLE, TESS. 1997. *Genealogy and Fiction in Hardy: Family Lineage and Narrative Lines* (Basingstoke: Macmillan)

PALAU Y DULCET, ANTONIO. 1949. *Manual del librero hispano-americano: bibliografía general española e hispano-americana desde la invención de la imprenta hasta nuestros tiempos, con el valor comercial de los impresos descritos*, vol. 2 (Barcelona: A. Palau Dulcet)

PAN-MONTOJO, JUAN (ed.). 1998. *Más se perdió en Cuba: España, 1898 y la crisis de fin de siglo* (Madrid: Alianza)

PAQUETTE, GABRIEL. 2015. 'Introduction: Liberalism in the Early Nineteenth-Century Iberian World', *History of European Ideas*, 41.2: 153–65

PARDO BAZÁN, EMILIA. 1891. 'Blanca de los Ríos', *Nuevo Teatro Crítico*, 1.8 (August): 85–91

—— 1964. 'Casi artista', in *Obras completas (novelas y cuentos)*, ed. by Federico Carlos Saínz (Madrid: Ediciones Aguilar), pp. 1691–93

—— 1999. *La mujer española y otros escritos*, ed. by Guadalupe Gómez Ferrer (Madrid: Cátedra)

―――1999. *Obras completas*, ed. by Darío Villanueva and José Manuel González Herrán (Madrid: Fundación José Antonio de Castro)

PAREDES MÉNDEZ, FRANCISCA. 2007. 'Las hijas de Don Juan de Blanca de los Ríos y otros textos: donjuanismo y flamenquismo vs. regeneración nacional', *Espéculo: Revista de Estudios Literarios*, 35, <https://webs.ucm.es/info/especulo/numero35/bdlrios.html> [accessed 20 August 2013]

PARTZSCH, HENRIETTE. 2014. 'The Complex Routes of Travelling Texts: Fredrika Bremer's Reception in Nineteenth-Century Spain and the Transnational Dimension of Literary History', *Comparative Critical Studies*, 11.2–3: 281–93

PASCUAL DE SANJUÁN, PILAR. 1864. *Preceptos morales para la infancia: basados en hechos históricos* (Barcelona: Juan Bastinos e Hijo)

―――1869. *La moral de la historia: colección de cuadros históricos con su aplicación moral al alcance de los niños* (Barcelona: Juan Bastinos)

PASCUAL MARTÍNEZ, PEDRO. 2000. 'Las escritoras de novela corta', in *Mujeres novelistas en el panorama literario del siglo XIX*, ed. by Marina Villalba Alvarez (Ciudad Real: Universidad de Castilla-La Mancha), pp. 67–94

PEIRÓ, IGNACIO. 1995. *Los guardianes de la historia: la historiografía académica de la Restauración* (Saragossa: Institución Fernando el Católico)

PÉREZ, JOSEPH. 2006. *Los comuneros* (Madrid: La esfera de los libros)

PÉREZ GALDÓS, BENITO. 1911. *Episodios nacionales: de Cartago a Sagunto* (Madrid: Perlado, Páez y compañía)

―――1957 [1870]. 'Observaciones sobre la novela contemporánea en España', ed. by José Pérez Vidal (Madrid: Afrodisio Aguado), pp. 223–49

―――2000 [1881]. *La desheredada*, ed. by Germán Gullón (Madrid: Cátedra)

―――2011 [1887]. *Fortunata y Jacinta: dos historias de casadas*, ed. by Francisco Caudet (Madrid: Cátedra)

PÉREZ GARZÓN, JUAN SISINIO (ed.). 2004. *Isabel II: los espejos de la reina* (Madrid: Marcial Pons)

PÉREZ VIEJO, TOMÁS. 2001. 'Pintura de historia e identidad nacional en España' (doctoral thesis, Universidad Complutense de Madrid)

―――2013. 'La representación de España en la pintura', in *Historia de la nación y del nacionalismo español*, ed. by Antonio Morales Moya, Juan Pablo Fusi Aizpurúa and Andrés de Blas Guerrero (Barcelona: Galaxia Gutenberg, Círculo de Lectores), pp. 479–92

Pousa, Luis. 2015. 'Cervantes, en los huesos', *La Voz de Galicia*, 14 June, <> [accessed 27 July 2015]

POYATO, JOSÉ CALVO. 1996. *La vida y época de Carlos II el hechizado* (Barcelona: Planeta)

POZUELO YVANCOS, JOSÉ MARÍA, and ROSA MARÍA ARADRA SÁNCHEZ. 2000. *Teoría del canon y literatura española* (Madrid: Cátedra)

POZZI, GABRIELA. 2000. 'Carmen de Burgos and the War in Morocco', *MLN*, 115.2: 188–204

PUENTE PEREDA, BELÉN. 2007. 'Periodismo y discurso en El Cuento Semanal' (doctoral thesis, Universitat de Barcelona), <http://tdx.cat/bitstream/handle/10803/4897/bpp1de1.pdf?sequence=1> [accessed 22 July 2018]

PUJANTE, CARMEN M. 2014. 'La retórica de la seducción en las novelas cortas erótico-pasionales de los años 20', in *Culturas de la seducción*, ed. by Patricia Cifre Wibrow and Manuel Gónzalez de Ávila (Salamanca: Ediciones Universidad de Salamanca), pp. 199–206

PUJOL DE COLLADO, JOSEFA. 1883. 'Revista madrileña', *La Ilustración de la Mujer*, 1 July

PULIDO MENDOZA, MANUEL. 2009. *Plutarco de moda: la biografía moderna en España (1900–1950)* (Mérida: Editora Regional de Extremadura; Cáceres: Universidad de Extremadura, Servicio de Publicaciones)

QUIROGA, ALEJANDRO. 2007. *Making Spaniards: Primo de Rivera and the Nationalization of the Masses, 1923–30* (Basingstoke: Palgrave Macmillan)
QUIROGA, ALEJANDRO, and FERRAN ARCHILÉS (eds). 2013. *La nacionalización en España* (Madrid: Asociación de Historia Contemporánea; Marcial Pons)
RAMÍREZ ALMAZÁN, MARÍA DOLORES. 2009. 'Pilar Contreras de Rodríguez: nuevas indicaciones bio-bibliográficas', *Elucidario*, 7 (March): 169–82
REAL ACADEMIA ESPAÑOLA. 1803. *Diccionario de la lengua castellana compuesto por la Real Academia Española, reducido a un tomo para su más fácil uso*, 4th edn (Madrid: Viuda de Ibarra)
REYERO, CARLOS. 1989. *La pintura de historia en España: esplendor de un género en el siglo XIX* (Madrid: Cátedra)
RICO, FRANCISCO. 2015. 'Con bandera y música', *El País*, 7 July, <http://elpais.com/elpais/2015/03/12/opinion/1426179143_555082.html> [accessed 27 July 2015]
RÍOS, AMADOR DE LOS. 1861. *Historia crítica de la literatura española*, vol. 1 (Madrid: José Rodríguez)
RÍOS, DEMETRIO DE LOS. 1861. *Tertulia literaria: colección de poesías selectas leídas en las reuniones semanales celebradas en la casa de don Juan José Bueno* (Seville: Del Porvenir)
RÍOS-FONT, WADDA C. 2004A. 'Literary History and Canon Formation', in *The Cambridge History of Spanish Literature*, ed. by David T. Gies (Cambridge: Cambridge University Press), pp. 15–35
—— 2004B. *The Canon and the Archive: Configuring Literature in Modern Spain* (Lewisburg, PA: Bucknell University Press; Cranbury, NJ: Associated University Presses)
RÍOS, BLANCA DE LOS. 1901. *Melita Palma* (Madrid: B. Rodríguez Serra)
—— 1902 [1901]. 'Por la República', in *La Rondeña: cuentos andaluces; El salvador: cuentos varios* (Madrid: Idamor Moreno), pp. 97–122
—— 1906A. *Tirso de Molina: conferencia leída por su autora en el Ateneo de Madrid el día 23 de abril de 1906* (Madrid: Bernardo Rodríguez)
—— 1906B. 'Tirso de Molina: recientes descubrimientos en Guadalajara y Soria', *Los Lunes de El Imparcial*, 1 October, p. 3
—— 1907A. *Las hijas de Don Juan*, El Cuento Semanal, 42
—— 1907B. *Madrid Goyesco*, El Cuento Semanal, 68
—— 1907C. 'La niña de Sanabria', in *Obras completas*, vol. 2 (Madrid: Idamor Moreno), pp. 5–88
—— 1910. *Las mujeres de Tirso [pseud.] conferencia leída por su autora en el Ateneo de Madrid el día 16 de marzo de 1910* (Madrid: B. Rodríguez)
—— 1911. *Afirmación de la raza: porvenir hispanoamericano* (Madrid: Centro de Cultura Hispanoamericana)
—— 1915A. 'Mujeres de la Historia: Las patriotas de la Independencia en Cádiz', *Blanco y Negro*, 26 December, pp. 10–15
—— 1915B. 'Mujeres de la Historia. La madre de San Fernando', *Blanco y Negro*, 15 August, pp. 14–18
—— 1928. *El enigma biográfico de Tirso de Molina: conferencia leída por su autora en la Real Academia de Jurisprudencia y Legislación, el 30 de abril de 1928* (Madrid: Alberto Fontana, San Bernardo)
Rodríguez, María Pilar. 1998. 'Modernidad y feminismo: tres relatos de Carmen de Burgos', *Anales de la literatura española contemporánea*, 23.1/2: 379–403
ROMERO, EUGENIA R. 2010. 'A Stranger in My Own Land: Sofia Casanova, a Spanish Writer in the European Fin de Siècle by Kirsty Hooper', *Hispanic Review*, 78.1 (Winter): 127–30
ROMERO TOBAR, LEONARDO. 2010. 'Colombine, biógrafa de Larra', *Arbor*, 186 (June): 183–89

Rosario Delgado, María del Pino. 2012. 'Ideología y re/creación en la literatura infantil española de la segunda mitad del XIX y primer cuarto del XX', *Garoza: revista de la Sociedad Española de Estudios Literarios de Cultura Popular*, 12: 66–77

Rosenstein, Leon. 2009. *Antiques: The History of an Idea* (Ithaca, NY, & London: Cornell University Press)

Roth, Norman. 2002. [1995]. *Conversos, Inquisition, and the Expulsion of the Jews From Spain*. Madison & London: University of Wisconsin Press

Sáinz de Robles, Federico Carlos. 1975. *La promocion de 'El Cuento semanal': 1907–1925* (Madrid: Espasa-Calpe)

Sala, Carlos, and Deva Salas. 2015. 'Habla el último descendiente de Cervantes', *El Mundo*, 8 February, <http://www.elmundo.es/cronica/2015/02/08/54d50684e2704ef3288b456f.html> [accessed 27 July 2015]

Salle, Sarah T. 2002. 'Revisiting El Encubierto: Navigating Between Visions of Heaven and Hell on Earth', in *Werewolves, Witches, and Wandering Spirits: Traditional Belief and Folklore in Early Modern Europe*, ed. by Kathryn A. Edwards (Kirksville, MO: Truman State University Press)

Sánchez Álvarez-Insúa, Alberto. 1996. *Bibliografía e historia de las colecciones literarias en España (1907–1957)* (Madrid: Libris)

Sánchez Dueñas, Blas. 2013. 'Preocupación patriótica y compromiso nacional en las escritoras españolas finiseculares a traves de la prensa', in *Escritoras españolas en los medios de prensa, 1868–1936*, ed. by Ivana Rota and María del Carmen Servén Díez (Seville: Renacimiento), pp. 237–66

Sánchez-Llama, Iñigo. 1999. 'Representaciones de la autoría intelectual femenina en las escritoras isabelinas del siglo XIX peninsular', *Hispania*, 82.4: 750–60

Santisteban y Delgado, Joaquín. 1927. *Historia cronológica y biográfica de Almería: de los corregidores, gobernadores, alcaldes, regidores y concejales desde 1493 hasta 1927* (Almería: C. Peláez)

Scanlon, Geraldine. 1986. *La polémica feminista en la España contemporánea (1868–1974)*, 2nd edn (Madrid: Akal)

Scott, Joan Wallach. 1999. *Gender and the Politics of History* (New York: Columbia University Press)

Seco Serrano, Carlos. 2002. *La España de Alfonso XIII: el estado, la política, los movimientos sociales* (Madrid: Espasa Calpe)

Sepúlveda, Ricardo. 1888. *El corral de la Pacheca: apuntes para la historia del teatro español* (Madrid: Fernando Fé)

Serrano Asenjo, Enrique. 2002. *Vidas oblicuas: aspectos teóricos de la "Nueva Biografía" en España (1928–1936)* (Saragossa: Prensas Universitarias de Zaragoza)

Simón Palmer, María del Carmen. 1991. *Escritoras españolas del siglo XIX*. (Madrid: Castalia)

—— 2010. 'Carmen de Burgos, traductora', *Arbor, Ciencia, Pensamiento y Cultura*, 186 (extra no., June): 157–68

Sinclair, Alison. 1977. *Valle-Inclán's Ruedo ibérico: A Popular View of Revolution* (London: Tamesis)

Smith Rouselle, Elizabeth. 2014. *Gender and Modernity in Spanish Literature: 1789–1920* (New York: Palgrave-Macmillan)

Soguero García, Francisco Miguel. 2000. 'Los narradores de vanguardia como renovadores del género biográfico', in *Hacia la nueva novela — Essays on the Spanish Avant-Garde Novel*, ed. by Francis Lough (Bern: Peter Lang), pp. 199–217

Soufas, C. Christopher, Jr. 1998. 'Tradition as an Ideological Weapon: The Critical Redefinition of Modernity and Modernism in Early 20th-Century Spanish Literature', *Anales de la literatura española contemporánea*, 23.1–2: 465–77

STARCEVIC, ELIZABETH. 1976. *Carmen de Burgos: defensora de la mujer* (Almería: Librería Editorial Cajal)
STAVANS, ILAN. 2015. 'The Downside to Digging Up Cervantes', *The New Yorker*, 19 March, <http://www.newyorker.com/books/page-turner/the-downside-to-digging-up-cervantes> [accessed 27 July 2015]
STEINBERG, DEBORAH L. 2000. 'Reading Genes/Writing Nation: Reith, "Race" and the Writings of Geneticist Steve Jones', in *Hybridity and its Discontents: Politics, Science, Culture*, ed. by Avtar Brah and Annie E. Coomb (London & New York: Routledge), pp. 137–53
SUÁREZ GALBÁN, EUGENIO. 1982. 'Sobre dos novelas cortas recuperadas de Carmen de Burgos', *Ínsula*, 436 (September): 7
TOLLIVER, JOYCE. 2011. 'Politics and the Feminist Essay in Spain', in *A Companion to Spanish Women Studies*, ed. by Xon de Ros and Geraldine Hazbun (Woodbridge & Rochester, NY: Tamesis), pp. 243–56
TORRECILLA, JESÚS. 1996. *La imitación colectiva: modernidad vs. autenticidad en la literatura española* (Madrid: Gredos)
TORRES GONZÁLEZ, BEGOÑA. 2010. 'Hablando con los descendientes de Carmen de Burgos', *Arbor*, 186 (extra no.): 169–81
TOYNBEE, POLLY. 2015. 'Britain Mourns a Monster — Because He Was a King. Richard III's Burial Was Absurd', *Guardian*, 26 March, <http://www.theguardian.com/commentisfree/2015/mar/26/britain-king-richard-iii-tyrant> [accessed 27 July 2015]
UGARTE, MICHAEL. 1994. 'The Generational Fallacy and Spanish Women Writing in Madrid at the Turn of the Century', *Siglo XX/20th Century*, 12: 235–50
—— 1998. 'Carmen de Burgos ("Colombine"): Feminist Avant la Lettre', in *Spanish Women Writers and the Essay: Gender, Politics, and the Self*, ed. by Kathleen M. Glenn and Mercedes Mazquiaran de Rodríguez (Columbia: University of Missouri Press), pp. 55–74
UNAMUNO, MIGUEL DE. 1902 [1895]. *En torno al casticismo* (Barcelona: A. Calderón & S. Valentí Camp)
—— 1968. 'El porvenir de España (1898–1912)', in *Obras completas*, vol. 3 (Madrid: Escelicer), pp. 637–77
URÍA, JORGE. 2008. *La España liberal, 1868–1917: cultura y vida cotidiana* (Madrid: Síntesis)
VALIS, NOËL M. 1989. 'The Novel as Feminine Entrapment: Valle-Inclán's Sonata de otoño', *Hispanic Issue*, 104.2: 351–69
—— 2002. *The Culture of Cursilería: Bad Taste, Kitsch, and Class in Modern Spain* (Durham, NC: Duke University Press)
VALLE-INCLÁN, RAMÓN. 1927. *La corte de los milagros* (Madrid: Rivadeneyra)
VÁZQUEZ RECIO, NIEVES. 1998. 'Las hijas de Don Juan (1907) de Blanca de los Ríos: fin de siglo y mirada femenina', in *Don Juan Tenorio en la España del siglo XX: literatura y cine*, ed. by Ana Sofía Pérez-Bustamante Mourier (Madrid: Cátedra), pp. 379–403
VEGA, MARIANO ESTEBAN DE. 2013. 'La nación en las Historias Generales de España', in *Historia de la nación y del nacionalismo español*, ed. by Antonio Morales Moya, Juan Pablo Fusi Aizpurúa and Andrés de Blas Guerrero (Barcelona: Galaxia Gutenberg, Círculo de Lectores), pp. 435–49
VICENTE, LAURA. 2010. 'Del gabinete perfumado a la redacción del periódico: marisabidillas en la Barcelona de finales del XIX', in *Il Congreso virtual sobre historia de las mujeres* (Jaén: Asociación de Amigos del Archivo Histórico Diocesano de Jaén), <https://dialnet.unirioja.es/descarga/articulo/4095892.pdf> [accessed 20 August 2013]
VILLARES, RAMÓN, and JAVIER MORENO LUZÓN. 2009. *Restauración y dictadura*, in *Historia de España*, ed. by Josep Fontana and Ramón Villares, vol. 7 (Barcelona: Crítica; Madrid: Marcial Pons)

WEIGEL, SIGRID. 2006. *Genea-Logik: Generation, Tradition und Evolution zwischen Kultur- und Naturwissenschaften* (Munich: Wilhelm Fink)

WILSON, MARGARET. 1969. *Spanish Drama of the Golden Age* (Oxford & New York, Pergamon Press)

WOLOSKY, SHIRA. 2010. *Poetry and Public Discourse in Nineteenth-Century America* (New York: Palgrave Macmillan)

WOOD, JENNIFER J. 1999–2000. 'A Woman Writing War in 1909: Colombine in Melilla', *Letras Peninsulares*, 12.2–3: 373–85

WRIGHT, SARAH. 2007. *Tales of Seduction: The Figure of Don Juan in Spanish Culture* (London: Tauris Academic Studies)

YETANO LAGUNA, ANA (ed.) 2013. *Mujeres y culturas políticas en España, 1808–1845* (Bellaterra: Universitat Autònoma de Barcelona)

YUVAL-DAVIS, NIRA. 1997. *Gender & Nation* (London & Thousand Oaks, CA: Sage Publications)

YUVAL-DAVIS, NIRA, and FLOYA ANTHIAS (eds). 1989. *Woman, Nation, State* (New York: St. Martin's Press)

ZAPATA-CALLE, ANA. 2011. 'En la guerra de Carmen de Burgos: crítica del proceso de nacionalización e imperialismo español en Marruecos', *Decimonónica*, 8.2 (Summer): 91–112

ZAPLANA, ESTHER. 2005. 'War, Militarism and the Feminine "Habitus" in the Writings of Rosario de Acuña, Carmen de Burgos and Emilia Pardo Bazán', *Bulletin of Spanish Studies*, 82.1: 37–58

ZARAGOZA, JOSÉ. 1858. *Discursos leídos en las sesiones públicas que para dar posesión de plazas de número ha celebrado desde 1852 la Real Academia de la Historia* (Madrid: los Señores Matute y Compagni)

ZERUBAVEL, EVIATAR. 2012. *Ancestors and Relatives: Genealogy, Identity and Community* (New York: Oxford University Press)

ZORRILLA, JOSÉ. 1978 [1849]. *Traidor, inconfeso y mártir*, ed. by Ricardo Senabre (Madrid: Cátedra)

ZUBIAURRE-WAGNER, MAITE. 2003. 'Double Writing/Double Reading Cities, Popular Culture, and Stalkers: Carmen de Burgos "El perseguidor"', *Revista Hispánica Moderna*, 56.1: 57–70

—— 2012. *Cultures of the Erotic in Spain: 1898–1936* (Nashville, TN: Vanderbilt University Press)

INDEX

Alas, Leopoldo 18, 22, 79, 80
Alba, Duchess of 126–27, 129
Álbum Iberoamericano, El 40, 80
Alfonso XII xi, 17–18, 27 n. 11, 33, 48, 56, 65, 74, 107
Alfonso XIII xi, 13, 18, 25, 27 n. 11, 74, 75, 83, 87, 128
Amadeo I of Saboya 17, 56, 86, 99, 123
americanismo 58, 71 n. 1
angel of the hearth 70
Asensi, Julia de:
   A.S.M el Rey D. Alfonso XII 56
   El aeronauta 34
   El retrato vivo 40–41
   La hija de Villoria 40
   Tres amigas 37, 38, 41–44, 69, 78
   Victoria y otros cuentos 55
Ateneo de Madrid 12, 68
Azaña, Manuel 150–51
Azorín 80, 116

Baroja, Carmen 143
Bastinos, Editorial 31, 44 n. 2
Bécquer, Gustavo Adolfo 27 n. 10, 77, 106
   El rayo de luna 81–82
Biblioteca de Autores Españoles (BAE) 34, 35, 36, 39
Biblioteca Mignon 79–80
Biblioteca Nueva 145–46
Biblioteca Universal 34–37, 39, 44, 45 n. 11, 57 n. 6, 79–80
Bieder, Maryellen 21, 60
Blanco, Alda 21–22
Blanco García, Francisco 31–32, 60
Blanco y Negro 116
Blasco Ibáñez, Vicente 80
   La maja desnuda 93–94, 96, 125
Böhl de Faber, Cecilia, *see* Caballero, Fernán
Burgos, Carmen de:
   Confidencias de artistas 113
   El tío de todos 23, 107, 133
   El último deseo 130
   Fígaro (revelaciones, 'ella' descubierta, epistolario inédito, numerosos grabados) 115
   Gloriosa vida y desdichada muerte de Don Rafael del Riego 116–17
   Hablando con los descendientes 106, 107, 111, 118, 150
   La incomprensible 130
   La malcasada 111
   La mujer moderna y sus derechos 107

   Los huesos del abuelo 107, 149–52
   ¿Quiere usted comer bien? 110

Caballero, Fernán 22, 31, 62, 70
Cádiz Cortes 14–15
Cánovas del Castillo, Antonio 17–19, 116
Carlist wars 6, 16, 27 n. 8, 32, 48–49, 56, 65, 107, 141
Carlos I 15, 47–48, 52, 55–57
Carlos II 97
Casanova, Sofía 12, 16, 36, 42, 44, 59, 73 n. 12, 77, 80, 89 n. 6, 108
casticismo 104 n. 4, 105 n. 5
castizo 10, 15, 21, 68, 104 n. 6
Cervantes and Realism 21, 36, 64, 66, 121, 150
Chacel, Rosa 143
Contemporáneos, Los 79, 145
Coronado, Carolina 12, 36
Cuento Semanal, El 79, 92–93, 97, 104 n. 1
cursi 10, 21

Danvila y Collado, Manuel 49, 55
Darío, Rúben 150
Darwin, Charles 9, 139
degeneration 7
   Max Nordau 9, 24, 71, 96–97
Disaster of 98: 25, 74, 94, 97
Don Juan 57 n. 4, 60, 69–73, 72 n. 11, 73 n. 12, 76, 89 n. 6, 93

Echegaray, José 71
   O locura o santidad 91–92
education, female 29–33, 44 n. 1, 144
El desdén, con el desdén 75, 81
Espina, Concha 118
Exposición Nacional de Bellas Artes 11, 57 n. 1, 127–28

Felipe IV 97
Fernando VII 13, 48, 112–13, 117
Fitzmaurice-Kelly, Jaime 20, 60

Generation of 98: 8, 58, 100, 131 n. 2, 134, 138
germanías 47, 49, 52, 54, 55 48, 54, 57 n. 1
Gimeno de Flaquer, Concepción 40, 74
Gómez, Matilde 33
Gómez de Avellaneda, Gertrudis 3, 116
Gómez de Baquero, Eduardo 93

Gómez de la Serna, Ramón 109–10, 140, 145
　La maja desnuda 125
　'Prólogo' in Carmen de Burgos, *Confidencias de artistas* 113
Goya, Francisco 25–26, 62, 69, 93–97, 99, 119, 120–21, 123–26, 131 n. 2, 132, 154
Grassi, Ángela 21, 70
Greco, El 62, 121, 129, 131 n. 2, 132
Guerra de la Independencia Española, *see* Spanish War of Independence

Ilustración de la Mujer, La 38–40, 63–64, 78
Isabel The Catholic 12, 16, 42, 44, 61, 64, 83, 89
Isabel II 13, 16–17, 20–21, 24, 27 n. 5, 9 & 10, 31–32, 39, 46, 48, 69, 99, 141

Kirkpatrick, Susan 7–9, 23, 64, 109, 121, 130, 143
krausism 30

Lafuente, Modesto 14, 19, 20, 27 n. 14, 35, 83, 141
Larra, Mariano José de 60, 106, 108, 110–11, 114–16, 118, 143, 146
Lejárraga, María de la O 75, 89 n. 3

maja 25, 69, 90, 93–102, 194 n. 3, 120–21, 124–27, 129
majismo 94, 104 n. 2 & 4
mantilla 90, 94, 99–101, 105 n. 6 & 7, 125–27, 129
María Cristina of Bourbon-Two Sicilies 13, 16, 69, 72 n. 9
María Cristina of Habsburg xi, xiii, 11, 18, 25, 74–75, 87
Mariana Pineda 114
Martínez Sierra, Gregorio 75, 89 n. 3
Menéndez y Pelayo, Marcelino 19–20, 60, 67–69, 101
Modernism 26, 70, 79, 88, 108, 128, 130
　in Spain 23
　women and 23, 109, 145
Molina, Tirso de 36, 60, 65–69, 72 n. 8, 85–86, 103, 107–08, 115, 117–18

National Exhibition of Fine Arts, *see* Exposición Nacional de Bellas Artes
novela corta 6, 23–24, 76–80, 89 n. 6, 114, 119 n. 3
Novela Corta, La 79, 116
Novela Pasional, La 120, 131 n. 1
novella, *see* novela corta

Pardo Bazán, Emilia 22, 23, 34, 36, 42–45, 44 n. 3, 45 n. 6, 60, 65–66, 77, 89 n. 6, 108, 115
　Casi artista 143
　La mujer española y otros escritos 42–43
　Nuevo Teatro Crítico 60
Pascual de Sanjuán, Pilar 31, 41

Pérez Galdós, Benito 21–23, 57 n. 2, 77–80, 86–87, 93, 99, 108, 123, 139–40, 145, 147 n. 1
　Doña Perfecta 78
　Episodios nacionales: de Cartago a Sagunto 57 n. 2
　Fortunata y Jacinta 139, 147 n. 1
　La desheredada 86–87, 99, 123–24
　'Observaciones sobre la novela contemporánea española' 21
Pi i Margall, Fracisco 56, 57 n. 2, 117
Prado, Museo del 26, 97, 120–25, 128–31, 136
Pujol de Collado, Josefa 38–39, 63–64

Quixote, Don:
　as national archetype/trope 36, 64, 69, 83

Raza Española 58
Real Academia de la Lengua Española 65–66, 118–19, 119 n. 8, 135, 147 n. 2
regeneration 8, 25, 27 n. 5, 30, 62, 74–76, 91, 94, 100–01, 105 n. 5, 107, 116
Restoration xi-xii, 9, 11, 17–18, 27 n. 11, 74
Revolt of the Brotherhoods, *see* germanías
Riego, Rafael del 106, 108, 110–11, 112, 113, 117–18, 146
Ríos, Blanca de los:
　Las Hijas de Don Juan 60, 69–71, 72 n. 11
　Las mujeres de Tirso 68, 69, 118
　Margarita 78
　Por la República 63
　Romanticismo 76
　Sangre española 70, 104
Ríos, José Amador de los 20–21, 35, 58, 60–62, 65, 89, 114, 122
Romero de Torres, Julio 125, 127

Saéz Melgar, Faustina 21
Saint Teresa of Jesus 12, 36, 42, 44, 45 n. 6, 64, 95, 113
Sinués, Pilar de 21–22, 31, 63, 70
Spanish War of Independence 13–14, 18, 93–94, 118, 153

Unamuno, Miguel de 8, 80, 100, 138, 147 n. 5
　En torno al casticismo 104 n. 4

Valera, Juan 8, 79
　Juanita la Larga 77
Valle-Inclán, Ramón del 23, 27 n. 10, 70, 79–80, 88
Velázquez, Diego 25, 62, 96–97, 105 n. 5, 121, 128, 131 n. 2, 154

Zamacois, Eduardo 79
Zorrilla, José 46, 77, 81, 106, 116, 150
　La pasionaria 78
　Margarita la Tornera 78
　Traidor, inconfeso, mártir 52–53

www.ingramcontent.com/pod-product-compliance
Lightning Source LLC
LaVergne TN
LVHW061252060426
835507LV00017B/2027